The Asian Gang Revisited

Also available from Bloomsbury

The Asian Gang Revisited

Changing Muslim Masculinities

Claire E. Alexander

BLOOMSBURY ACADEMIC
LONDON • NEW YORK • OXFORD • NEW DELHI • SYDNEY

BLOOMSBURY ACADEMIC
Bloomsbury Publishing Plc
50 Bedford Square, London, WC1B 3DP, UK
1385 Broadway, New York, NY 10018, USA
29 Earlsfort Terrace, Dublin 2, Ireland

BLOOMSBURY, BLOOMSBURY ACADEMIC and the Diana logo
are trademarks of Bloomsbury Publishing Plc

First published in Great Britain 2024

A catalogue record for this book is available from the British Library.

A catalog record for this book is available from the Library of Congress.

ISBN: HB: 978-1-3503-8412-5
       PB: 978-1-3503-8413-2
       ePDF: 978-1-3503-8414-9
       eBook: 978-1-3503-8415-6

Typeset by Integra Software Services Pvt. Ltd.

To find out more about our authors and books visit www.bloomsbury.com
and sign up for our newsletters.

This book is dedicated to the memory of my father,
John Leonard Alexander,
and my birth mother,
Chhanda Datta

Contents

Acknowledgements

This book has been a long time in the making, and the debts I owe to so many people have accumulated along the way.

First, most and always, my love and thanks go to the men from 'the Asian Gang' projects. It has been a privilege and a joy to have known you across the past quarter-decade, and to have been part of your lives, close-up or at a distance. Thank you for sharing your journey with me – I hope I have at least partially repaid your time, your patience and your trust.

Shahin, Zohar, Humzah, Hanif and Silver read drafts of the chapters along the way, and I want to acknowledge their generosity and insights. Alas, the blame for any errors or misinterpretations lies with me.

I want to thank Shahin and Humzah's families, who welcomed me into their lives and their homes. I particularly want to thank Auntie, Shahin's sisters and 'the dots', who are my Bengali 'family of choice', and whose love and support has been than I could have ever wished for. I also want to send love to 'Ana' and her children, whose friendship has been an anchor across difficult years.

Thanks are due to the ESRC, who funded my 2011/12 study, and have never once queried why the book took so long to appear. I'm grateful to colleagues at the LSE and Manchester for many conversations as the project and the book took shape – and particularly to Manchester for giving me sabbatical time to complete the manuscript. Thanks are also due to Mark Richardson and Elissa Burns at Bloomsbury for their enthusiasm and support in bringing the book to press.

Many colleagues have supported this work through occasional – or incessant – conversations across the years. I am particularly grateful to Yunis Alam, Ajmal Hussain, Remi Joseph-Salisbury, Caroline Knowles, Nasar Meer, Shamim Miah, James Rhodes, John Solomos and Derron Wallace, who read draft chapters and who were unfailingly kind. Thanks are due too to Rashida Bibi, Dharmi Kapadia and Julia King, who assisted with bits of research for context, and Siobhan O'Neill, who helped me get the manuscript into shape.

I have benefitted from the support, patience and occasional badgering of many friends and colleagues along the way, including Suki Ali, Alice Bloch, Bridget Byrne, Aditya Chakrabortty, Joya Chatterji, Brian Heaphy, Sundeep Lidher, Vanessa May, Kate Reed, Ruth Quinn, Shirley Summers, AnnMarie Sylvester-Charles, Meghan Tinsley and Gary Younge. Wendy Bottero and Chris Orme deserve an honourable mention for their (usually) unfailing tolerance in the face of my chronic procrastination.

Thanks to Suki Dhanda for her wonderful cover photos, for both 'Asian Gang' books, whose evocative images, nearly twenty-five years apart, capture the sense of continuity and change that I have struggled to put on the pages that follow.

The past decade has been one of huge loss and change, with the death of my mother and father, younger sister and birth mother. I want to send my love and thanks to my big sister Carole and my niece Victoria and her four beautiful girls, Isabel, Rosie-May, Caitlyn and Ivy, for always being there through the best and worst of times. Finally, I want to acknowledge the two great loves of my recent life – my beautiful little cat-neighbour, Malibu, who started visiting in lockdown and helped me get started on the book, and my lovely rescue-diva Lilo, who arrived in February and has been doing her furry best to stop me finishing it.

Revisiting 'The Asian Gang'

Two Weddings and the Rebirth of 'The Asian Gang'

This story starts where most end – with a wedding. Or, in fact, two weddings. The first took place in November 2009, the marriage of Hanif to Khadija. The marriage was arranged – Hanif had met Khadija only a few months before, when he had taken his mother on Hajj. Khadija was there with her father and brother, and the families had spent time together during the pilgrimage, and stayed in contact on their return to the UK. When I first met Hanif in 1994, he was thirteen. At the time of his marriage, he was twenty-eight and worked as a solicitor for a prestigious firm in central London. Khadija had just turned twenty-two, and had recently finished a degree in psychology at a London university – in fact, as part of her studies, she'd even read *The Asian Gang* (2000) – and was training as a primary school teacher.

Many of Hanif's old friends – and protagonists of *The Asian Gang* – were at the wedding, resplendently decked out in matching gold *sherwanis* to accompany him to the stage as part of the groom's wedding party. In 2009 at least, the core of this group was still very close, and had remained so in the decade since *The Asian Gang* was published. I used to refer to them as 'the little ones' – and that is still how they are described by some – though they were then all in their late twenties, mainly married and some had children of their own. Hanif was, in fact, one of the last to marry from that group – his best friend Jamal was to be married the following weekend, which left only Ismat, who remains unmarried even until today. At that time, Jamal had just started work in a bank near the Stoneleigh Estate. His marriage had been hastily arranged, after a disastrous love affair, and he told me at Hanif's wedding that his wife-to-be, aged twenty-four, was very sensible, though he confessed, slightly coyly, that he really preferred older women. Sayeed, the third of this very close trio, had been married for some time – his marriage, to a cousin, was arranged in Bangladesh. Sayeed had two children, and worked then, as now, as a bus driver. He had become very religious in recent years, since his father's death, and sported an impressive beard that made him look rather fierce, belying his very gentle nature. Others of that friendship group were also there, some with their wives; several of the 'older lot' were there too, as friends of Hanif's older brothers Shahin and Khalid, as well as some of the people I had worked with in the SAYO youth project, including Yasmin and Silver. It was a meeting of the clans. Some were missing, of course, notably Ifti, who was serving three years in prison for dealing drugs, but had drifted away from the group after leaving school. Nevertheless, this core group of seven or eight friends had remained very close in the last decade, through college and university, and the early years of work, marriage and family.

The second wedding took place seven months later, in June 2010, at an Arts Centre in South West London. This time, it was the marriage of Zohar to his girlfriend of fifteen years, Humaira. Zohar and Humaira had met just as I started the interviews for *The Asian Gang* in 1995, and theirs had been an epic romance of star-crossed love, feuding families, community conflict (Humaira is of Pakistani descent) and, finally, love triumphant. Zohar was then in his early thirties and worked as a senior youth co-ordinator in London – work he had been doing for fifteen years. He had recently started a charity with Silver and other former colleagues from the SAYO project working with young people in Bangladesh.

The wedding was small by Bengali standards – only around 400 people. Nevertheless the Stoneleigh contingent, past and present, were there in force. Zohar was one of what was referred to as 'the older lot' when I began my research, a group then aged between eighteen and twenty years. Now in their early to mid-thirties, all were married and most had children, although none of the wives and children were in evidence on this occasion. Big Hanif told me, rather shamefacedly, that they had decided to keep this to a 'boys only' night – a chance to catch up with friends they had not, in some cases, seen for some time. The diversity amongst this group was starker in some ways than with 'the little ones': around the table were Big Hanif and Mustafa, both working as bus drivers; Humzah, recently married and returned from Bangladesh, and working in his family's takeaway; Liaquot, who was working as a cab driver; Jadil, who owned a successful pub near the river; Salman, who was working in an insurance call centre. Salman told me he wanted to open a bar but his younger brother Sayeed had refused on religious grounds. Also at the table was Shahin, who was working in a City law firm specializing in employment law – the only one there with his partner, Emma, also a solicitor. The little ones were not so much in evidence because, as Shahin explained, Zohar did not have a younger brother who would have been the necessary link for the invitation – only Hanif and Khalid had come with their older brother Shahin, and a couple of Zohar's former colleagues from the play service were also there. Unspoken age and peer group distinctions meant, however, that they sat on a different table, with Yasmin, who had also been invited, though there was a lot of informal interaction, as well as some sneaking off to have a quiet cigarette out of the view of older eyes.

It was at Zohar's wedding that the idea to revisit *The Asian Gang* project was born. As I sat with the 'older lot', reminiscing about the previous fifteen years and longer, listening to the well-worn jokes and gentle teasing that seems to pass for communication amongst this particular group of men, and fielding some quite pointed questions about the earlier book – how it had sold (ok, for an academic book), how much money I had made (none, I assured them), what had changed and why I didn't write another one – the decision was an obvious one. I was particularly struck not only by the changes that were apparent across the time I had known these men, the differences between them that the intervening years had wrought or highlighted, but also the enduring sense of connection which brought them together at this time and in this place to celebrate Zohar and Humaira's marriage. Of course, this occasion was one of many similar events across the years – other weddings, Eid Day celebrations, the occasional funeral, the increasingly rare 'boys' nights' out – but it was the first time I had seen many of this group, and seen them together, for several years. Unlike 'the little ones', when I first met them, 'the older lot' were already more disparate and more loosely connected, with a broader age range, and wider social and geographical mobility – by virtue of age, and cars, largely. These differences had become more marked over the years and stood in contrast to the still tightly knit brotherhood of friends visible at Hanif's wedding – though this too was to change in the following years. Nevertheless, the sense of affection, concern and care was still tangible and interwoven with shades of nostalgia for the young men they had been and the battles they had faced and fought together.

In this case, literally. Around the table were a number of men who had been involved in the long running series of fights in 1995, which had started with the attack on Shahin, then aged seventeen, outside the West London College, where he was studying A-levels. He was set upon by a group of a dozen young men, armed with baseball bats and iron bars, which put him in hospital for three days with stitches and a gash on his leg, and gave him a limp that lasted for several months. This incident had led to a number of escalating retributive attacks, culminating the following year in an ambush of the main ringleader, Rahul. These events were described in *The Asian Gang* (2000), and will be discussed further in Chapter 5, but were resonating throughout Zohar's wedding. Zohar's bride, Humaira, had met Shahin at the same college in 1995 and had been introduced to Zohar at that time. Shahin, in fact, was then dating Humaira's younger sister. Mustafa, who had been the main person involved in organizing the revenge attack, and had later assumed sole responsibility for it, received a sentence of six years. When I interviewed him in 2012, he told me that if he had known the sentence he was going to get, he would perhaps have reconsidered. However, he also reflected that his time in prison had allowed him to explore his religion more and had 'saved his life'. Since his release, he had moved away from the Stoneleigh Estate, married and started working as a bus driver.

The afternoon of Zohar's wedding, Shahin picked me up from home and we went to his flat, in a neighbouring block to Zohar's, to meet Emma. Although it was already late afternoon, and the wedding was due to start, across London, at 6.00 pm, Zohar was wandering around the car park outside the flats, still dressed in sweatpants and a T-shirt. Mustafa was with him, as were Liaquot and Jadil. I had not seen Mustafa for over ten years, not since he had been in prison, and had not known him well when I was doing the research, partly because he was a little older than Shahin and rarely attended the youth club, and partly I had always been a little afraid of him. Mustafa then had been practically silent, and he had a reputation for being very short-tempered and violent. In fact, I believe it was he and Liaquot who had once smashed the windows on my car when I was working in the youth club, after a disagreement. We were waiting for Zohar, sitting in Shahin's flat and having tea and snacks, while the men talked about their families, their gym routines and, memorably, what shampoo was good for one's scalp. Mustafa had recently shaved his head because, he confessed, he was losing his hair. He is a big fan of organic products. There was no discussion of the earlier events, although there was some coded speculation about whether some of their erstwhile antagonists – who were related to Humaira – would be at the wedding, and some slightly shamefaced laughter about their youthful indiscretions. The general consensus was that they were, of course, now all grown-up family men, and above any revisiting of these past conflicts. At the same time, though, it was clear too that there was a strong sense of a shared history that still mattered, but differently to the way it had mattered and expressed itself fifteen years earlier.

It was the complexity of these connections, the continuities and discontinuities, which intrigued me. Part of this was a reflection on the biographies of the individuals themselves, but also of the group as a whole, in the fifteen years since the first project: on their transition to adulthood and different choices and trajectories that this encompassed;

on the fractures and fissures; on distance travelled; and what remained of the friendships and hopes and ambitions of their younger selves, and what had been lost along the way. These more personal stories are, of course, deeply enmeshed in the broader social and political environment of their growing up, which saw the transformation of 'the Asian gang' through the first decade of the new Millennium, nationally and globally. Indeed, these young men – *my* 'Asian Gang' – came of age against the backdrop of suspicion, criminalization, securitization and the War on Terror, at home and abroad, and their personal (and collective) troubles are necessarily inseparable from the public issues which both surround and produce them, and which render the lives of these men at once hypervisible, and profoundly invisible. As with *The Asian Gang* originally, it is the encounter between the individual and the social, agency and the structures that produce and constrain it, which forms the core of this work, and which shapes the sociological and ethnographic imagination of 'the Asian gang'. Now, over two decades from the original project, and nearing twenty-five years from the publication of *The Asian Gang*, the need to revisit this work and to trace the lives of its participants across the intervening years seems not just intriguing but necessary.

Enter, The Asian Gang

Sociological research, and ethnography in particular, is always late to the scene – confined to a rear-view analysis of events that have already passed, if not been fully understood. At its best, perhaps, it can illuminate hidden connections, or map out emerging features of a known terrain and indicate new directions, but it most often feels like screenshot of a moment always already 'out of date' (Cohen 1980: i). Nevertheless, as Stan Cohen notes in his introduction to the second edition of his iconic *Folk Devils and Moral Panics*, one can argue for a 'piece of historical reconstruction as having implications somewhat beyond the immediate and topical' (Cohen 1980: i). As Cohen originally noted in 1972, new folk devils are always emerging and moral panics are constantly created, and recreated – but while the process (the 'how') is remarkably consistent, the content (the 'who' and 'what') and the context (the 'when' and 'why') bear scrutiny. While Cohen too lightly dismisses these as 'ephemera', it is worth reflecting that the consequences for some designated folk devils are far-reaching and enduring, well beyond the framing of the original moral panic itself.

As it turned out, 'the Asian gang' as folk devil and moral panic proved both short-lived and remarkably resilient. Indeed, the life cycle of 'the Asian gang' pretty much mirrored that of my first research project, weaving earlier concerns around race, religion and deviant masculinities (brown men with beards) to coalesce in the idea of 'the gang' in the early 1990s. 'The Asian Gang' folk devil reached its heyday in 1994–6,and was inescapably formative to my British Academy postdoctoral research, which ran, officially at least, from 1994 to 1997. By the time the book was published in 2000, 'the Asian gang' was already fading to anachronism.

Nevertheless, 'the Asian gang' captured a significant moment of transformation in the imagination of British Asian communities which has had enduring consequences, laying the foundations for future incarnations of, particularly, Muslim folk devils, which were to dominate the landscape of the new Millennium. Importantly, 'the Asian gang' fractured the complacent homogeneities of the 'Asian community' to reveal not only the national and ethno-religious boundaries within this imagined community but also differences around gender, generation and class. Accounts of 'the Asian gang' slide opportunistically between a focus on race/ethnicity (Asian), national origin (Pakistani and Bangladeshi) and religion (Muslim), indicating the relative newness, and conceptual uncertainty, of this emerging split. These internal divisions were apparent from the mid-1980s onwards, when concerns focused on the emergence of the so-called 'Muslim underclass' (Modood 1992, Modood et al 1997, Alexander 1998), and which placed socially and economically disadvantaged Pakistani and Bangladeshi communities in the spotlight. Tariq Modood thus points to the increasing distinction between Indian and East African Asian (implicitly Hindu and Sikh) communities as 'achievers' and Pakistani and Bangladeshi (majority Muslim) communities as 'believers' (1992: 43). He also notes the emergence of gendered and generational pathologies, which were crucial to the imagination of 'the Asian gang', and specifically the growth of a new 'anxiety about a possible trend of criminalisation among young Pakistanis and Bangladeshis' (1997: 147). It is important to note the ways in which ethnicity (and, by implication, religion) is used as the default condition – the ur-explanation – for all other forms of differences within the communities formerly known as 'Asian', subsuming class, migration and settlement histories and patterns, gender and generation. At the same time, explanations for both 'the Muslim underclass' and 'the Asian gang' pivot crucially on the same evocation of 'culture' (family, values, tradition, gender roles) that were used to explain the earlier success of 'Asian' communities (Modood 1992, Parekh et al 2000, Alexander 2002). One might argue, in fact, that 'the Asian gang', and by the extension, 'the Muslim underclass', embodies the dark side of the 'model minority' myth.

Of course, 'the Asian gang', even at its height, never captured the imagination of the academy, the press or the public, in the way that earlier 'Black' folk devils had done, and would continue to do. It remained a local folk devil, lurking in the confines of ethnically dense urban communities: an Asian problem, of little concern or interest to those outside of those communities. In fact, in the late 1990s, when I was seeking a publisher for *The Asian Gang*, the task was much harder than for my first book, on Black youth, *The Art of Being Black* (1996). As one commissioning editor from OUP told me, Asian youth were simply 'too dull' (Alexander 2004b). Leaving aside here the implications for work on 'race' and whose experience is deemed interesting (i.e. saleable), and in what form (i.e. attractive to an imagined white readership, who presumably like their race research with more ghetto-fabulous grit), her response also reflected the dominant focus of research and publication on British Asian communities at the time, which was largely fixated on arranged marriages, language practices, gift giving and religious rituals

(Benson 1996). Despite the brief flirtation with 'Asian cool' (Banerjea & Banerjea 1996), and the seminal theoretical challenges of *Dis-Orienting Rhythms* (Sharma, Hutnyk & Sharma 1996), which exploded the 'fourth wall' of empirical research on Asian communities in Britain, this more inward-looking, apolitical and culturalist approach remained, and indeed remains, dominant. Asian youth (and particularly young men) were either viewed as indistinguishable from the culture of their parents or 'caught between cultures' (Anwar 1998) and in crisis – defined through either cultural 'excess' or cultural 'lack': both problematic and both 'dull' (Alexander 2002, 2018).

'The gang' challenged these conventional culture-bound accounts of Asian youth identities, by highlighting internal differences/conflicts around gender and generation, but particularly around religion. Nevertheless, while the visibility of Asian youth, *as* youth, is to be cautiously welcomed, the *ways* in which they became visible were inevitably more problematic. First, the focus on 'the gang' erased a longer and important history of Asian youth participation in the anti-racist/Black struggle from the 1970s, most notably through the Asian youth movements, which cut across ethno-religious lines, and formed alliances with other minority and left-wing groups (Alexander 2010, Ramamurthy 2013, Virdee 2014, Alexander et al 2016). Second, while there are a few media accounts of 'Sikh gangs' through this period and some academic work on Hindu nationalist youth groups (Bhatt 2001), the focus is very much on the problem of 'Muslim' youth. This focus was discernible from the late 1980s, emerging from the nascent discomfort around the disruptive public presence of Muslim men in the aftermath of the *Satanic Verses* affair in 1989 and the protests around the first Gulf War in 1990 (Alexander 1998), but was to consolidate through the lens of 'the gang' in the 1990s. Third, as I argued in *The Asian Gang*, the symbol of 'the gang' wove together multiple and interlocking pathologies – around race/ethnicity/religion, gender and generation, as well as class (which was not a focus of the book but perhaps should have been) – to place 'Muslim young men in the spotlight as the epitome of crisis and cultural atrophy' (2000: xiv). The only available image of Asian/Muslim young men was one of unremitting negativity, alienation/alienness and threat.

As with the focus on Black youth and 'mugging' previously (Hall et al 1978), however, this particular incarnation of a racialized moral panic tells us more about Britain, and its contemporaneous moment of social, economic, political and cultural crisis – in the aftermath of Thatcher and nearly two decades of the 'Little Englander' nationalism, deindustrialization and decline, the death of 'society' and the un/settled 'multicultural drift' of a reluctantly globalizing Britain (Hall 2000, Hesse 2000) – than it does about Asian or Muslim young men.

Indeed, Asian/Muslim youth themselves remained largely absent from 'the gang', or from wider British society – a blank canvas for projected paranoias rather than a rounded portrait. *The Asian Gang* was my attempt to redress this balance – to make visible the lives of Asian young men, within their own terms, but with an eye to how these lives were shaped through and by the negative discourses of 'the gang' – to humanize the folk devil.

Though, as it turned out, *Goodness Gracious Me* (BBC 1998–2001) got there sooner, and with better jokes. And by the end of 2001, no one thought Asian youth were dull.

2001: Millennial Folk Devils and Moral Panics

The spring and summer of 2001 marked the advent of 'the Asian gang' onto the national stage, with a series of 'riots' across the former milltowns of the north of England. Starting in Bradford in April and Oldham in May, and followed by smaller clashes in Leeds and Burnley in June and Bradford (again) in July, the events were greeted with the usual public and political expressions of horrified surprise and outrage. This response was partly perhaps due to the recurrent historic amnesia which infects the British press and polity whenever 'race relations' erupt through the patriotic blindness to racial inequality. It was partly too because of the geography of the 'riots', outside of the urban centres where minority communities were imaginatively located (and which was to presage future – whitewashed – concerns over the plight of the post-industrial 'left behind'), and partly, perhaps, because the violence finally shattered any illusions of passive, compliant and largely autonomous Asian communities. The 'riots' marked a shift from 'the Asian gang' being an 'ethnic' or a 'community' matter to a societal problem – if not a societal responsibility. As I have argued earlier (2004a, 2005), the coverage of 'the riots' bracketed the events from the broader context of social and economic decline, and racialized hostility that marked the run-up to the conflicts. This included the activities of the National Front and police discrimination locally (Allen 2003, Bagguley & Hussain 2008) and, nationally, the toxic political rhetoric around asylum seekers and Muslim 'self-segregation' (Ouseley 2001), which was to lay the groundwork for the later state-sanctioned 'hostile environment' policy (Jones et al 2017). The 'riots' also posed significant challenges for the New Labour government, whose celebration of 'chicken tikka masala' and the urban multiculture of 'Cool Britannia' seemed worlds away from the terraced houses and narrow streets of Glodwick or Manningham, or the images of burned-out cars and masked young men with petrol bombs.

Nevertheless, the continuities with earlier conceptions of 'the Asian gang' are clearly apparent, rehearsing tropes of masculinity-in-crisis and 'between two cultures' generational conflict, and linking these to patterns of criminalization, notably around drugs, 'no-go areas' and 'turf wars'. Indeed these links can be traced back to an earlier 'riot' in Bradford, in 1995, which shaped 'the Asian gang' folk devil (Keith 1995, Alexander 2000), and are recurrent images in the more recent debates around 'gangs', knife crime and 'postcode wars' discussed as follows. The reduction of protest to criminality – or what then Home Secretary David Blunkett dismissed as 'sheer mindless violence' (cited in Allen 2003: 23) – had clear and immediate consequences in the heavy sentencing for the Bradford 'rioters'. However, its roots lie in the longer criminalization of Asian young men through the 1990s (Webster 1997) and their increasing visibility in the criminal justice system (Clancy et al 2001, Spalek & Wilson 2002).

As with 'the Asian gang', the 'riots' were fundamentally enmeshed in discourses around ethnicity and culture. While 'Asian' remained the predominant label, it became largely interchangeable with Pakistani (and to a lesser extent, Bangladeshi), while both were in turn now recoded through the common lens of religion – specifically 'Muslim' – though more as a cultural than religious marker. The government reports on the 'riots' focus predominantly on ethnicity and 'culture', reifying ideas of 'parallel lives' (Cantle 2001), 'self-segregation' (Ouseley 2001) and the need for 'cohesive communities' (Denham 2001), which have continued to define the experiences of marginalized Asian/Muslim communities and set them apart from both their white working-class neighbours and broader society (Bagguley & Hussain 2008, Waite 2021). It also, of course, works to homogenize and demonize whole communities on the basis of a perceived shared ethnic or religious identity. Chris Allen has noted, thus, that what Herman Ouseley described as the 'undeniably unfair and possibly racist' sentencing of the rioters in Bradford (in Wainwright & Dodd 2002) amounted to 'community sentencing' (2003: 46), serving as a warning to the broader British Asian/Muslim community. Importantly, between the 'riots' and the sentencing, the landscape had shifted dramatically with the attacks on New York on 11th September that year, and the launch of the War on Terror (2003: 46). That this 'war' was declared on Muslims at home, as well as abroad, was made starkly apparent in the sentences and Blunkett's defence of them as '*a genuine reprisal* but also a message to the community' (in Travis 2002, my emphasis).

The events of September 2001 thus saw the definitive shift from 'Asian' to 'Muslim', and from ethnic community to 'suspect community' (Hickman et al 2011). It also saw the demise of 'the Asian gang', and its reincarnation in three new post-Millennial folk devils – 'the terrorist', 'grooming gangs' and 'the [Black] gang'. Nevertheless, the DNA of 'the Asian gang' can be traced throughout, and across, these new folk devils.

The Asian Gang Goes Global: Good Muslims, Bad Muslims and the War on Terror

The attacks on New York, the Pentagon and Washington on 11 September 2001 were to reconfigure relations between 'the West' and its Muslim 'others', foreign and domestic, in dramatic and enduring ways. The past two decades have presided not only over conflicts and proxy wars which have transformed the landscape of the Middle East, Asia and Africa, and have sent ripples – and people – across the increasingly fortified borders of Europe, Australasia and the Americas but have redrawn the internal borders of national identity, citizenship and belonging in hitherto unimaginably draconian ways. In Britain, it is hard to conceive of the infiltration of the hostile environment into housing, health and welfare services, or the expansion of the Prevent agenda across the education system from primary schools to universities (Miah 2017), without a broader sense of the country being in a state of undeclared civil war with sections of its own, racially and religiously marked, population (Kundnani 2014). The punitive stripping of citizenship from British Muslims, increased use of deportation or extraordinary rendition, the use of solitary confinement in prisons, the internment of refugees in immigration camps at home and the state abandonment of 'jihadi brides' in refugee camps abroad testify to the legal and structural dehumanization and demonization of British Muslims, set against a broader cultural and political shift to the (far-)right in a bid to preserve an imagined national unity at all costs (Kapoor 2013, 2018, Abbas 2021).

It is important, of course, to recognize the longer roots of this enduring 'crisis', and the ways in which race and religion have overlapped in the service of political expediency at home and imperial privateering abroad for a millennium (Meer 2013). As Mamdani argues (2004), the roots of the current stand-off between 'the West' and political Islam can be traced to colonialism and the proxy conflicts of the Cold War, routed through global pathways and inflected through national-historical particularities to take shape in idiosyncratic and localized formats (Sayyid & Vakil 2010). Drawing, often explicitly, on Huntington's controversial 'clash of civilisations' thesis (1996), the War on Terror rehearses and extends existing concerns about British Muslims as an incipient 'fifth column' from the late 1980s onwards, but it must also be linked to broader and longer historical discourses and fears rooted in the imperial venture, or back as far as the Crusades. It is not accidental that the language of the Crusades has been deployed or evoked by politicians across the spectrum to support the War on Terror, from Tony Blair's war in Iraq to David Cameron's 'muscular liberalism'. As I have argued elsewhere (2017), the more spectacular 'events' of the War on Terror need to be placed against this historical and discursive racist hinterland, which resurrect and re-present ideas of medieval cultures, barbarism and timeless antagonism to an imagined 'West', interwoven with 'modern' racist and Orientalist discourses emerging from colonialism and post-war migration (Meer 2013).

This ideological hinterland constitutes a powerful commonsense repertoire of anti-Muslim stereotypes and sentiments that can be tracked into contemporary Islamophobic discourse and practice, from the everyday surveillance and internal bordering of Muslim communities (Hussain 2013, Miah 2017, Abbas 2019) to the criminalization, persecution and 'unmaking' of British Muslim citizens (Kapoor & Narkowicz 2019) in the name of 'national security'. Such extreme forms of state violence against British citizens are rendered unexceptional, even mundane, through the conjuring of racist tropes, such as images of the nameless (brown, male, young) hordes at the 'breaking point' of pre-Brexit Europe (Stewart & Mason 2016) or the dog whistle Islamophobic rhetoric of Muslim women as 'Ninjas' or 'letterboxes' (Dearden 2019a).

The links between these contemporary images and their recent-historical racial/ethnic antecedents are clear, whether in the hooded, masked (brown, male, young) rioters in Oldham or Bradford or the invisible women/brides, whose foreign cultures and language practices were accused (by Bradford MP Ann Cryer) of 'importing poverty' (Wainwright, Perkins & Travis 2001) and reinforcing 'parallel lives'.

This is clearly apparent in the configuration of 'the Muslim terrorist' through the 2000s, and especially in the aftermath of the July bombings in London in 2005, which saw the emergence of the 'home grown' (brown, male, young) terrorist (Kundnani 2014). A vitriolic comment article by Alice Miles in *The Times* the week after the attack lays the blame firmly at the feet of a putative Muslim 'community':

> Forget the mourning and tear into those *Muslim ghettos* instead. Force them to open up. Make the imams answer. Tell them to let their women speak ... We should insist that *they cannot continue in a state of alienation from the rest of society.*
>
> (Miles 2005, my emphasis)

In reality, none of the bombers was from a 'Muslim ghetto' – assuming these even exist (Finney & Simpson 2009): three were British-born and had higher or further education qualifications, two were married with children, and all were integrated socially and culturally into their broader community (Home Office 2006). Nevertheless, the recourse is to notions of 'parallel lives', urban segregation and community/ collective failure that draws heavily on racialized repertoires, which can be traced back through the 2001 'riots' and 'the Asian gang' of the 1990s, to the late 1970s and fears around Black (African-Caribbean) youth violence (Alexander 1996, Keith 2009, Hussain 2013).

The slippage between the individual, the community and a wider putative religious, ethnic or racial identity has been an enduring feature of the portrayal of ethnic minorities in Britain, and particularly of young men (Alexander 2004a, 2006, 2014, 2016), as can be seen, above, in the aftermath of the 2001 riots. The idea of 'community sentencing' is both very clear and particularly problematic in relation to the figure of the Muslim 'extremist/terrorist', who stands at once as the embodiment of individual anomie/agency and collective pathology – or what Michael Gove referred to as the 'swamp' in which extremist 'crocodiles' were said to swim (Duggan 2014). This ambiguity is clear in the official report on the 2005 bombings to the House of Commons, which described the background of the bombers as 'largely unexceptional' – 'Little distinguishes their formative experiences from those of many others of the same generation, ethnic origin and social background'. The three Pakistani-descent bombers, Khan, Tanweer and Hussain, grew up in Beeston, Leeds, which the report describes as 'deprived ... but there is little to distinguish it from many poorer areas of Britain's other big cities' (Home Office 2006: 13). While the report strives to de-sensationalize the events and the perpetrators, it nevertheless reflects an uneasy, and seemingly irresolvable, tension between positioning the attackers as both a part of and apart from their ethnic, social, cultural and religious milieu – as at once 'unexceptional' and yet capable of extreme and exceptional violence. The question of 'why these?' too easily becomes 'if these, then why not others, or why not all?'

This syllogistic fallacy seems to be the cornerstone of the government's counter-terror strategy, which positions all Muslims as part of one homogeneous 'suspect community'. Where this maps onto older understandings of race and ethnicity – as with the focus on South Asian communities in urban or peri-urban contexts – this has facilitated the surveillance and criminalization of whole communities, as with the spycams affair (Hussain 2013) or the 'Trojan Horse' furore (Miah 2017), both in Birmingham (and not coincidentally, perhaps, Britain's largest ethnic minority-majority city). The rolling out of the Home Office Prevent Strategy in public services, prisons, schools and universities, and across the charity sector, serves to criminalize British Muslims and has been heavily criticized as both discriminatory and counter-productive (Cohen & Tufail 2017) – tantamount to what Kundnani describes as 'racial and religious profiling' (2014). The targeting of individuals 'at risk of radicalisation' (Home Office 2011: 6) becomes inseparable from broader concerns around community integration and cultural difference. The Home Office Prevent Strategy, published in 2011 thus asserts that its success 'depends on a successful integration strategy' (Home Office 2011: 6). As Cohen and Tufail note (2017), the Prevent duty on public authorities exactly mirrors the language of the public sector 2010 equality duty, seemingly oblivious to the incompatibility of these two obligations. Or, perhaps, the Home Office is simply being ironic – as in the wielding of 'fundamental British values' to deny basic human and legal rights to Muslims, or the championing of free speech to no-platform Islamic events in Universities, or to encourage supposedly self-segregating, traditional, culture-deficient parents to surveil their (too globally wired, too modern, too tech-savvy) children's internet usage. Indeed, the elimination of 'Googling While Muslim' (as my friend Wendy Bottero evocatively terms it) is a key plank in the Prevent Strategy.

The undergirding principle of Prevent comes straight out of the Black-Youth-In-Crisis handbook – the reification of ethno-racial community, and the assertion of cultural conflict and inter-generational identity crisis (CCCS 1982, Alexander 2006, 2014). The Strategy asserts – ignoring the vast swathe of research and writing that poses a counterpoint –

> Some recent academic work suggests ... that some second or third generation Muslims in Europe, facing apparent or real discrimination and socio-economic disadvantage, can find in terrorism a 'value system', a community and an apparently just cause. We note that organisations working on Prevent have also found evidence to support the theory that *identity and community are essential factors in radicalisation.*
>
> (Home Office 2011: 18, my emphasis)

This version of ethno religious community and identity crisis draws directly on older incarnations of 'the gang' and offers the illusion of legibility and control, of 'placing' the individual in a cultural framework with bounded and knowable features, located geographically and visibly distinct (skin, beard, dress). Nevertheless, the figure of 'the terrorist/ extremist' offers some uncomfortable challenges to this discourse, not least in exceeding the boundaries of ethnicity or race (as with the July 2005 bombers), and their insertion into complex trans- and multi-national pathways of political and ideological mobilization (Bhatt 2013, Hussain 2013, 2014). Even within the UK, the contours of the British Muslim community are diversifying (Alexander, Redclift & Hussain

2013). While religion featured for the first time in the 2001 Census, the inclusion of the category 'Arab' for the first time in 2011 suggests a recognition that the previous ethnic classifications of Pakistani and Bangladeshi were no longer sufficient to address the question of who and where Britain's Muslims are (Jivraj & Simpson 2015) – and where the possible threat might lie. It is worth noting, for example, that the 2017 Manchester Arena bomber was a local man of Libyan descent. As Abbas (2019) has also noted, this concern has been reinforced and conflated in recent years with the migrant and Syrian refugee crisis.

Recent years have also seen a re-gendering of the figure of the 'terrorist/extremist'. As noted above, Muslim women have most often been seen either as the victims or the perpetuators of backward patriarchal cultures, reflected in the ongoing obsession about forced marriage, Muslim women's bodies (FGM) and dress (from burkhas to burkhinis) (Rashid 2016, 2017). The rush to 'save' Muslim women from 'brown men' has forged an unholy alliance of politicians, (white) feminists and the far right (Bhattacharyya 2008), while failing to engage with Muslim women themselves. More recently, however, and particularly with the case of Shamima Begum and her fellow 'jihadi brides' from Tower Hamlets who left to join ISIS in Syria in 2015 (Shackle 2016), there has been the withdrawal of even this opportunistic and neo-Orientalist paternalism. Boris Johnson's 'bankrobber' and 'letterbox' jibes are a clear indication of the shift in perspective; more stark is the denial of citizenship to Begum's children and the (possibly illegal, probably lethal and certainly inhumane) abandonment of Begum herself, and other young women, by the British government (Dearden 2019b).

Meanwhile, the consequences of such everyday Islamophobia are endured by its victims, very often Muslim women – Tell Mama, for example, reported that the week after Boris Johnson's 'Ninja' and 'letterbox' comments saw a 375 per cent increase in the numbers of hate crimes reported against Muslims – while its perpetrators wield the dual defence of 'free speech' and 'humour' (Telegraph Reporters 2018). Some joke.

Grooming Gangs: Gender, Culture and Ethnicity

If the 'Muslim extremist/terrorist' reflects the dominant reincarnation of 'the Asian gang', but also reconfigures it in significant ways, the conventional tropes associated with 'the Asian gang' – ethno-cultural, gendered and generational dysfunction and societal threat – can be traced in a more recent moral panic: the 'grooming gang'. The 'grooming gang' hit the headlines in January 2011 with the case of Rotherham, although there are less well-publicized cases of sexual exploitation of teenage girls, where the perpetrators were mainly South Asian, reported as far back as 2005 (Gill & Harrison 2015). In 2014, in response to the Jay Report on Rotherham, Channel 4 News claimed that there were twenty-seven such cases from 2005 to 2013, concentrated particularly in the northern former milltowns, but also in Derby (2010), Telford (2012), Ipswich (2013), Oxford (2013) and Peterborough (Worrall 2014) – areas with relatively small South Asian communities. It was, however, an article in *The Times* by journalist Andrew Norfolk in January 2011, on 'on-street grooming' in Rotherham, which proved decisive in framing the 'grooming gang' moral panic. Norfolk wrote,

> For more than a decade, child protection experts have identified a repeated pattern of sex offending in towns and cities across northern England and the Midlands involving groups of older men who groom and abuse vulnerable girls aged 11 to 16 after befriending them on the street.
>
> (*The Times* 2011)

The article continues 'Most of the victims are white and most of the convicted offenders are of Pakistani heritage', and points to a 'culture of silence' around the 'criminal pimping gangs' due to 'fear of being branded racist' (*The Times* 2011). The sense of wider societal threat and conspiracy was underscored the following May, 2012, when nine Pakistani-descent men were convicted of sex trafficking and rape of underage girls in the neighbouring Greater Manchester town of Rochdale.

The cases of Rochdale and Rotherham provide the parameters for the 'grooming gang' folk devil, coalescing fears around race, (inter-racial) sex, secrecy and institutional fear/paralysis which have come to define 'grooming' as an 'Asian/Muslim' crime. The framing of these events follows the course of a classic moral panic (Cohen 1980): the role of the media in the definitional/inventory stage (Asian perpetrators, white victims, child abuse, institutional fear/conspiracy); prediction (as with later cases in Newcastle or Huddersfield) or retrospective classification (as in the twenty-seven cases identified by Channel 4 above); and symbolization (particularly through the physical signification of racial difference) (Gill & Harrison 2015). It continues through the intervention of agents of social control and moral entrepreneurs (the police and criminal justice system, the commissioning of official reports, such as the 2014 Jay Report and the 2016 Casey Review, both on Rotherham and on the role of MP Sarah Champion). Finally it leads to its broader social ramifications, including the redefinition of child sexual exploitation (CSE) (Cockbain 2013), the use of deportation to strip convicted offenders of their citizenship (Home Office) (McCann 2018) and the ongoing intensification of Islamophobic rhetoric and violence (notably by the EDL and Tommy Robinson).

It is significant that 'on-street grooming', or 'grooming', is not a distinct criminal offence but is a subset of CSE (Cockbain 2013). Like 'mugging' before it, however, the term has come to stand for a very particular, 'street-based' crime (and the idea of 'the street' is itself always-already highly racialized) (Hall et al 1978), which is inseparable from the perceived race/ethnicity of the perpetrator (Cockbain 2013, Gill & Harrison 2015, Cockbain & Tufail 2020). This works to 'define out' similar crimes where the perpetrators are white (or the victims are non-white) and reinforces the association of 'grooming gangs' with South Asian men. As Ella Cockbain argues, the Child Exploitation and Online Protection Centre's (2013) assessment of CSE reflects this definitional circularity, distinguishing between two types of group-based abuse: type 1 (community based or 'localized grooming' which targets vulnerable victims) and type 2 (abusers with a long-standing interest in abuse of children [paedophile 'rings']). She notes that this division itself reflects the role of the media in shaping the official response to CSE definitions, and works to carve out 'grooming gangs' from broader societal patterns of sexual abuse (much like 'honour killings' are distinguished from domestic violence). Based on data from police and children's services, and excluding familial, peer-on-peer, professional or online abuse from the definition of Type 1 offences, the report found that, where ethnicity was known (31 per cent of cases), 46 per cent were South Asian and 49 per cent white. Nevertheless, the Channel 4 ironically named 'FactCheck', asserts, 'According to the best available data, Asian men make up 75 per cent of "Type 1" group abusers, who target children and young women because they are vulnerable' (Lee 2017). A similar report from the Office of the Children's Commissioner in 2012 similarly showed disproportionate representation of Asians in the statistics for CSE in England, at 33 per cent (compared to 45 per cent of white offenders), but was limited to offenders acting in groups (Berelowitz et al 2012), and only focused on limited geographical areas (Cockbain 2013).

If the data is, as Cockbain asserts of the OCCE report, 'often confused and incoherent, exacerbating methodological shortcomings and understandable data deficiencies' (2013: 27), it is also largely irrelevant, except in its purpose of reinforcing existing 'confirmation bias' (2013: 28). Indeed, the belief in an 'Asian model' of CSE transcends the inconvenience of mere facts through an appeal to longer-standing colonial ideas of Asian/Orientalist/Muslim sexual predation and threat (Said 1978, Bhattacharyya 2008, Salter & Dagistanli 2015, Tufail & Poynting 2016). This can be clearly seen in the media coverage following the *Independent Enquiry into Child Sexual Exploitation in Rotherham*, otherwise known as the Jay Report, published in August 2014. The report estimates that over 1400 children were victims of CSE in the period 1997–2013, and points to a systemic collective failure by the police, social services and the borough council to protect vulnerable children, particularly those in the care system. The report states, carefully:

> In a large number of the historic cases in particular, most of the victims in the cases we sampled were white British children, and the majority of the perpetrators were from minority ethnic communities.

(p 35)

The report argues later, however, in the section on 'Issues of Ethnicity', that 'there is no simple link between race and child sexual exploitation, and across the UK the greatest numbers of perpetrators of CSE are white men' (p91). As Waqas Tufail has noted (2015), only one of the Report's fifteen Recommendations mentioned race or ethnicity, and in the vaguest of terms: 'The issue of race should be tackled as an absolute priority *if* it is a significant factor in the criminal activity of organised child sexual abuse in the Borough' (p118, my emphasis). It is worth reflecting on the use of the conditional conjunction 'if' in this sentence. Nevertheless, it was this speculative 'Recommendation' which formed the core of the media frenzy that followed, with the report both being seized on for 'proof' of the role of ethnicity and attacked for its 'whitewashing' of the issues (Tufail 2015).

The issue of race and ethnicity is central to the construction of the 'grooming gang' folk devil in three ways: first, in the opposition of Asian (male) perpetrators and white (female) victims; second, as a way of attacking anti-racism, multiculturalism and 'political correctness' and promoting Islamophobic discourse and practice; third, through the focus on 'culture' as central to facilitating the abuse. Each of these facets spotlights ethnicity/religion/race as the overarching framework, while rendering other explanations invisible or irrelevant. As the Jay Report notes, the focus on white British girls has erased the victimization of South Asian women and girls, a pattern repeated in the Rochdale case (Cockbain 2013, Salter & Dagistanli 2015, Cockbain & Tufail 2020). Jay records a pre-history of abuse amongst the Pakistani community in Rotherham which was similarly ignored by relevant agencies, although the report falls back on problematic culturalist narratives of silencing and the need for female 'empowerment' in addressing these issues, effectively 'blaming the victims' for the spread of the abuse outside of the 'community' (2014: 95). At the same time, the 'grooming gang' has legitimated a toxic public and political rhetoric, attacking South Asian/Muslim communities as a whole, under the guise of 'speaking out' about uncomfortable truths stifled by the multicultural mantras of political correctness. Rotherham MP, Sarah Champion, then Shadow Minister for Women and Equalities, was forced to resign after writing in *The Sun* newspaper in 2017:

> Britain has a problem with British Pakistani men raping and exploiting white girls … For too long we have ignored the race of these abusers and, worse, tried to cover it up. No more. These people are predators and the common denominator is their ethnic heritage.
>
> (Swinford & McCann 2017)

Champion's words echo the rhetoric of Far Right groups, such as the English Defence League, whose leader, Tommy Robinson, was jailed in July 2019 for breaching reporting restrictions during the prosecution of a Huddersfield 'grooming gang' in Leeds, during which he launched an hour-long tirade against 'rape jihad gangs' and called for 'vigilante action' (Dearden 2019c). Far-right groups, like National Action, have formed an uneasy alliance with white feminists in the name of 'protecting' (white) women and children against the Muslim predator threat. A report by the government agency, Commission for Countering Extremism in October 2019, argued that 'grooming gangs' were used as a key recruitment tool at local marches, focusing on the threat as exclusively linked to 'Muslims' (Dearden 2019d; see also Gill & Harrison 2015).

More significant, and perhaps more worrying, is the way in which the idea of 'grooming gangs' as a specifically and uniquely Asian/Muslim phenomenon has been mainstreamed in the media and political discourse, most notably through the appeal to entrenched, 'commonsense' ideas of cultural difference. In the aftermath of the Rochdale case in 2012, then Children's Minister, Tim Loughton, asserted that 'It is important that we do not shy away from difficult issues around culture' (in Bingham 2012) and that 'closed communities' had allowed the offences to go unreported (Doyle 2012). Meanwhile, former Home Secretary Jack Straw, whose 2006 comments on Muslim 'veils' had already proved controversial, used the Rochdale sex abuse case to suggest that the abusers were simply young men 'fizzing and popping with testosterone' who were unable to find an 'outlet' with girls from their own community. *The Telegraph* quotes Straw:

> These young men are in a western society, in any event, they act like any other young men, they're fizzing and popping with testosterone, they want some outlet for that, but Pakistani heritage girls are off-limits ...
>
> So they then seek other avenues and they see these young women, white girls who are vulnerable, some of them in care ... who they think are easy meat.
>
> (Prince 2012)

Leaving aside the many jaw-droppingly problematic aspects of Straw's account – from the dismissal of sexual abuse and rape as natural youthful high spirits or natural male sexual appetite, or the misrepresentation of the abusers as young single men, or the assumption that Muslim women were somehow to blame for denying sexual access/rights to 'their' men, to the denigration of the victims as 'easy meat' – the focus on culture works to collectively construct South Asian masculinities as sexually deviant, and as distinct, from, and incapable of dealing with, the (seemingly natural) sexual freedoms of the West (Salter & Dagistanli 2015). In perhaps the most surreal intervention in the discussion, Tudor- historian-turned-gang-expert David Starkey was reported as stating that the abusers were 'acting within their cultural norms' – 'entrenched in the foothills of the Punjab or wherever it is' – and that they were insufficiently inculcated in the history and culture of England (Paton 2012). This religio-culturalist explanation was further legitimated by controversial 'counter-extremism' thinktank the Quilliam Foundation in their report on 'Grooming Gangs', published in 2017, which argued, 'the majority of these offenders are of *Pakistani origin with Muslim heritage*' and 'goes on to discuss and analyse these *cultural and religious contexts* in order to explain why this demographic features so prominently in this specific crime' (Gibbs 2022, my emphasis).

As with the terrorist folk devil, the 'grooming gang' conjures the spectre of absolute cultural difference, which slips easily from the individual to the group to the 'community'. 'Community' here, in particular, layers ethnicity with place: it is significant that the 'grooming gang' moral panic takes shape in the same communities which after the 2001 'riots' were defined through discourses of self-segregation and cultural alienation. These discourses were rehearsed anew in the 2016 Casey Review of 'Opportunity and Integration' in 'isolated and deprived communities', which were themselves defined, with circular logic, as those marked by immigration, segregation (viewed exclusively through the lens of ethnicity/religion) and exclusion. Casey notes the 'worrying' perpetuation of 'cultural and religious practices in communities that are not only holding some of our citizens back but run contrary to British values and sometimes our laws' (2016: 5). She positions women and children as 'the targets of these regressive practices', before, 'reluctantly', placing 'some communities under the spotlight – particularly communities in which there are high concentrations of Muslims of Pakistani and Bangladeshi heritage' (2016: 5). As with 'the terrorist' there is a conflation of nationality, ethnicity, race and religion, and slippage from Pakistani through Asian to 'Muslim', from 'culture' to 'religion' – a terminological flexibility that facilitates the seamless inclusion of other 'grooming gang' incidents involving diverse immigrant (e.g. Romanian and Albanian 'grooming gangs') and non-Asian Muslim groups.

Re-Raceing the Gang: Black Youth, Knife Crime and County Lines

Meanwhile, back in the city, 'the gang' re-emerged in an earlier re-racialized form, as a retro-pastiche of 'the mugger'. As I argued earlier (2000), 'the Asian gang' was itself built on a series of commonsense assumptions about Black youth, from the 1970s onwards, which brought together ideas of raced, gendered and classed dysfunction and threat, intricately bound to ideas of the urban and the street, where racialized youth were (un)imaginatively located (Hall et al 1978, Keith 2009). Where 'the mugger' individualized social marginalization and criminalized resistance, 'the Asian gang', and its post-Millennial update, collectivized the threat and linked it explicitly to ideas of 'culture'. This was, in turn, to shift the focus from social structure to cultural difference (envisioned as discrete and, often, opposed causalities), and from 'race' and racism to ethnicity and identity.

Through the 1970s and until the late 1980s, Black (African-Caribbean) youth were the face of Britain's public enemy, while Asian youth were largely viewed as unproblematic or invisible – at least as far as wider society was concerned. However, these roles were reversed from the late 1980s, as the focus turned to unassimilable Asians, and riotous Muslims. With the growing concern over Asian/Muslim youth through the 1990s, Black youth were publicly (at least) rehabilitated and integrated into (partial) Britishness (Alexander 1996, 2018). Where Asians were positioned as anachronistic, inward-looking and traditional, Black Britons were embraced as hypermodern, trans-Atlantically networked and at the cutting edge of cultural identity and cultural production (Alexander 2002).

This new, and superficially positive, visibility worked to deny entrenched forms of inequality and discrimination confronting Black British communities, in education, employment and, particularly, in the criminal justice system, where Black young men remain over-represented (Phillips & Bowling 2017, Williams & Clarke 2018, Byrne et al 2020, Wallace 2023). The New Labour promise of post-Millennial racial equality enshrined in the Macpherson Report (1999) and the Race Relations Amendment Act (2000) has remained largely unfulfilled. Despite the unprecedented presence of Black people in national culture and institutions – including government, media, sport and, latterly, the monarchy – the everyday lives of the majority of Black British youth in the first two decades of the Millennium have been blighted by institutional neglect, at best. At worst, they have been subject to increasingly stringent forms of organizational surveillance and control, from the waxing and waning of avowedly discriminatory stop and search policies and the setting up of gang risk registers (Williams & Clarke 2018) to the establishment of metal detectors and police in schools (Joseph-Salisbury 2020). As the recent Windrush scandal has made apparent, the citizenship of Black Britons remains as precarious as their South Asian Muslim counterparts – subject to the 'hostile environment', citizenship stripping, state-sanctioned violence, imprisonment and deportation (De Noronha 2020). At the same time, Black communities have become increasingly diverse, both through the exponential growth of mixed-race families (Joseph-Salisbury 2018) and new forms of migration, particularly from Africa (Shankley, Hanneman & Simpson 2020), transforming the category of 'Black youth' even as it envelops them into pre-existing stereotypes, policies and practices.

This iterative and centripetal process is clearly apparent in the re-emergence of 'the gang' in the mid-2000s, and its more recent incarnation in the moral panic around 'knife crime', 'postcode wars' and 'county lines'. It is perhaps significant that where the 'Asian' in 'The Asian gang' was a necessary ethnic qualifier, the ethno-racial signifier of 'the gang' remains implicit – and implicitly unnecessary. As with 'the mugger' beforehand (Hall et al 1978), the terminology of 'the gang' was always already racially designated, drawing upon long-standing and commonsense understandings of Black youth identity and crisis (CCCS 1982, Alexander 1996, 2016). As with mugging too, these racialized discourses are imported, largely wholesale, from the United States, where they are inextricably linked to ideas of the urban/ghetto, the underclass, crime and violent inter- and intra-ethnic conflict (Alexander 2008). In fact, in 2009, then Conservative Shadow Home Secretary Chris Grayling was reported as claiming that 'in many parts of British cities ... *The Wire* has become a part of real life' importing a 'culture of deprivation, harm, addiction and failure' and creating 'a nightmare of drugs, gangs and organised crime' (Watt & Oliver 2009).

The moral panic around 'gangs' can be traced in two main, but connected, phases – from 2007 to 2008, in which the trope of 'the gang' was central, and again in 2017 to the current time, with a focus on knife crime (Mason 2019), postcode wars and, latterly, 'county lines' drugs gangs. Central to both is the focus on Black (male) youth identities, and on the seemingly inextricable matrix of raced, gendered and generational dysfunction that this embodies.

The first phase of the post-Millennial 'gang' moral panic reached its peak in 2007–8, and was focused largely on London. The year 2007 had seen the deaths of twenty-seven teenagers in London from gun and knife crime; the following year saw a rise to thirty teenage deaths – mainly racialized minority young men, with a majority from African and African-Caribbean backgrounds. A now-defunct website by Citizens Report UK counted 152 teenage murders in London alone between 2005 and 2013. Central to the reporting of these deaths was the idea of 'the gang'. Take, for example, eighteen-year-old Henry Bolombi, who had, according to *The London Paper*, arrived in 2002, having 'fled war torn Congo in search of a safer life in Britain' (Summers 2008). Henry was the first stabbing victim of 2008, murdered in the early hours of New Year's Day. The *Daily Mail* heralded Henry as the victim of a 'vicious *"postcode war"* between rival London *gangs*' ('London's gang wars claim the first teenage victim of 2008' (2008), my emphasis). It was reported further that Henry, also known as 'Black H', had a series of convictions for robbery and assault using knives and was the leader of a 'gang' labelled variously in the press as the 'Cage boys', 'the Africa Boys' (*Evening Standard* 2012) or '123' ('Teenager is stabbed to death on busy street' (2008)). The *Daily Mail* was quick to place the death as part of 'The knife and gun crime wave … thought to be centred around rival teenage gangs fighting for territory in deadly acts of violence' ('London's gang wars claim the first teenage victim of 2008' (2008)).

'The gang' then becomes a baseline for understanding the deaths – it functions as both motif and motive – the perpetrators of violence are almost always described as 'a gang' and the victims themselves are assumed to be members of 'a gang' or at least participants in a seemingly ubiquitous, if ill-defined, 'gang culture'. Attributions of 'gang' membership, linked to highly racialized and classed ideas of the 'inner city', thus link to questions of 'culture', which fuse youth culture with broader notions of Black cultural dysfunction, centred on family failure and hyper-masculinity. Press coverage of teenage murders throughout 2007 and 2008 point to websites, 'tags', musical tastes and photos as signs of 'gang association', irrespective of broader proof. Clearly to be young, male and Black is enough.

While the definition of 'the gang' remains elusive and contested (Alexander 2008), the term has become inseparable from race. In April 2007, Tony Blair stated: 'The black community ... need to be mobilised in denunciation of this gang culture that is killing innocent black kids. But we won't stop this by pretending it isn't young black kids doing it' (in 'Blair action pledge on gang culture' (2007)). As with the 'community sentencing' of Muslim communities, the slippage between 'Black kids', 'gangs', 'criminal cultures' and 'the Black community' serves to collectivize the problem as one specific to, arising from and potentially encompassing, the Black community as a whole. Or, as the *Daily Express* captioned it, 'Black kids to blame for Knife and Gun Murders, says Blair' (Hall 2007).

As with the 'grooming gang', 'the gang' passed swiftly from media fantasy to policy reality. In May 2007, the Metropolitan Police Service (MPS) published a 'Response to Guns, Gangs and Knives in London', which identified 171 active 'gangs' in London, which estimated that 50 per cent of their identified 'gangs' were African/Caribbean, and the majority of others from racialized minority backgrounds. This was followed by a sharp increase in police activity across a number of cities and with a range of targeted interventions involving schools and social services. In February and again in August 2007, first Tony Blair and then Gordon Brown convened 'emergency summits' around gangs and gun crime, with the government announcing 'a three point plan' focusing on policing, courts and community prevention ('Three-point plan to tackle gun crime' (2007)). In September, Home Secretary Jacqui Smith announced a £1 million 'Tackling Gangs Action Programme' launched the following year, which established a dedicated national 'gang' unit focused on 'hotspots' – London, Greater Manchester, Liverpool and Birmingham – all, not coincidentally, urban areas with a large Black population (Stratton & Agencies 2008). The following year saw the extension of stop-and-search powers (Wintour 2008), while the use of 'joint enterprise' in 'gang-related' convictions, particularly for Black and Asian men, has grown exponentially across this period (Williams & Clarke 2016, 2018).

The 'gang' issue continued to expand across the noughties and beyond. A report in 2009 by Conservative thinktank the Centre for Social Justice estimated in a study called 'Dying to Belong' that somewhere between 20,000 and 50,000 teenagers were members of violent gangs. In 2011, the Home Office invested over eight million pounds in the 'Communities against Guns, Gangs and Knives' programme. The government website also provides handy hints on recognizing whether your child is in a gang – which includes being withdrawn, having a new nickname, using new slang or hand gestures, changing their clothes to look like their friends and 'tagging' schoolbooks (Home Office 2013). Or what I think of as being a teenager.

The 'raceing' of 'the gang' raises a number of problems. First, it collectively implicates and criminalizes all Black young men and, as noted above, the whole Black community. Second, it reduces the complex ethnic profile of the violence – which in 2007 included white, Asian, mixed-race and Turkish victims and perpetrators – to a simple one-dimensional attribute of 'Blackness'. Third, the focus on race homogenizes 'the Black community', erasing differences between African, Caribbean and Black British experiences, and eliding any distinctions between new migrant or second- or third-generation communities. What binds these disparate individuals, groups and events together is 'the fact of blackness', to use Fanon's (1967) powerful term, naturalizing and essentializing issues that beg a more nuanced social, political and historical understanding.

A second significant feature of 'the gang' is the conflation of 'race' and 'culture'. Culture here functions as the default explanation for the violence blurring ideas of culture as a way of life, culture as a form of production and consumption, culture as identity and culture as ethnicity/community. All are primarily defined through notions of deviance, of pathology and of failure. This is most clearly apparent in the criminalization of Black youth cultural forms from rap and hip-hop to garage to grime and, most recently, drill music. The focus on youth cultural production works to position 'urban youth' as a threat to wider British society – as spreading out from the inner city to suburban (implicitly white) youth. This idea of Black culture as infection or epidemic can be clearly seen in David Starkey's inciteful *Newsnight* comments in the wake of the 2011 'riots':

> The whites have become black. A particular sort of violent destructive, nihilistic gangster culture has become the fashion and black and white boys and girls operate in this language together. This language which is wholly false, which is this Jamaican patois that has been intruded in England and that is why so many of us have this sense of literally of a foreign country.
>
> (Quinn 2011)

As Starkey's comments suggest, the understanding of youth violence as an urban phenomenon inseparable from race has now formed a new common sense, which has entrenched the idea of 'the gang' at the heart of political rhetoric and policy practice in policing, education and criminal justice. In recent years, as Ian Joseph and Anthony Gunter have argued in their Runnymede publication, *Gangs Revisited: What's a Gang and What's Race Got to Do with It?* (2011), the proliferating 'gang industry' has naturalized this discourse to such an extent that it has proved impossible to imagine urban youth outside of the 'gang' framework. More seriously, it hinders attempts to effectively tackle problems of youth violence without recourse to racialized stereotypes, particularly in relation to the disproportionate impact on Black young men themselves – as victims and perpetrators, or, indeed, simply as (the majority of) young people socializing, hanging around or doing nothing 'on road'.

The ubiquitous power of 'gang' discourse can be traced in its most recent incarnation, in the moral panic around knife crime, post-code wars and county lines, which has dominated the deadlines particularly since 2017. Headlines in 2019 suggest that this year saw a peak in knife crime (Badshah 2019), although it should be noted that knife crime was only recorded by the police as a separately identified offence since 2008 (Grimshaw & Ford 2018) – a policy innovation itself linked to the 'gang' crisis. Despite the fact that there is no statistically significant link between ethnicity and carrying a weapon (Brennan 2018, Mason 2019) and that a key driver of knife crime was most closely linked to poverty and deprivation rather than race and ethnicity (Mason 2019), the crime itself remains indelibly racially marked. As Gary Younge argued in 2018, following the *Guardian*'s year-long analysis of knife crime, *Beyond the Blade*:

> Almost every time the term 'knife crime' appeared in the national press last year … it was referring to black kids in London … So the term is not used to describe all crimes committed with knives, just those where young black men in London are involved. Much like 'mugging' once only denoted black street crime and 'street grooming' only refers to Asian sexual predators, 'knife crime' is a racialized construct.
>
> Working on the assumption that gangs – another term generally reserved for black kids – are driving the rise in knife crime, politicians tend to call for stiffer sentences and tougher laws, and target cultural expressions most popular with black youth …
>
> Still, if we are talking about 'knife crime in Britain', it cannot be reduced to race and culture in the capital – but very often has been. Half of the children killed by knives in Britain are not in London; of those, only around 15% have been black in the last decade. Indeed, taken as a whole, two-thirds of the young people killed by knives in Britain, including London, are not black.
>
> (Younge 2018)

Despite efforts to reframe knife crime as a 'public health issue' (Younge 2019), the myth of 'the gang' has proved unsurprisingly enduring and adaptable. Indeed, the attempt to frame the issue more broadly has, ironically, reinforced the idea of 'the gang' as a form of infection. Take, for example, the report in the *Daily Mail* in 2016, which announced the arrival of 'supergangs': 'The drug lords of Middle England: London's most feared criminal gangs invade England's green and pleasant shires' (Dowling 2016). Quoting both this article and Younge's argument that the 'knife crime crisis is national' as proof, a teacher-training site, asking, 'how can we address gang culture in schools?' asserts:

> the gang 'crisis is no longer an urban issue ... the Super Gangs have invaded ... All students are now at risk either as victims, as perpetrators or both.
>
> (Warner 2018)

The Afterlives of 'the Asian gang'

Over two decades into the new Millennium, it seems 'the gang' has lost none of its power to thrill our imagination and chill our policymaking and practice. Indeed, the crucible of fears around race and ethnicity, masculinity and youth, spiced with newer (and older) elements of religious terror and (under)classed entropy, has proved remarkably resilient to the passage of time, the by-now-mundane presence of generations of Black and Asian people, and the presentation of decades of empirical evidence to the contrary. Itself a staging post for a longer narrative of racial, national and post-imperial crisis, the spectral presence of 'the Asian gang' can be easily traced into the current moment, with little or no change in the intervening twenty-plus years. Less a 'zombie category' than Frankenstein's monster, the Black youth folk devil has retained its use as a way of constructing, categorizing and controlling successive generations of Black and Asian young men, grafting new forms onto older 'commonsense' fears around racial difference – what John Solomos and Les Back have referred to as a 'scavenger ideology' (1996).

While the idea of 'the gang' seems to go from strength to strength, with (necessarily, perhaps) only fleeting reference to the everyday lives of its putative subjects, what is less clear is how it shapes these lives. Certainly, 'the gang' continues to shape the understandings and experiences of Black and Asian British youth in a myriad of tangible ways, drawing on and reinforcing ongoing patterns of racialized and classed inequality – as discourse and practice, 'the gang' cannot simply be shrugged off or ignored. This was a key lesson of the original *Asian Gang* project, which explored the ways in which this then-new(ish) folk devil impacted the young men it supposedly captured. The book tried to show how 'the gang' constrained, but could not fully contain, the lives of these young men and how, in turn, they confronted, played with and exceeded its limit(ation)s. Very much a snapshot of a point in time, the project and book captured the stereotype and its object/ subjects at the point of encounter: Asian young men, image and counter-image.

This begs two important questions: What happened next to 'the gang' as idea, and what happened to the young men? While this chapter has attempted to sketch some routes for the former, the rest of the book is focused on the second question. It will be for others to trace the lived experiences of contemporary Black and Asian youth in the shadow of these new folk devils: this book is concerned with how it feels to grow up through, and out of, 'the gang', to come to adulthood as Asian/Muslim men against the changing backdrop of 'the gang' and its post-Millennial formations. Where Black and Asian men are most often imagined solely through the lens of youth – as if transfixed in a perpetual arrested development – this book traces the lives, loves and journeys of the original 'Asian gang' across the past two decades and as they changed from boys to men. Revisiting some of the topics of the original project – friendship and family – and exploring some new ones – work, marriage, religion – this book tells the story of what The Asian Gang Did Next.

2

Changing the Setting

Stoneleigh Estate, February 2020

Mid-morning, on a rainy and cold Saturday just before Storm Ciara was to batter London, I took a bus south of the river to the Stoneleigh Estate. Tucked out of view in a corner of a busy intersection of a number of major arteries into the City, the Estate was relatively deserted. A young woman in *niqab* pushed a buggy along Abbey Street with another small child in tow, and a couple of older Asian men with beards looked at me curiously as I snapped some photos of the local mosque. Otherwise the red brick buildings and the surrounding streets were quiet. It was my first visit back to the Estate since 2012, which was itself a fleeting trip, and I had rarely been back since I had moved out of the area in the early noughties.

On the fringes of large-scale regeneration in the borough, I was struck by how little the Estate had changed, from the outside at least, in the twenty-five-plus years since I had done the first research. The businesses along the main road at the entrance to the Estate were the familiar mix of fried chicken shops and barbers, though the new Latin American bar and Lebanese restaurant and the Polish supermarket testified to changes in the people living there. A shiny glass-fronted estate agent spoke too to some more substantial transformations to the area, and to the regeneration that bordered the Estate. On the turn-in to Abbey Street, a block of new flats, mirrored by a just-completed block at the far end of the road promising 'luxury living', suggested some attempt at gentrification at the edges. The businesses on Abbey Road itself were the same mix of old and new – the youth employment project and an Asian supermarket, both shuttered behind grills, both familiar. Adjacent, a more recently renovated whitewashed block of supermarkets, newsagents, hardware stores and another glass-fronted estate agents, sandwiched between two pubs, one stubbornly shabby, the other closed for renovation. I was delighted to see that the 'Nigerian phone box' was still in place, and still in use, though the crumbling stone wall where the 'little ones' used to sit has been replaced by an attractive walled flower bed. That time in the morning, and in February, it was not clear whether a new generation of young men, or women, spent time there, nor could I see evidence of the police surveillance camera that was in place during my earlier fieldwork.

Across the road, the old Philip Sidney primary school and the Thomas More secondary school, where the SAYO youth project had been based, had been combined into a shiny new academy school, which still sported a banner from 2018 'Celebrating 10 years of success'. While 'the mound' of the old secondary school is still visible behind the walls, the locked gates are now built on the site of the old car park, where in the mid-90s the 'older lot' were most usually to be found in their cars, smoking and listening to music. Another new block of flats, also gated and locked, takes up the rest of the site, across the road from the older red brick council blocks. Further up, and in the tiny square where the adventure playground was housed, the road is dominated by the Mosque. During my first project, it was a small, squat building, home to only several hundred of the mainly Bangladeshi local men. In the past twenty years, the Mosque has expanded, including an Islamic cultural centre and a section for women – its website claiming space for 2500 Muslims. The building is elegant, with long windows and imposing wide steps to the entrance, and stands opposite to the adventure playground, which looks shuttered and neglected in contrast – and would later be demolished.

Across Abbey Street, Gaol Park, named because of its historical connection to the local courthouse and debtors' prison, has been renovated to include a newly tarmacked basketball court and a picnic area with seating. It looks smaller than I remember – when the Asian gang boys would use it for impromptu summer cricket matches, inspired by the Cricket World Cup, or when we held a football match there during the launch for *The Asian Gang*. Or perhaps my memory is at fault. Some of the now no-longer-so-young men still meet there regularly for Saturday football, or spend time there after Friday prayers.

Abbey Street was where I mainly remember spending time with 'the Asian gang', when we were not in the youth club. The street curves NW-SE along one end of the Estate, bordering the 1930s council blocks. The estate itself is divided by two parallel streets, and the flats face inwards around paved or grassed courtyards, five or six storeys high, with narrow balconies linking the front doors. By contrast with the shiny new builds, or the elegant Edwardian terraces which flank the estate, the red brick blocks are dark and grimy, the wooden window frames chipped and splintered. The community centre looks untouched from when I was last there, two decades earlier. The morning of my visit was quiet, but it was possible to hear the sound of construction above the hum of London traffic, and it was impossible not to notice looming towers that hem the estate on three sides, including the distant shiny glass of the Shard to the East. Across the main A-road, a cluster of glass-fronted high rises speak to the massive investment that, to date, seems to have left the Stoneleigh untouched. Other estates from my first project have been demolished completely. The concrete pre-fab house that I rented from Silver for eighteen months during that time, across the road from the Stoneleigh Estate, was now a building yard, described by in 2015 as 'a shipping container village of temporary restaurants and pop-up pilates classes' (Wainwright 2015) and largely unchanged since then. The Stoneleigh Estate seems marooned within this bigger transformation; at once unchanged and at the edge of an encompassing and encroaching regeneration: an urban village (Tonkiss 2005) within the fast changing global city.

The Changing Same: A Portrait of a 'Great Estate'

Of course, change is inescapable, for the Stoneleigh and its inhabitants; and at least the Estate's distinctive red brick blocks have not been slated for demolition, unlike its more architecturally brutalist neighbours. Indeed, the Stoneleigh was recently targeted as a pilot for the 'Great Estates Programme', which will see nearly £1 million of investment across seven estates across the Borough aimed at improving the material infrastructure of the buildings. Certainly, the need for investment is clear – the Estate remains one of the most deprived areas of the Borough, which itself ranked, in 2019, 43rd out of 326 local authorities in terms of indices of multiple deprivation (although this was an improvement from its top ten position at the start of the Millennium).[1]

More Ward, where the Stoneleigh Estate sits, reflects both continuity and change: when I was doing fieldwork for my 'Asian gang' project in the mid-1990s, the Ward already had an established 'reputation for serious deprivation' (Poverty Profile 1996), and was the fifth most deprived ward in the Borough. In 2019, the Ward ranked 13th (out of 23).[2] The Ward has seen significant changes in population. In the mid-1990s, More Ward had a population of just over 9,000 people; by 2001 this had risen to over 13,000, and peaked in 2015 at 16,200.[3] A Ward Profile of 2017 estimated a population of 15,670 people, of which 50 per cent were of Black, Asian or Minority Ethnic descent (BAME) – an increase from 31 per cent at the time of my first study, and slightly above the current Borough average (45.8 per cent)[4]. Of these, the largest group is Black (23 per cent) while Asian/Asian British comprised 17 per cent (considerably above the Borough average of 9.4 per cent)[5]. About 8.5 per cent of the Borough population described themselves as Muslim. On the Stoneleigh Estate itself, over 50 per cent of the 1500 inhabitants were BAME, 14 per cent of Bangladeshi origin (a decrease from 18 per cent when I conducted my original research), and nearly a quarter self-identified as Muslim (ACN 2010).

Interestingly, the age profile of the Ward has increased over time, with over 17 per cent aged over 65 (compared to 8.3 per cent across the Borough), and a decline in the proportion of under 15s, from 20 per cent in 1991 to 14 per cent in 2018. This is a sign perhaps of the increasing influence of regeneration and new, more affluent arrivals into the area, or of a static and ageing population. The former possibility is underscored by the change in housing tenure in the past thirty years: in 1991, 75 per cent of the ward lived in social housing, and 10 per cent in private rented accommodation; by 2011 these figures were 43 per cent and nearly 30 per cent, respectively. Home ownership had nearly doubled across the same period from just over 13 per cent to nearly 26 per cent,[6] while unemployment nearly halved. The latter explanation is suggested by persistent pockets of deprivation, with 15 per cent of dependent children living in low-income households, and 16 per cent of the population classified in the most deprived quintile nationally. Between 2011 and 2018, the crime rate has decreased, but remained consistently higher than the Borough average.[7] However, given the dramatic population increase, and the increasing wealth of its newer inhabitants, the social and economic condition of the Stoneleigh Estate's longer-term residents remains opaque.

Some things have not changed however – notably the dominant representation of the Estate as marked by deprivation and social problems: the 'Great Estates' plan, for example, states that Stoneleigh 'Residents have raised concerns regarding crime and anti-social behaviour, in particular *rival youth gangs* with the [neighbouring] estate' (my emphasis)[8]. A 2010 report by Active Communities Network notes that 'the area has witnessed violent and gang related incidents, and in the past young members of the Mosque have been targeted for gang membership' (p26). 'The Gang', it seems, is a definitional constant – an unchanging same – even twenty years on.

Of course, many of the participants in the original 'Asian Gang' study never lived on the Stoneleigh Estate itself, even at the time of my research. About half of my interviewees lived on the Estate itself, while the rest lived in other parts of the Borough but were tied to the area through the local primary and secondary schools, or through family. In the past twenty-five years, most of those who had once lived on the Estate had moved out, often outside the Borough, most usually to the south and east of the City. Only one of the men I interviewed for the second project, Big Hanif, lived on the Estate, and he had moved there from his family home in a neighbouring ward comparatively recently. Nevertheless, the Estate holds a significant emotional place in their lives: many still attend the local mosque, or have parents or siblings locally; many still play football together in the area, or meet nearby to celebrate Eid and other occasions; and there are Facebook and WhatsApp groups which link the lives of the men across time and space. As will be explored in Chapter 5, Abbey Street and the Stoneleigh Estate still feature strongly in the imagination of its erstwhile denizens.

For myself, not so much. Visiting Big Hanif for an interview in 2012, I realized belatedly how significant the Estate was in shaping the experiences of the young men through the years of my study, and how this had not featured in the fieldwork itself, except as backdrop. This was partly because my time with the young men took place largely in the school and youth club, or along Abbey Street, rather than in the courtyards of the Estate itself. The interior of the Estate was the place of family and community, which I skirted, partly through choice and partly because of my own positionality – as a woman, non-Muslim, non-Bangladeshi – which made entry into those private spaces difficult. My focus was on the 'public life' of the young men, which can be rationalized, post hoc, as engaging the public discourses around 'the gang', but which also overlooked the more intimate spaces of family and how these shaped their experiences and choices. Some of these missing elements came out of the later interviews – struggles with parents or siblings, with poverty and violence, the importance of religion – in part because the young men themselves were now reflecting on these things, and in part because my relationship to the young men, and the issues, had also changed in the intervening years.

What was also apparent, though, was how their teenage years were shaped by the materiality of the Estate itself. Walking to Big Hanif's ground floor flat, in one of the courtyards, I was struck by the lack of public space between the blocks, and the way the inward-looking balconies loomed forbiddingly over any outsiders. My sense of being visible – and surveilled – was reinforced about ten minutes after I reached Big Hanif's flat. As we chatted in the kitchen while he made me tea, a Bangladeshi neighbour knocked on the door, asking for his wife (whom she had clearly seen leaving the flat on her way to college just before my arrival), and peering over Big Hanif's shoulder accusingly. While we both laughed at the absurdity of the encounter, it did make me think about what this level of surveillance would have felt like for the young people, then and now, who could not do their growing up away from the prying eyes and predeterminedly damning judgements of their families and neighbours. In fact, as became apparent in the later interviews, the young men were adept and inventive at carving out space – literal and metaphorical – for their activities away from the community, their parents, and each other (although this would have been harder, I imagine, for their sisters). This gave an additional significance to the youth club, but also made clear the bigger picture in which the club formed only a comparatively small part and which was, in hindsight, necessarily missing from the earlier study. As (little) Hanif was to comment to me about the book some years after its publication – 'I can see why you wrote it that way, but I don't think that it was *quite* right'.

After 'The Asian Gang': Endings

The project book, *The Asian Gang: Ethnicity, Identity, Masculinity*, finally appeared in the early summer of 2000. We marked the event with a launch in the hall of the Stoneleigh Estate Play Association, which sat slightly back from Abbey Street, adjacent to the Mosque. There was food and music, and most of 'the little ones' and some of the 'older lot' drifted in, though not for long enough for me to give my beautifully crafted thank you speech. We later headed across the road to Gaol Park, for an impromptu football match between the SAYO footballers and a hastily scratched-together team of some academic friends who had come for the launch and the youth workers (who, unsurprisingly, were soundly trounced). Afterwards, each of the young men were given a copy of the book. One of the little ones, Hanif, told me later that as they left, a group of older white men, outside one of the nearby pubs, had shouted racial abuse at them. He continued, laughing, 'So we went to Shafiq's house, to put the books down, because we didn't want to get them damaged, and then we came back out and beat them up'.

For me, the publication and the launch marked the end of my involvement with 'the, Asian gang' – at least as research project. Or, perhaps *an* ending – one of several, in fact. The funding, from the British Academy had ended in 1997, but my involvement with the SAYO youth project continued for at least another two years. The youth project itself was severely impacted by restructuring of the Borough's youth provision in the late 1990s and when I was writing the conclusion to the book in October 1999, all of the staff I had worked with during the research had moved on, as had most of the members. Sher Khan and Silver moved to youth projects elsewhere in London, and Yasmin later followed Silver to North London and then to work in housing in East London. My own involvement with the project was curtailed when I took up a temporary lecturing post at Southampton University. As the young men grew older, started work and college, the focus of their time shifted away from the club and the Estate, and the new cohort, I think, simply did not feel the same commitment to the project. By the time of the launch, the project had officially closed.

The closure of the youth club arose from broader, external structural changes – primarily around the defunding of statutory youth provision, coupled with a move away from dedicated provision for ethnic minorities, towards an emphasis on social cohesion. Reflecting back on the project in 2012, Silver commented:

> I think a number of things happened ... there was an impact by local people, non-Bengali people, who were saying 'what about youth provision for other young people' ... and they couldn't see the value in

it. So there was an issue around 'what about inclusion issues?' ... That coupled with the Council making strategic decisions to water down services, to find integrated ways of working, to add value.

Or as Sher Khan noted, 'Well, they say it's funding, whether that's true or not ... and it was that whole thing of "it's an Asian youth club"' (2012).

In some ways, the project also fell victim to its own success: the first Asian youth club on the Stoneleigh Estate had been established in 1988 to provide a safe space for local Bengali young women, and later young men, to address their exclusion from mainstream youth provision and their daily experience of racial violence. Through the 1990s, the discourse of 'the gang', and a series of violent confrontations between the local Bengali young men and white racists, shifted the discourse from 'need' to 'problem', with a focus more on containment and the threat being posed by the Asian young men. By the time I began my fieldwork in 1995, the reputation of the project as a place for 'troublemakers' (Hashim, interview 1996), or its members as 'corrupted' or 'bad' (S Ahmed, interview 1996) had become accepted by the local Bengali community, the wider neighbourhood, as well as the police and youth services. The project aim, as Julia, one of the original founders of the project told me in her interview in 1996, was 'just to keep them off the street' (see Alexander 2000 chapter 3).

After some troubled times, the arrival of Yasmin marked a turning point for the project, and under her direction, SAYO became an exemplar of what good youth work could be, and could achieve. The Duke of Edinburgh awards, the fashion show, the trip to Tunisia, the football project were the visible highlights of a broader, less visible network of initiatives, which supported the young men into training, further education, paid play work and developed their management skills. As Silver suggests, above, however, this high-profile work led to antagonism – often explicitly racialized – from neighbouring estates, where the provision was less ambitious and less successful. Indeed, these tensions were already apparent when I was doing my fieldwork. At the same time, it shifted the perception of the Stoneleigh Asian youth away from being a problem that needed dedicated support: a shift that coincided with the increased focus on non-statutory, targeted area-based crime prevention. Silver, who moved to a senior youth work role in another London borough, commented:

> The whole social education, the whole youth empowerment, the whole development of young people through choices and youth work model became less and less significant and targeted work, working with referral systems, working in targeted hot spot areas. Crime prevention work.
>
> (2012)

Ironically, then, the youth provision set up to engage 'troublemakers' and 'bad' boys was finally defunded and replaced by initiatives explicitly focused on crime prevention, because the young men who attended were no longer considered 'bad' enough.

Sher Khan, who had been with the project first as a volunteer, and then as a paid worker, was part of the project from its early days under Yasmin, and remained until the project formally closed. In our interview in 2012, he still felt sadness about the demise of the youth club:

> I think it's really sad, it was such a good thing, and then it just came to a total standstill … Everyone on the Stoneleigh felt it. All the kids, even the staff … it was really up there, really making positive change and everything and then suddenly a good thing came to an end and the kids had nowhere to go. So, really, it fell down a hole.

Nevertheless, both he and Silver felt that the project had made significant and enduring changes to the young men who passed through, both as workers and as members. Silver reflected:

> I think it changed their lives … It certainly changed my life … It shaped who I was. It opened my eyes to the world and gave me the opportunities, but in the same way it did for me, I think it did it for most of those young people who had the opportunity to spend a sustained amount of time with us … It shaped who they were. It challenged their thinking. It increased their aspirational levels, self-confidence, self-worth, self-value … People who lived there at the time felt it. You couldn't just speak it, you felt it.
>
> (2012)

Like Silver, Sher Khan spoke passionately about how his own life was shaped through the youth project:

> If it weren't for SAYO and that bit of voluntary work I'd done, I wouldn't be where I am today. Because today, I'm working in schools, and I'm working with young offenders, I'm working with behaviour support.
>
> (2012)

He continued:

> What did the boys get? I think they got a lot ... I think they were at that junction where they didn't know where to go .... And I think as a team and as a project we ... sort of opened up their eyes to avenues and options, and we gave them options. 'This is what you can do ...' It was a time for change for the whole Asian community, for young people to break into other fields, and I think they've done that now, in the greatest possible way ... and I think that's all because of the project .... Once it closed down, there was nothing for the next generation, and probably the next generation.

Several of the SAYO members echoed Sher Khan's sentiments. In particular, a number of the older lot, who had formed the senior management team on the project, spoke of the ways in which the youth club had shaped their aspirations. Zohar, who had worked as a volunteer youth worker and then as a play worker, joined the project's senior management team and underwent training provided by the Council:

> I used to do a bit of youth work ... and then I had to go and do all that training. And it helped, because you look back and I went ... here and there, and I enjoyed it. I thought, because I used to always help people, give back to people. I was part of that, to do something ... and I loved it ... I don't want to do anything else.
>
> (2012)

Zohar went on to work with Kickstart, and then to co-found an organization focused on empowering young people through sport. Fifteen years on, his organization is a multi-million-pound national organization, with over forty staff members and Zohar himself as chief executive. A 2010 report cites his experience of the SAYO project as formative to this work. In a conversation in July 2020 Zohar told me that the project, and its workers, had been central to his career aspirations and choices, and that he hoped that his organization would open up similar opportunities for a new generation of urban young people.

Shahin similarly spoke of the significance of the youth project in keeping him focused after he had been forced to drop out of college:

> I think the youth club helped me as well in terms of keeping focused, because, if that wasn't there, what do you do? So at least you're engaged in that … So I think without that encouragement and support, my life could have gone in a different direction, and having good people around you helps. Because obviously, like yourself, Yasmin of course, and Silver, because Silver had been to university … I don't think there were many that … nobody went to university … And he was working, and he was doing his degree at the same time. And so I remember thinking to myself, you know, that's possible. You can still maintain a part-time job and also go to university.
>
> (2012)

Mohammed, one of the little ones, who went on to study law, also commented:

> I think it definitely kept us out of trouble at one point, but I think yourself, Yasmin, you know, it was quite nice to socialize with you guys and just speak to you generally about bits and pieces. So I think it did have an effect, it was like a hub … yes, it was quite instrumental.
>
> (2012)

As Zohar noted, and will be discussed in Chapter 4, many of the youth project members went on to work in play or youth provision themselves, for shorter or longer amounts of time. Some, like Zohar or Khalid, or indeed Silver and Sher Khan, remained working in this sector, and established their own careers, while others, like Shahin, used the skills they learned and the contacts and experience they gave to move on to new areas while retaining a strong commitment to the area and the ethos of 'giving back'. In some cases, as Shahin suggests, the impact was more nebulous – opening up ways of seeing and imagining, or getting advice on universities and careers (which, in my memory, they often ignored), seeking support during encounters with the police or the courts. For others, again, the impact was probably negligible – a place to hang out, see their friends and have some fun. It would be misleading too to think of the youth club as the sole formative influence during this period. As I only realized fully later, the club was a focal point – as Mohammed calls it, a 'hub' – but it was only one of a number of spaces in which the lives of 'the Asian gang' intersected, and paused, before moving on to other places, other encounters and other times.

As Sher Khan suggests, above, the youth club always had nebulous boundaries, and the commitment of both staff and members often overspilled its official contact hours – something that was, in my later view, both a strength and a weakness. Sher Khan recalled,

> We were always there for them, whether it was daytime, night-time, we were always on the phone, you know. And because we were local, you were always going to bump into them, and if they ever needed me, I was always only at [his restaurant] and they could always pop in there, all hours.
>
> (2012)

For the youth workers, the boundaries between work and home became increasingly blurred. In the aftermath of a particularly difficult relationship break-up, which took place while I was conducting the first round of interviews, I was forced to leave, and sell, my flat, and for several weeks slept in Yasmin's living room, and spent most of my time with her at the youth project. Temporarily homeless, I then moved into a concrete pre-fab house on the edge of a neighbouring estate (now demolished), which Silver had recently bought and I furnished. When I started lecturing at Southampton and was commuting to and from the university, I would often come home, or downstairs, to find Silver and Sher Khan sat in the kitchen, chatting and smoking weed, and Sher Khan would call his restaurant and tell them to make me food (concerned, I think, about my inability to cook). The SAYO management committee would occasionally meet in the living room of the house, and I suspect Silver occasionally used the house for romantic assignations with his many girlfriends.

Perhaps inevitably, given the levels of intimacy, relationships sometimes became strained. Over time, tensions increased between members of the team, and as the project itself became more enmeshed with other organizations, such as SEPA and Kickstart, with a reorientation away from the Asian youth project towards more generic, sports-based provision, and with my new lecturing role, my own position became more marginal.

At the same time, the bonds we had built up with the project members also worked to prevent new, younger members coming through. As some staff members moved on, Yasmin recruited Shahin and Zohar to work in the project, but their position as 'older brothers' in the community made some of the little ones uncomfortable, and the next generation nervous. Ironically, perhaps, the familiarity of the project and its people eroded the sense of space and freedom that it had initially offered, replicating some of the weaknesses of its earlier incarnations (see 2000, Chapter 3). Ultimately, though, the original members grew up and moved on – 'just busy now' as Sher Khan commented – and the staff team simply seemed to run out of energy. Yasmin, in particular, who had been the driving force and vision behind the SAYO project, lost interest and, as the council cut funding, moved out of the borough and eventually out of youth work completely. As time went on, she cut ties with myself and lost contact with many of the young men, although our paths would occasionally cross at weddings. The last time I saw her, in fact, was at Zohar's wedding in 2010.

After 'The Asian Gang': Beginnings

There is a point at which ethnography ends, and becomes, simply, life. For me, the book launch marked the end of my 'formal' connection with 'the Asian gang', but not with the young men themselves. The connections that were made in the youth club, and spilled out to other settings during its final years, laid the foundations for my ongoing relationships with a number of the young men – some more constantly than others, admittedly – and it is impossible to imagine the past two-plus decades without their presence in my life. While with most, the connections have been sporadic and second-hand – with occasional catch-ups at weddings, or during Eid festivities, or when they were driving my bus home, or meeting by chance in the street, or with occasional, unexpected email requests for references – others have become entwined with my life on an everyday level.

These connections have grown, changed and, in some cases, faltered, over the past twenty years, strengthening some ties, building new ones, losing others. They are particularly linked with two sets of brothers – Ifti and Humzah, and Hanif, Khalid and Shahin – but have grown to include their wider families, including their parents, sisters, nieces, wives and now children. Although these voices do not appear in the current book – its focus remains on 'the gang' – their presence is an integral part of the stories of the young men, and of my relationship with them. They shape my understanding of the 'bigger' lives of 'the Asian gang', foregrounding aspects that were hidden or overlooked in the original project, and which we revisited second time around, with different eyes. The shift can perhaps be characterized as one from the 'public' to the 'private' lives of 'the Asian gang', from the open spaces of the street and the club to the insides of houses, from the hypervisible to the invisible.

This shift can be clearly traced too in my photo albums (now relics from the days when people still took actual photos). These early albums covered the five years I worked at the SAYO project, capturing important and mundane moments as they grew from teenagers to adults, changing hairstyles, leaving school, getting cars. Jamal once commented that these albums captured 'all the years of our growing up'. Even in these albums the portrait progressively narrows and focuses on the young men that formed the heart of the book: they carry hints too of the future pathways my relationships would take after the project ended. The later pages develop this story – they are largely made up of pictures of smiling sisters and nieces, of camera-shy mothers, of glittering sarees and salwars for Eids and weddings, of birthday cakes and candles, of little girls growing into beautiful young women, of beards and marriages and wives and, towards the end, a new generation. They are, most often, pictures of interiors, of home, of family.

While they tell part of a story, this is a highly selective and episodic one – it gestures towards a longer and deeper relationship, but it also elides some of the more difficult moments that these journeys encountered. This was particularly true of my relationship with Ifti, Humzah and their family, whose presence in my life was dominant in the early years after the closure of the SAYO project, but which became increasingly distanced, apart from two important and precious ongoing connections, with Humzah and Ana (Ifti's wife).

I first met the eldest of Humzah and Ifti's sisters, Tahiya, very early on in my 'Asian gang' project during the brief life of the *Salam Bhano* project, the sister-project to the original *Salam Bhayo* project, which later became the SAYO youth club. Tahiya was one of the original members of the project, along with Sayeed's older sister, Sultana, and one of the most regular attendees. I remember her as quiet and reserved, though not unfriendly. At that time the family still lived on the Stoneleigh – indeed, their father, along with Zohar's father, had been one of the earliest arrivals to the area. The family moved in 1995, a short time into my fieldwork, when Tahiya and her younger sister, Tasnim, were victims of a racist attack outside a local doctor's surgery on Abbey Street. The event caused shock in the Bengali community on the Estate – in fact, I think the first time I plucked up courage to speak to Humzah was to express my sympathies to him and his family after the attack. The family were moved, for their protection, from their small flat on the Stoneleigh to a new three-storey, five-bedroomed Housing Association property about fifteen minutes away from the Estate. Curious about the women who were an increasing part of her sons' lives, Humzah and Ifti's mother invited Yasmin and me to visit quite soon after they moved in. I remember clearly sitting in the boys' bedroom with the brothers and sisters watching a Bollywood film when some former neighbours – three elderly Bangladeshi women – arrived to see the house. They entered the bedroom without knocking, opened all of the cupboards, exclaiming loudly about the mess, and then told

Humzah that he was not properly dressed (in a T-shirt and jeans). I think I gaped. Humzah simply shrugged.

Their mother, who was only five years older than I was, later asked me if I could help Ifti with his schoolwork, and I became a regular visitor to the house. Ifti, however, was always a reluctant student, and he would contrive to find things to distract me – music, films, gossip – and I, never a natural teacher, was happy to go along with his plans. We soon gave up any pretence of study and I would often drop round at weekends or evenings just to see the children. The family set up was, I think, an unusual one. The parents were largely absent – the father was often out at the mosque, and the mother spent a lot of time in her room, or with neighbours. The children, four girls and three boys in total, seemed to function largely autonomously, rarely spending time with either parent. The older girls, Tahiya, Tasnim and Kalima, who were aged fifteen, twelve and nine when I first got to know them, were welcoming, affectionate and lively, and I soon came to spend most of my visits with them. They welcomed me partly I think as a distraction from the boredom of being at home, and partly because they thought I was rather lost. On reflection, I think perhaps they were right.

Over the next several years, I became a regular fixture in their lives. We would go to the cinema and (window) shopping in the clothes and jewellery shops on Green Street, to visit family friends, and, as they got older, out for meals on Brick Lane for Eid or for birthdays. I remember taking Tasnim and Tahiya to the South Bank for the Millennium fireworks, and regretting it, in the terrible crush of people. Once, after a particularly difficult time, when Humzah was stabbed in an altercation with some local boys, and after leaving hospital had become very depressed, I took him and the two oldest girls to Suffolk for a long weekend break – their first visit to the British seaside. More usually, however, we would sit at home and talk, while they educated me on Bollywood cinema and music (they were delighted to see my photograph with Bollywood actor Salman Khan) and on being a proper Bengali.

My original relationship with Humzah and Ifti melted into this broader familial matrix once the project ended, and I came to see quite a different side to both young men from the one they presented outside. Humzah, in particular, who was taciturn and a little forbidding when in public, was talkative and affectionate with his siblings – particularly Tasnim, with whom he was very close. In the early days, we would watch Hindi films together, with Humzah translating for me. As time went on, and the girls became independent young women, there were evident tensions, especially between Humzah and Tahiya, which often led to arguments. After his stabbing and as he grew older, Humzah was more withdrawn and often depressed, and had difficulty holding down work. He would often spend most of his time at home in his bedroom playing computer games, and was out all night with his friends. He and I became close friends over this period, and I was often employed as intermediary – sometimes the only person he would talk to when things were particularly bleak. Mostly, though, we would hang out, talking, or sit and play 'Tomb Raider' on his play station for hours on end. After I stopped going to the house, he would regularly phone or drop by and see me. After his marriage, we saw each other less often, but were – and are – still in contact, usually by phone, and more recently by email and text.

It is hard now to reflect on my relationship with Ifti in the immediate years after the project closed without it being marred by the things that happened later, and which broke all of our hearts. Ifti was one of the little ones I was closest to. As a teenager he was cheeky, confident and always, seemingly, in trouble at school and outside. Fiercely protective of his friends and family, charming and funny, Ifti seemed to have an unerring knack for being in the wrong place at the wrong time, and for always being caught out. He had a reputation as a troublemaker, even when young and even amongst his friends, and yet a seemingly inexhaustible supply of self-belief and optimism that, in his mind, made him indestructible.

Although Ifti was my initial route into the family, and was much loved by his siblings, as time went on, he was rarely at home and seemed to lead an entirely separate life outside which none of us knew much about and which he never discussed. One of the complications of his 'outside' life was brought 'home' in 1999, when Ifti became involved with a Turkish-Cypriot young woman, Ana, who fell pregnant and left home to be with him. His parents were shocked and unsupportive, even after the couple married and their son, Kerim, was born. It would be two years later, after pressure from Humzah and Tahiya, that Ana was introduced to his parents and allowed to come to the house.

It was around this time that my relationship with Ifti's family came to an end. The brothers were around less, and as the sisters had grown older they developed their own lives outside the home. As Tahiya became more independent and started work, I also discovered that she had been using me as an alibi to cover for her own activities, saying she had been with me when she had been out with friends and, later, boyfriends. While I sympathized with her desire for freedom and autonomy, I also knew this placed me – an unmarried, non-Bangladeshi, non-Muslim woman – in an extremely vulnerable position should anything be discovered or go wrong. With these shifts, and with my own work life taking up more time, I stopped visiting the house as often; on the occasions I visited, Tahiya and Tasnim were often out and eventually I withdrew completely.

I kept in contact with Ifti and Ana, however, when the couple moved into a local authority flat several miles away. At one time, stuck for several months between house moves, I rented a room in their flat, and became close to Ana and Kerim, although Ifti was rarely at home. It later became clear that Ifti had been dealing drugs for some time (see Chapter 4). For the next few years, as his relationship with Ana foundered, Ifti was in and out of jail several times, had a child with another woman and struggled with drug use. When I interviewed him in 2012, he had recently been released from his latest stint in jail and was back with Ana, with whom he had a daughter, Zahra (aged 2) and then another son, Kadir. Shortly afterwards, however, his problems with drugs resurfaced and his marriage to Ana ended badly. When I last saw him, a couple of years later on the bus, he told me he had struggled with heroin addiction and had been homeless for several months but was, he assured me with typical bravado, back on top of his game. I have not seen him since.

My relationship with Shahin, Khalid and Hanif's family started around the same time, and in the same way, as Ifti and Humzah's but could not be more different in its journey. Having heard about us from her sons, Shahin's mother invited Yasmin and I to their house for lunch a couple of years before the project closed. A widow, with two daughters who were then estranged from the family, she welcomed us immediately and we soon became regular visitors for Eid Days and other family celebrations. When Yasmin moved away from the project, she stopped visiting, so I continued to visit alone, and fell in love with the whole family. In the early days, the three brothers lived with their mother, older sister Munira, her husband and their three daughters, all in primary school. Another daughter was born a couple of years later. The extended family lived together in small three bedroomed duplex on a red brick council estate near the river – the three brothers all shared a bedroom on the ground floor – and the house was crowded and noisy and happy. The brothers were devoted to their nieces, whom Shahin referred to, affectionately, as the 'rug rats' (but I came to think of as 'the dots'). Their mother, whom I called Auntie on her insistence, was a quiet and reserved woman, who did not speak much English (although I suspected understood a lot more than she let her sons know), but was warm and caring and generous. She would show her affection through cooking mountains of amazing food and feeding any unsuspecting visitors to near-death.

After the birth of their fourth daughter, Munira and her family finally moved to their own flat nearby, and my visits were spread between the two homes. I visited regularly, especially for Eid and for birthdays, and before Christmas, and the dots would come to my house to decorate my Christmas tree and to the cinema to watch the early Harry Potter movies. Over the years, the brothers were more absent, as they went to college and university, or were at work, but I saw each of them often (and always on their mother's or the dots' birthdays) and they would keep me updated on all the things happening on the Estate and with their friends. On Eid, and occasionally at other times, the other 'Asian gang' boys would drop round while I was visiting the house, and we would catch up.

Across the past twenty years there have, of course, been changes and moments of crisis: several years after I had met the family, the two absent sisters, Rukhsana and Amna, reconnected with the family. For many months, Khalid left home to live with a girlfriend and their baby daughter; Shahin moved to his own flat, to spend more time with his English girlfriend, Emma, whom he later married; Hanif, the youngest, went on Hajj with his mother, where he met his future wife, Khadija. Both families moved from the estate to buy houses further south; Shahin started his own law firm; the brothers have married and have children. The dots have grown from little girls to beautiful, self-assured and articulate young women, graduated from university, started work, married (apart from the youngest, Rabia) and started their own families. In 2019 they sent me a birthday card made up of some of the photos we took together over the past two decades, mapping their growth from childhood to adulthood (while I, of course, had barely aged). In the summer of 2020, they invited me for lunch in Dum Biryani, off Oxford Street, and insisted on paying, which finally brought home to me the reluctant realization that they were no longer children.

My relationship with the brothers, and the family, was always very different from that with Ifti and Humzah's family. I very rarely met with the brothers individually and alone – I think I can probably count on one hand the times when that happened (when Shahin wanted to talk to me about his relationship with Emma, or when he recently visited Manchester for work, and took me out for dinner) – and always in the shared living areas, though we had plenty of time to talk during my visits to the family or when they dropped me home afterwards. At the same time, though, our lives and interests became more entwined – Shahin and Hanif would talk to me a lot about their legal work, and their increasing interest in Islamic politics and identity; they arranged for my researcher to interview their mother and uncle for my 'Bengal Diaspora' project (Alexander et al 2016), and we had long conversations about race and religion, racism and Islamophobia, which has shaped my thinking on these issues for the past two decades. In 2017, Shahin came with me to the launch of the Runnymede report,

Islamophobia: Still a Challenge for Us All, and we discovered we had several mutual contacts at the event; on a couple of occasions he told me that his clients (academics, always anonymous) had read *The Asian Gang.* Much of the time, we would talk about the Stoneleigh young men and what was happening with them – the brothers were my main source of information about 'the gang' over the past twenty years – and they were the ones who facilitated my second interviews with the group in 2012. More than that, though, it was watching the brothers grow from teenagers to adults – from boys to men – through the trials and tribulations and transformations of these years, individually and as part of the post-9/11 generation of British Muslims, that convinced me of the importance of revisiting the earlier study more formally than I had ever expected or planned.

Our relationship has, of course, been centred on the thousands of mundane moments of shared history: of eating together (*a lot* of eating together), talking, laughing, arguing (they are a noisy, boisterous and opinionated family when they get together), occasionally worrying, swapping gifts and jokes and stories. These interactions, ordinary but also important, have underpinned my life across the many changes of the past two decades. My house is full of birthday and Christmas presents from the family – a woven footstool from Tunisia, a painting from a holiday in Turkey, perfume, sarees, candles, cushions from Morocco, a decorative bronze-coloured platter, which hangs on my kitchen wall, cookery books. One of my most precious pieces of jewellery is an Indian gold ring, studded with tiny roses, which the family gave me on a birthday many years ago. These objects are the tangible 'evidence' of the unseen relationships of care and acceptance which, I think, the family take for granted, but which I, certainly, do not. As someone who is most often on the edge of things, looking in – personally and professionally – I treasure these ordinary 'family' moments. I treasure too the support that the family have given me through some difficult times – when my younger sister died suddenly in 2014, the family sent flowers to my parents, and again when my mother died only a few weeks later. When my father died in 2018, the brothers offered to come with me to his funeral, so I would not be alone; and when my birth mother died a few months later that same year, their mother hugged me and told me she had cried for me (I think the only person who had done so). She said, 'I am your mother now.'

An Unexpected Ethnography: Revisiting 'The Asian Gang'

If, at a certain point, ethnography becomes life, what happens when what has been, simply, 'life' becomes ethnography (again)? While it is true that the earlier project laid the foundation for the relationships I have sketched above, and framed my ongoing interest in its participants, my concern and curiosity soon left any ethnographic purpose behind and became more personal than professional. It was never my intention to return to this project, though seeing how the young men's lives developed over the years was an endless source of fascination and discussion for me with friends and colleagues, and, of course, with the young men themselves.

As noted in Chapter 1, the idea for a formal revisit of the project came out of a discussion at Zohar's wedding in 2010. I applied for research funding soon afterwards, and was awarded one year's money by the Economic and Social Research Council for the academic year 2011–12, to cover my time and transcription costs for repeat interviews with the core members of the original project. Interviews took place through the winter and spring, with all but three of the original main participants. Of those three, I was unable to contact one, Faruk, although I knew he was working in a local hospital as a radiographer, and another, S Ahmed, was hiding out from the police in Bangladesh. Only one, Ismat, refused to be re-interviewed, and would give no reason, though his friends Jamal and Sayeed speculated dismissively that it was because 'his life hasn't changed at all since that time, so he's got nothing to say'. I also decided to add a number of new interviewees – individuals who had been in the background of the original project but whom I had come to know in the following years and whose lives captured illuminating aspects of the group's experiences, growing up. These were mainly drawn from 'the older lot', and included Jadil, 'Big' Hanif, and Mustafa, but it also included M, who was, in age, linked to the middle group (Khalid's and Shakiel's cohort) but had been an ad hoc member of the older lot, and a long-time friend of Shahin's. In 2012, M was in his first year of a twenty-year jail term for drug offences in a high security prison, where I visited to do the interview. The other interviews took place in a variety of settings: Jadil's pub, their homes, cafes, my home. The interviews lasted between two and eight hours and covered the areas explored in the following chapters: education, work, friendship, love and marriage, religion. For the original participants, we took the last interviews as a starting point, and followed their lives from school or college onwards, though we also circled back to look at friendships and family, particularly relationships with their fathers, in the light of their later lives. For the new interviewees, whose early lives I knew less well, the focus was broader, but also more focused on particular 'issues' and questions – especially around work and friendships.

While in some ways this book is a 'what happened next', it is not, and cannot be, a sequel, except perhaps in (loose) chronological terms, and in terms of some continuity of its subject(s). It is a very different kind of study, built on foundations that are, in some ways, deeper, and in others more tenuous, and fragmented, and opportunistic. Obviously, it is not a classic ethnography, which relies on 'being there', both spatially and temporally, as participant and observer, as well as, later, interpreter/translator (Coleman 2010, Collins & Gallinat 2010, Fassin 2017, Behar 2020, McGranahan 2020). But nor is it a simple return to the field, which suggests distance and separation (what Collins and Gallinat term as 'life at least once removed'). Perhaps it should be best understood as (auto)biography or 'memoir' (Behar 2020: 52), which traces multiple stories as they intersect with my own, as author. Certainly, doing the interviews as well as writing this book has been a way of revisiting my own past and my own journey as much as those of my informants – as a form of what Davis and

Davis (2010) call 'subjective time travel'. Yet much of what follows is reliant on the testimonies of others, for which I was, in the most part, absent. It is not, then, based on 'fieldwork' – as partial and limited as that is (Alexander 2000, 2004b) – unless one takes the span of now over twenty-five years of multiple and entwined lives, encounters and experiences as 'the field'. Because I never expected to revisit the study, this field (and certainly the past twenty-five years) remains largely uncharted, by myself and others; it lacks the immediacy of 'being there', or 'being seen', and relies on what Collins and Gallinat call 'head notes' – embodied memories and salvaged experiences reconstructed as the 'truth' of what happened. While some of the events recounted in the following chapters happened 'in real time' – where I was present or heard about them as they were unfolding – these went unrecorded, filed away in my memory, or of the individuals involved or, occasionally, as collective folklore. Much of what follows – work, love, family – happened 'off-stage' and is narrated through the perspective of the protagonists, often much later and with the benefit of a decade and a half of accumulated experience. Hindsight, it turns out, is less 20:20, and more a combination of selected memory, selective forgetting and post-hoc rationalization.

Memory is, of course, a notoriously unreliable witness to the past, most usually suited to the needs and vagaries of the present (Alexander 2013, Coleman 2010). As Ruth Behar has noted, ethnography can never capture present events; it is always 'in the past', the pursuit of 'irrecoverable' truths (1996: 7). This is also true even in 'traditional' fieldwork, where the reflexivity and positionality of the researcher is mirrored in the active self-portraiture of one's informants and where ethnography is (co)constructed 'after the fact' (Coleman 2010). Or as Khalid told me during his interview in 2012, 'reading that book, everybody lied about everything, their life; and that's just people'.

'The field' here, then, is perhaps understood more as a patchwork or collage, constructed through multiple embodied and sensory touchstones, through story and rumour, jokes and uneven, sedimented knowledge. Simon Coleman (2010) has described this not as a place but as 'plays of social relationships', which are 'pieced together out of the observations of the present as well as the observations of the past': as a space of 'emergence' or 'becoming'. Nevertheless, there are points at which these narratives coalesce and pause to form a picture. In the current study, these points of coalescence are threefold: the time of the original interviews and fieldwork (1994–2000), the interviews in 2012 and the time of writing (2020–22). Between (or alongside) these times, these fragments of lives shift and reconfigure, sometimes weaving through my own life, most usually not. What appears here, then, is a kind of salvage ethnography, which reconstructs after-images of 'the gang', filtered through multiple narratives (mine and theirs) and the lens of my own, uncertain memory and changing biography. At the same time, what is termed 'episodic' or 'autonoetic' memory (Coleman 2010, Collins & Gallinat 2010) can be woven into, or read against, 'semantic' memory, or ways of knowing, to lift its significance out of vagaries of the purely subjective or personal into the shared structures of the social.

The pitfalls of such an exercise are manifold and daunting: balancing the recognition of the always-already partial and subjective ways of 'knowing', with the commitment to ethnography as a 'necessary form of witnessing' (Behar 1996: 5, McGranahan 2020); acknowledging that ethnographic research and writing is irrevocably mediated through the self and the selves of others, in a process of 'co-construction' (a popular term which belies its precarious and unpredictable contours in practice), while challenging the broader structures of power that demand their 'truths' simple and impersonal; re-presenting the lives of people you know and love in all their complex humanity, without making them ordinary or heroic or foolish or, occasionally, selfish or vicious; and resisting the temptation to airbrush contradictions and bad choices or betray their trust – what Behar describes as 'the fear of observing too coldly or too distractedly, or too raggedly' (1996: 3) – and knowing that you are bound to fail. There are more practical and ethical issues too: what to do with the 'illicit' knowledge I have acquired over the past twenty years, both directly and through hearsay, but for which there has been no formal 'consent'? What stories and secrets are mine to share, and what should be left untold? What to do about the many people who appear as important, but silent, interlocutors in the lives of the interviewees in the pages that follow? How to write about the profligacies of youth (and adulthood) knowing that they may be read by friends, siblings, wives, nieces, children?

At this point in the writing, I have no real answers. There are some practical safeguards, of course: not including things that my interviewees asked to be kept in confidence (surprisingly few, actually); excluding anything that might do them tangible harm; editing out some of the more bizarre or salacious or delightful moments if they do not add something concrete to the overall narrative – not simply stories, but stories with a point; re-checking details with the people involved; sending drafts to key individuals (Shahin, Hanif, Humzah and Zohar) and relevant sections to others; and being open and reflexive about the process of analysis and writing and my own position as author – 'Acknowledging the heart' (Behar 2020: 49). As Carol McGranahan argues, ethnographers are 'the guardians of other people's stories' (2020: 3), and this guardianship requires accountability and authorial honesty, engaging with an ethics of practice that balances what energizes the research with the need to honour those it represents (Behar 2020: 50), and the demands of its multiple possible (and as yet unimagined) audiences (Fassin 2017).

I have written elsewhere about ethnography as reflecting both the 'impossibility' and the 'necessity' of academic research on race and ethnicity (2004b): as providing a lens, however fractured and imperfect, into the lives of those others who, as argued in Chapter 1, are often the objects of assertion and control, but more rarely appear as fully human. At the same time these are not simply stories of people, nor of their unreliable narrator, but of individuals located within particular historical, social, political and cultural contexts (Goldstein 2020) – individuals who are shaped by, and shape, these contexts; who push back the boundaries of how and by whom they are 'seen'; and who illuminate new ways of being, and seeing and thinking and acting. Ethnography, as

Willis and Trondman have argued, provides 'some kind of voice' (2000) to 'tell stories that matter, and to share new insights about the human world that might change it for the better' (McGranahan 2020: 3). To witness. To understand. To illuminate. To tell. To change.

Leaving School

Spring/Summer 1997

In the summer of 1997, the 'little ones' left Thomas More School for good. Their 'graduation' was marked by their National Record of Achievement (NRA) ceremony, held in the circular assembly hall in the heart of the school campus. My photos of the time show the young men dressed smartly in their uniform black trousers, white shirts and black ties with a (clearly co-ordinated, non-uniform and, I suspect, deliberately subversive) splash of gold, awash in hair gel, and smiling broadly as they collected the maroon, gold-embossed folders, which contained the official record of their school lives. Faruk, who was in the year below, had come to wish his friends farewell and carried a bunch of red carnations (though for whom, neither the photos nor my memory recall), and Ismat, who attended a different school, can be seen lurking in the background. Several of the photos show the young men with their arms around their mothers or sisters, resplendent in sarees and headscarves, beaming with pride. None of their older brothers attended, and only one father, Sayeed's, a gentle and shy man who accompanied Sayeed's mother, a woman so terrifying that on the couple of occasions when she visited the youth project looking for her sons, the young men (including the 'older lot') had been known to hide behind the pool table to escape her. They are standing rigid and unsmiling on either side of their son, who towers several inches above them, his arms folded across his body in a classic 'gangsta' pose, his usual wide grin on his face. In others, the young men cluster together on the hall steps, arms around each other's shoulders, NRA folders proudly on display, some staring moodily into the camera, others clearly trying not to laugh.

Nearly twenty-five years on, the pictures seem rather melancholic – a snapshot of the as yet-undaunted optimism of sixteen-year-olds, for whom the world seemed full of possibilities and opportunities, untold riches and untrammelled success. When I interviewed them earlier in the academic year (September–November 1996), they all told me of their post-school plans – GCSEs, college, university and then a job 'in an office'. What kind of office was, for most, unclear and even unimportant, perhaps even unimaginable. This dual sense of possibility and impossibility was captured poignantly by Sayeed, who told me, 'I want to become a bank manager. Or a pilot. Something like that' (1996). Only Hanif had a clear sense of what he wanted – to be a lawyer. Others simply hoped for a 'good job' (Mohammed interview 1996), which Shakiel defined as 'a business-type job – you know, wear a suit, go to work, come back with your briefcase, have a nice car and everything' (1996).

Rereading the interviews now, I am particularly struck by how opaque the future loomed for these young men and how, caught up in the present(ism) of the ethnography, I had overlooked both the uncertainty that awaited them, and the personal and social histories that shaped and constrained their ambitions and choices. While there was optimism, there was also a sense of fatalism: as Hanif noted, 'half of them will say it like, yeah we're all going to end up in restaurants anyway, so fuck the GCSEs' (1996). Given the high levels of unemployment within the Bangladeshi community through the 1990s (Modood et al 1997, Alexander 2000) and even until today (Clark & Shankley 2020), such fatalism was not without foundation. Indeed, it could be seen at first-hand in their own families. The fathers of all but one of the young men were unemployed; most were in their sixties, and had worked in the textile or leather factories of East London, as tailors or machinists, and had retired through ill health. One, Zohar's father, had owned a company making clothing for department store C&A and Top Shop, but was now retired. Sayeed's father had worked in a steelworks near Manchester before moving to London to be near family when the factory closed, while Hanif, Khalid and Shahin's father had also worked in a steel factory before retiring after a heart attack. He passed away several years before I met the brothers. Only Ifti and Humzah's father, who was in his forties, had worked in a restaurant (an 'English' restaurant, they were at pains to tell me), but even he had given up work to devote himself to religious duties at the local mosque, relying on state benefits and his children to support him. None of their mothers did paid work outside the home, though Humzah's mother used to work from home, sewing underwear for Top Shop (and about which she had some very disapproving comments).

The attraction of an 'office job' could then be seen, at least in part, as a desire to avoid the poorly paid, heavy manual labour their fathers had mainly undertaken, and which had exacted a heavy toll, financially and in terms of health. Their parents also played a key part in shaping their sons' youthful ambitions, as much for the wider family and the broader community as for their sons themselves. As Mohammed told me,

> They really want me to do well, to set an example to my little brothers and sisters and then like go on to further education. Because in the Asian community, like if your child is a judge or a barrister or a solicitor, you earn a lot of respect. People think, 'Ah, they have worked hard for their children'.
>
> (1996)

This was particularly important for those, like Mohammed, who were the eldest son. Ismat echoed, 'They want us to do good, turn out good for the future, you know, get good jobs, support the family' (1996). Such expectations were not, however, always in line with what the young men wanted for themselves: Ismat, for example, continued,

> My dad's already got a plan for me to become a doctor. I said no, I don't like science anyway but he's planning for me to become a doctor. I said alright, we see what happens ... I ignore him totally. But I don't know really what I want to be – something to do with computers, and that's all I know so far.

If a job 'in an office' was the collective ambition, albeit ill-defined, there was a very clear shared sense of what they did *not* want: a job in a restaurant. While the kinds of work their fathers had done had long ceased to be an option, the restaurant trade was, and is, dominated by Bangladeshi men (Alexander 2010, Alexander et al 2020), and was viewed by all as the epitome of failure. Ismat told me,

> I don't want to work in a restaurant. Basically all the Bengali old people that I know have worked in a curry house, in a restaurant somewhere in their life … because they haven't been doing good in school and so they always turn to a restaurant.

Mohammed similarly commented, 'It's like when everything's failed, that's when you go to a restaurant … when you hear someone's working in a restaurant, you know they just done nothing right' (1996).

Nevertheless, several of the young men thought that this would be an inevitable destination for some of their friends (though not, of course, themselves): as Ismat prophesied, 'I've got a feeling some of us are going to turn to a restaurant sooner or later' (1996).

None (or all) of these uncertainties or ambitions can be read into the sixteen-year-old faces of the little ones on their 'graduation' day, nor could their futures be read in what they hoped and feared for themselves, or their friends. The choices and constraints, stumbles and determination, and the random chances and events that marked the following years were as yet unwritten, but would unfold in ways which shaped all aspects of their lives – their friendships, marriage plans, even, for some, their faith – and which will be explored in future chapters. This chapter and the one that follows trace the routes through education and employment that 'the Asian gang' took after leaving school, and into adulthood. This chapter follows their first steps from school into college, and the fracturing of these schoolboy ambitions which took place during the first two years, before focusing in on the experiences of those few who went on to higher education. The chapter that follows explores their entrance into the world of work, and their pathways from college to career, which captures the transformative years from eighteen to their early thirties. While some of these routes were what were hoped for, or expected, or feared, most cannot be so easily charted, and the journey is perhaps the most important, and intriguing, element. As sixteen-year-old Hanif reflected, enigmatically, 'Everyone has an ambition when they're small about "yeah, I want to be in an office and all this". But I don't think it's going to work out for all of us, because of the way a few of us are heading' (1996).

Starting Out

Frankly, there were times when I worried that the little ones would not make it out of Thomas More School alive – literally and spiritually. Their time at the school, particularly from Year 9 onwards, had been marred by constant violence, in school and outside. This was compounded by the hostility of the school administration and the local police towards the Bengali young men, who were demonized as 'a gang', subject to continual suspensions and exclusions in school, and stop and search outside it. *The Asian Gang* was an exploration of the representation and the reality of this moral panic, revealing the complex and shifting nature of the construction, and the ways in which the young men inhabited and contested its fictions. But its very real impact on the lives of the young men was palpable, and often visceral. I quickly learned not to ask about the various scars that all of the young men carried, which usually elicited a story that began 'yeah, this boy hit me with a brick/ belt buckle/Lucozade bottle …' I tried, but failed, not to worry over the convoluted routes and feints that they had to take to avoid being attacked getting to or from school on a daily basis, or even moving between lessons while on campus. That the young men themselves took this routinized violence and harassment for granted – as a fact of life – was almost the worst thing. That they came to school anyway was astonishing. Their school life often seemed like a scene from *Lord of the Flies* restaged on an inner-city housing estate. Certainly they were not simply passive victims: they fought back, individually or collectively, and were proud of it; they were, I am sure, sometimes the instigators; they bunked lessons; and they could be noisy, challenging, disruptive, lazy, rude. They were also charming, street- and (some of them) book-smart, caring, thoughtful, funny, sometimes naïve, undeterred, hopeful. Teenage boys, in fact. That they came out of school with any of that hope, ambition and determination still intact is something of a miracle.

Some of them even came out with qualifications.[1] Of the 'little ones' who 'graduated' in 1997, Mohammed, Hanif and Jamal passed eight or more GCSEs at grades A-C; Ismat, whom I did not reinterview in 2011/12, also left with good GCSEs. Ifti and Sayeed did not pass any exams – or as Sayeed said, fifteen years later, 'I did take a few GCSEs but I don't know what are the results to be honest with you. I probably failed all of them' (2012). Nevertheless, all headed to college – Hanif, Jamal and Mohammed to study A-levels, Sayeed and Ismat to begin BTecs in Leisure and Tourism, and Ifti to start a diploma in Business Administration. For all of them, college promised a new start – a break from the conflicts that scarred their final years of school and a next step in meeting their own, and their families', ambitions for the future.

In most cases, what this meant in tangible terms was unclear – as Mohammed said, 'I never actually knew what I wanted to be in my life … I didn't think that far ahead, you know. I just thought, I'm going to college and that was fine … that's an achievement in itself' (2012). Where for Mohammed, college was a first step on an unknown road, for others, it was simply something to do: as Sayeed stated later, going to college was 'just one of those things, you know, everyone's going … I should have started working' (2012). Jamal, who had done well in school but by his own admission 'couldn't be much bothered' to study, expressed some frustration at the apparent lack of any alternative route: 'it's almost like there's an obligation for you to do it … you had to go to university, and then that's the only way you could get a job … that mentality' (2012). Of the group, only Hanif seemed to have a clear sense of what he wanted to achieve from further education – he commented, 'Everyone went to college … but it was just something to do for most people' (2012). Acknowledged by his friends as the most academically inclined and hard-working, Hanif had aspirations to enter the law profession even in school:

I always wanted to go into law, so even when I look at my NRA folder, [Head Teacher] would say 'I'm sure Hanif will make a great lawyer one day'. So he already knew that's what I wanted to be … [but] I think it was more because my dad had said [it], you know.

While it was apparent that the young men felt the pressure of parental expectations around college and career, this was largely empty of content. It was the *fact* of college and the unspecified, but glorious 'office' career that would inevitably follow, rather than any particular course or its suitability to the interests and abilities of their sons, that was the overriding element. None of their parents had been to college or university themselves, and were unable to offer much advice. For many parents the sense of possible future careers was restricted to a few vocations – medicine, law, 'business'. Hanif recalled that his father had wanted Shahin, the oldest son, to be a doctor, and had suggested that Hanif become a lawyer, though he apparently had enough imagination (and humour) to suggest that his middle son, Khalid, who was not academically minded, should be 'a comedian'. Hanif did not say, and I did not ask, what his father wanted for his three daughters. Jamal claimed that he strongly felt the 'obligation' to go to college from his parents, and though he 'wasn't upset, obviously, for my mum and dad to push me to study', he did feel a strong pressure to succeed – though not enough, perhaps, to make him actually concentrate on his studies. When, after two years, he failed his A-levels 'miserably', he told me, 'Many times I caught my mum, I'd come home late in the morning and you know she's doing *fajr* prayers and she's crying … I definitely know I hurt my parents, well, definitely my mum in that sense' (2012). Looking ahead, he linked the expectation to study and succeed not only to future career but also to marriage:

I think, nowadays, it's a requirement … it's not more for the job that you're going to get or whatever. It's more to do with marriage … marriage proposals now is based on what you've studied rather than what you actually do, or who you are as a person.

For some, this lack of parental knowledge – if not support – brought particular challenges. Mohammed commented,

> I'm like the first person to ever go to college in my family ... and I think, with no disrespect to my parents, they just didn't focus me enough ... they didn't understand, like, the amount of work it takes, so it was quite normal for them to expect me to work part-time and at least manage myself as a minimum.

(2012)

Others felt torn between their own and their parents' desires for career success, and a more material imperative, around supporting their families financially, or simply making their own money. Jamal and Sayeed both noted that their fathers were more likely to want them to work rather than study: Sayeed told me, 'Like my mum would tell me, "yes, go study", but my dad would say "look, get a job"' (2012). They attributed this ambivalence, and their own, to a generational shift, from a migrant generation focused on work and sending money 'back home' to a second generation seeking firmer roots, better employment and material success in Britain (Abbas 2002). Mohammed mused, 'I don't think for people of my age group – you know, we're the second generation – the educational aspect was a key thing for parents and ... they just didn't focus me enough to thinking, if you can get this, you will achieve more in life' (2012). Sayeed also commented on the difference in attitude between his father and his older brother, who worked in Sher Khan's restaurant:

> I think the other thing is the older generation's getting older, and the new generation's coming up, so they have different mentalities and everything. You know, their children are going to go and study, whether or not ... So, it's about pushing the older generation out, basically, the mentality, 'oh, you know what, don't worry about studying just ... go and work' .... That's changed. I mean, like my older brother, he's like forty, he's telling his kids, encouraging them to go study, while our parents really didn't do that to us.

(2012)

Jamal, who had the natural analytical instincts of a sociologist, positioned himself as part of a 'third generation' where education was paramount:

> So, you know, the second generation Asians, they thought more financially. So for them to send their older son to college or university was seen as a waste of time because they needed financial help. So the older son usually tend to go to work, you know, Indian restaurant or whatever, and do that ... then the second son might go to college, you know. So like now we've become more affluent, we've become more established, so the priority of studying has become more because, you know, they can afford not to have that income.
>
> (2012)

Jamal's 'second generation' could include older siblings, even where only a year or two divided them from their 'third generation' brothers and sisters, and this was to become apparent particularly when they entered work. For those with older siblings, or cousins, who had already embarked on their own college or career paths, there were some examples to follow. Sayeed, for example, looked on his older sister, Sultana, who had completed her GCSEs at a local girls' school and was working in a high street bank, as a role model – perhaps where his 'bank manager' ambition came from. Ifti's older sister, Tahiya, had gone to college and then moved on to play work and later also to work in a local bank. Amongst the older lot too sisters were seen as role models: Shakiel, for example, had an older sister who worked in a local bank prior to marriage and two who worked in nursery education. Only one, Zohar, had sisters who had continued into university; his eldest sister worked as a primary school teacher and his youngest sister, seven years older than Zohar, later became a community worker (as Zohar himself did). It is interesting to reflect that in many cases the young men's sisters were more successful in education and post-school/college employment than their brothers (cf Dale, Shaheen, Kalra & Fieldhouse 2002, Niven, Faggian & Ruwanpura 2013, Alexander & Shankley 2020). It is true too, however, that, as with other minority ethnic and working class women, this apparent 'success' was often more a product of gendered divisions in employment classification than any material reality (see Mirza 1992). It also remains the case that there were, and are, significantly lower rates of employment for British Bangladeshi women in the labour market, showing a divergence between education and employment achievement (Ahmed & Dale 2011, Clark & Shankley 2020), although this picture is changing for later generations of British-born young women, as for their brothers (Dale 2002).

Relationships with older brothers were, in many cases, more complicated and constrained by the hierarchies of respect and authority (see Alexander 2000, Chapter 6), which made the giving and taking of advice an often fraught process. Jamal, for example, had an older brother who had done well at school and had studied 'something' in computing at university, but Jamal resisted his advice because he felt his more 'traditional' brother (1996) did not really understand his experiences: 'He's only, what, four years older than me … and my brother is very subdued, you know. He's very much like my father' (2012). Others, like Sayeed, felt that their older brothers had made poor choices themselves and were not in a position to give advice. His oldest brother had left school aged fourteen because of fighting, and had been working in Sher Khan's family restaurant for many years. Sayeed told me his parents used him as an example of his inevitable fate if he failed his education: 'They want me to do well, get a good job, but they think I'm going to end up in a restaurant' (1996). His middle brother, Salman, had left school with no qualifications, moved between poorly paid, temporary employment, dabbled in drug dealing and had developed a serious addiction, and had been in and out of prison. Ifti often defended his older brother, Humzah, who had dropped out of college and drifted in and out of low-paid and precarious work (with long periods of unemployment), from the demands of his parents, who expected him, as the oldest son, to support the family financially. In 2012, Ifti reflected, 'It was hard for him … I just guess it didn't go the way he planned all this'. Of the little ones, perhaps only Hanif followed the example of his older brother, Shahin, in going to college and then university to study law, but they did not seem to have discussed his choice or career plans until much later. In addition, Shahin's problems at college had stalled his progress, so the two developed their careers more in parallel.

Unsurprisingly, for the older lot, who had left school two or three years earlier, the ambitions and the obstacles were similar, and when I interviewed them in 1996, they had already encountered some potholes on the road to success. Shakiel, who had left school in 1995 with eight GCSEs, and was then at college studying for his A-levels, noted of his parents: 'They're really strict on me about going to college and that. They want me to go to college, get a degree or something. I want that too' (1996). For Shakiel, as the only boy in the family, the pressures and expectations were particularly great. He confessed of the 'business type job' his parents wanted for him: 'I find them jobs kind of boring.' Shakiel wanted to study sports science and become a PE teacher, but the A-level in sports sciences had been cancelled at his first college and was not available at his second, so he was struggling with subjects he did not enjoy. When we spoke in 2012, he told me that he completed two A-levels, in Sociology and Psychology, at Southwark College, and had felt pressured by his family into studying Computer Science at Westminster – a degree he hated. He told me:

> I really wanted to do the Sports Science degree, and everyone I spoke to were like 'why do you want to do it?' Because it was an odd subject at that time – like fifteen years ago, it was like almost doing a Home Economics degree, you know ... My family, my sisters and everyone, they'd say, 'Well, what's that?' It's not that you want to be like a masseuse or something like that. Because they didn't know what it was about. *I* didn't know what it was about.

His close friend, Khalid, left school with no GCSEs – he told me in 1996 that he was 'disappointed' in his results but shrugged 'that was because I didn't do any of my coursework. ... I really did bunk a lot'. He started a GVQ Intermediate course in Business Studies at Westminster College, but dropped out after a couple of months, and started work in McDonald's and in a local play centre. His mother, he said, 'was disappointed'. She said, 'What your dad wanted was him to see you going to college, going to Uni and all that but he never survived to see you do that, so I think you should have done it.' Positioned between two more academically minded brothers, Shahin and Hanif, he felt his perceived failure acutely: 'They [his brothers] probably think I'm a total disappointment', though he continued, 'It doesn't really bother me if they think that. If I get along with my life now … get a proper job or something, then that's alright. I'm not wasting my life or nothing'. When we spoke again in 2012, Khalid still felt this pressure:

> My brother [Shahin] was someone that was successful and I didn't want to be the person who breaks that chain … [but] he was just a year older than I am, so he wasn't old enough to support me in anything … because we was doing the same things. And even if he did, which he would have, I'm sure, it would not be in … the right way.

Shahin, in any case, had struggles of his own. Having left school with eight A-C grade GCSEs, he went briefly to Kingsway College in Camden ('we were just, "well, there's not much talent here"', he laughed in 2012) and then to Hammersmith College. He told me in 1996, 'I think I was the only Asian person that went on to do A-levels or any kind of BTec.' A few weeks ago, he sent me a video of his own NRA day and reflected that less than ten of his peers had left with more than five GCSEs, grades A-C, 'all BAME' (email, 25 March 2021).[2] Shahin completed a year of A-levels in Chemistry, Biology and Physics (perhaps to kickstart the medical career his father had wanted for him), but then switched to a GNVQ in Business and Finance and an A-level in Law. He told me in 1996,

> I didn't know what I was doing, do you know what I mean, and then Salman and everyone went to Hammersmith that year as well, and lots of other boys from Camden and Euston that I knew … it was corrupt! We didn't used to go there for study; it was just like a social club or something.

He left college mid-year, after the attack which hospitalized him for several days (see Chapter 5), and when I interviewed him in 1996, he was taking two A-levels, in Sociology and Psychology, in an intensive one-year course.

One of his closest friends was Zohar, who, unlike most of the young men, had not attended Thomas More School, but had grown up on the Stoneleigh Estate. He had attended a predominantly white school in a neighbouring borough and left with seven GCSEs, although he commented in 1996 that he felt he could have done better had he not been spending time with his friends. He went first to Westminster College to do A-levels in Art, English and Maths, but later dropped out and enrolled at Hammersmith College the same year as Shahin, where he completed a BTec National in Art and Design (and where he met his future wife, Humaira). He told me in 2012 that although he got a distinction in that course,

> I didn't pursue that because – I still love art today [but] … it's more, as you get older, you become less stupid. You don't want to go and hang out in the streets, you want to do things. I wanted to work in a bank, and get something that would pay well.

What emerges from the transition from school to college is a strong sense of uncertainty, confusion and the pressure of personal and familial expectations, which led, in most cases, to a series of false starts on the road to adulthood. For these young men, often forging new pathways for themselves and their families, the lack of readily accessible experience and role models was compounded by their reluctance to draw on what was available, underpinned by their own histories, insecurities and abilities. This meant that they viewed even the very few models of success in their families and communities – for example, Silver, who was one of the first British Bangladeshi young men in the area to go to University – as distinct and distant from their own, more difficult lives. In turn, for the little ones, the reluctance to learn from the older lot resulted in a kind of displaced Groundhog Day, which repeated the same choices and mistakes on a two-year delay.

Starting Over

With the benefit of hindsight, perhaps a key choice/mistake was the reliance on their immediate peer group in making their college choices. As with the older lot beforehand, the little ones initially chose their college, and sometimes their courses, because of their friends. Mohammed noted he picked Kingsway because 'at the time everyone else was going there and it just seemed the obvious choice' (2012), while Jamal recalled, 'At that time we was quite, you know, inseparable, so that mentality of us going to the same college was something that we probably unconsciously did' (2012). A primary consideration was being away from their own area – a chance to start over. Hanif reflected,

> It seemed as if the further you go, the better, and I think it may be probably from the concept of the older lot going to Hammersmith … And then you think you're in another area, you get to meet new people too. So you're just trying to distance yourself
>
> (2012)

Sayeed recalled that the friends had initially wanted to follow the older lot to Hammersmith: 'We were going to follow our older brothers' footsteps … they went, they told all these stories we used to hear. We were thinking yes, that's the college we want to go to … [but] I think [only] one of us got accepted, or something, the rest didn't' (2012). The group – Hanif, Jamal, Sayeed, Ismat, Mohammed – instead all headed together to Kingsway, and although they studied different courses, they socialized mainly together outside of classes. This support network had two drawbacks First, as Jamal noted, laughing, the social element dominated their college lives: 'I spent most of my time, rather than doing the homework, courseworks and doing my assignments, I spent it with these guys, you know … doing a lot of pastime activities, like smoking weed, stuff like that' (2012). His close friend Sayeed, who was in the interview with Jamal, chimed in: 'I would say that ruined his potential of doing, you know, going further in education.' Sayeed himself confessed: 'To be honest with you, I didn't really go there to study. I just went there for the crowd, you know, the friends and everything.' He rarely attended his course on leisure and tourism: 'I just attended three days. I made silly excuses and I just, you know, went in the canteen, just waiting for these lot to come down. Messing about with people in the common room, playing pool and things like that.'

Second, as had happened with Shahin and his friends at Hammersmith, the arrival of a tight-knit group of friends in a new area proved a provocation to the local Bengali young men, leading to a series of scuffles and then a major fight (see Alexander 2000). Sayeed noted,

> They thought we were new Asian boys come into their territory and start trouble … They were threatened by us, basically … especially these two, Jamal and Hanif, because of their hairstyles and whatever. Maybe they found them more good looking than them, who knows?

Hanif and Jamal were both strikingly handsome young men and had a very distinctive hairstyle, with gelled, spiked fringes that were very unusual for Bangladeshi young men at the time (and probably since). Hanif recalled,

> We had problems when we went to Kingsway because the local Bangladeshi kids there, the Drummond Street lot, they didn't take a liking to myself and Jamal because of our hair … and because there was these, you know, you had some Bengali girls in college that presumably liked us and they liked them … So then we had problems in college which wasn't good, because, you know, we'd gone to college to study and left some of these issues from your own area, and then you go there and you've still got things following you and because you was in another area, you had no control over things.
>
> (2012)

Although the conflict evaporated once the older lot intervened, several of the little ones expressed some disappointment that they had been unable to leave their more troublesome schoolboy reputations behind. Hanif told me,

> You're just trying to distance yourself, but no matter how much … it just sort of followed you and so every day in college was like … was that struggle going on, and there'd been a few incidents whilst we were at college in terms of fights that took place. So yes, that wasn't ideal.

Ifti, who had enrolled at a College nearer home, actually fared much better – or at least avoided the conflicts his friends had encountered (although this was most likely due to the fact he was rarely in college).

He had chosen not to go with his school friends to Kingsway – perhaps reflecting tensions amongst the group that were already emerging when they left Thomas More School (see Chapter 5). He told me that, like his older brother Humzah, he wanted to stay away from the bigger group to avoid being distracted. Humzah had started college in Tower Hamlets, with the initial aim of retaking his GCSEs, and avoiding the fighting and bunking that had marred his school life: 'I wanted to go somewhere far. I didn't want to – with all the things happening that time, I wanted to be somewhere [else]' (Humzah, interview 2012). When I asked him what had happened, he laughed 'Oh, it was as usual, made too many friends there, and doing the other stuff ... I made some new friends over there ... [and] at the end ... they just took us to the wrong'. The 'other stuff', he explained, was 'just fights, drugs ... mostly silly stuff', and by the summer he abandoned college for football in the park. While Humzah did have academic abilities and aspirations, Ifti – never strongly inclined to study, as I had discovered when I had rashly agreed to try and tutor him when at school – was focused more on 'business'. He mainly used his short time at college to start his fledgling drug enterprise (about which, more in the next chapter), something he traced to the local 'reputation' he had carried with him from school. He told me,

> Money's such a big thing in life and the way I saw it is, before I get to a certain age I just want to get rich and settled. I knew my grade wasn't [good] ....so I was doing a college business, because I knew that I had to recover in some way.
>
> (2012)

Moving on ...

Given what seems, even with hindsight, the slightly haphazard choices of course, college and imagined career that the young men made on leaving school, it was perhaps unsurprising that their first step into adulthood proved, in most cases, more of a misstep. Of the little ones, only Hanif completed his studies without detour, passing A-levels in Law, History and Sociology and moving on to study a degree in Law at Kingston University. His friend Jamal struggled with the shift to A-levels, starting courses in History, Sociology and Geography, then dropping Geography for Psychology in the second year. He finally took exams in History and Sociology – 'I failed miserably' he told me ruefully in 2012 – failed summer retakes, started over at Southwark College, followed by an access course through the Open University, but again dropped out. Hanif reflected, over a decade later:

> Jamal was always ... naturally very bright, unlike myself. I would never consider myself naturally bright, so I think I had to put more effort in ... But I think in college ... I adapted more and understood ... that you had to put more in ... and he never quite grasped that. And also at the time he was quite heavily involved in smoking and I don't think that helped him at all. And that was just one thing – he was changing subjects and then he just lost focus ... *[So] it just meant from an academic point of view there was no one else, it was just me left.*
>
> (2012, my emphasis)

Jamal was more direct: 'You know, reading, I really, really dislike reading' (2012). As time went on he found it harder and harder to return to studying, despite multiple attempts and his desire for a 'certificate'. The third of that very close trio, Sayeed, never even tried to pass his course, and embarked on a series of low paid, temporary jobs: 'I went from job to job. I didn't go back to college or nothing like that, or university. I've done pretty much everything' (2012). Ifti, as noted above, had already embarked on a different route. Mohammed did not take his A-level exams at Kingsway (though he did not say why), enrolled at Southwark for a one-year intensive course in Sociology and Psychology, but left before taking the exams to return to Bangladesh when his grandmother became ill. He recalled,

> I was a bit lost for direction ... I just knew there was a bigger world out there ... So I got some careers advice and basically the route that I

chose was to start university as a mature student … *I was on my own though – everyone else was doing their own things by that time.*

(2012, my emphasis)

Mohammed took an access course at Kingston College and entered the university as a mature student to study law – crossing with Hanif by one year. In addition to Hanif, only Ismat and another friend from the Stoneleigh Estate, Layaak (who was only a sporadic SAYO member, and whom I did not interview in 1996 or 2012), received their qualifications and moved on to university – both to study computer science.

A similar pattern emerged amongst the older lot. As noted, Humzah and Khalid both dropped out of college after only a few months, and drifted into part-time and temporary work situations. Shakiel passed his A-levels, but after resistance from his family about pursuing the desired Sports Science degree, he enrolled for a Computer Science degree at Westminster University – 'the worst decision I ever made', he lamented in 2012. Shahin eventually passed two A-levels, in Sociology and Psychology, and went to Middlesex University to study Law, while Zohar received a distinction in his BTEc National Art and Design course, but elected to take a Foundation course at Lambeth College, and then studied for a degree in Business Management at the University of East London.

As a stepping-stone from school to university or the world of work, then, college proved precarious – something to be endured or, very often, as a way of passing the time until adulthood caught up with them. Certainly, for those who entered it without a clear idea of a career already in place, college seemed to do little to help and, in some cases, hindered. Shahin, for example, noted that his decision to study law at university was discouraged by the college careers advisor:

> She said, 'Are you sure? You don't want to be a probation officer or a social worker?' … She said, 'Oh, you know, it's a very middle-class profession and most lawyers go to public school … it's going to be difficult'. And I think that motivated me. I just, in my mind, I wanted to prove her wrong.
>
> (2012)

... Moving Up ...

For those few young men who made it – Shahin, Zohar, Shakiel, Hanif, Mohammed – the move to university seemed to make relatively little difference to their lives outside. They all lived at home, worked part-time and largely socialized with their friends from the Stoneleigh Estate. In this, their experiences were consistent with those of their peers, set against a backdrop of expansion and restructuring of the higher education sector at that time. With the introduction of tuition fees to attend university in 1998, and the replacement of maintenance grants with loans from the 1999–2000 academic year, the experience of young people from more deprived backgrounds was markedly different from previous generations, such as my own. Claire Callender (2006) has noted that although in 2000–2001 (around the time the Stoneleigh young men were entering University), approximately one-third of young people in England and Wales entered full-time higher education, those from disadvantaged backgrounds were still under-represented (around 15 per cent of the student cohort). Vikki Boliver (2013) argues further that while funding changes did not negatively impact overall rates of participation in higher education, they did widen the gap in entry into more prestigious Russell Group universities for those from less privileged and ethnic minority backgrounds. Those from Pakistani and Bangladeshi backgrounds were over five times more likely to enter post-1992 institutions than Russell Group institutions across the decade from 1996 to 2006 (66 per cent versus 12 per cent respectively). Croxford and Raffe (2014) similarly note that across the period 1996–2010 working-class and ethnic minority students were more likely to study close to home and that South Asian students were disproportionately located in less prestigious post-1992 universities – a situation which continues today (Alexander & Arday 2015, Alexander & Shankley 2020). This was certainly true of the young men I worked with, who all stayed in London and in a range of post-1992 institutions (Middlesex, East London, Westminster and Kingston, respectively).

Against this backdrop, the biggest transformation was in what university 'meant' for the young men from the Stoneleigh Estate. When I left for university in the mid-1980s, it represented a chance to leave home, to make new friends, to explore new opportunities, to make a break and reinvent myself. I had a maintenance grant and during the vacations could claim housing benefit and unemployment benefit. By contrast, for the young men from the SAYO project, university meant business/life as usual: they all lived at home, they attended university as and when necessary, and took paid employment when they could, and they socialized, usually, with their former school and neighbourhood peers. It often seemed to me that university for them was more like a job than an adventure.

As with college, the choice of university and degree course seemed, in most cases, relatively random. This was in part due to the absence of role models locally. While most went to college, it was comparatively rare for young men from the area to aspire to university. Shahin noted that from the Bangladeshi families on the Stoneleigh Estate, only Silver had gone to university previously:

> I don't think there were that many … nobody went to university and I think that Silver was probably the only one from the guys I knew at Thomas More, that were older than me, that had gone to university.
>
> (2012)

Silver reflected on a rapid generational 'ripple':

> A lot of those young people were watching me at nineteen go to university at East London … And it had that ripple effect across the area, because parents and families, you know – Hanif's mum used to say, 'Look what Silver's doing' to Shahin, Ifti's family, Jamal's family.
>
> So I was one of the first people but then within three, four years, Shahin and that age group were at the universities, and Zohar's moving on. So then the new tier of role models were created and suddenly it was embedded – you go to university; of course you go to university.
>
> (2012)

Shahin noted that he had also been inspired by an older cousin, who had been the first in his family to go to university, and had qualified as an engineer: 'My dad ... spoke really highly of him and said, "I want, you know, when you grow up, I want you to be like him"' (2012). Shahin himself was less certain of what he wanted to do, or be. It was later, in college, that he had decided on a career in law – in part because of his problems there, and his recent experience of the trial of the young men who attacked him, though he also traced it back to a longer set of encounters with the police:

> I think a lot of it was through the problems we had as youths with the police ... We'd just sit hanging around on the Stoneleigh Estate and we would get stopped for no apparent reason. So there's a lot of stereotyping, and I think they just assumed these guys are hanging around, they must be carrying knives or ... you know, smoking drugs ... So I think that [it] was just generally seeing all the issues, the problems, growing up in the inner city.

Of the five who went on to higher education, only Shahin and his little brother Hanif seemed to have a clear sense of a career pathway through university. For the others, their choice of degree seemed to be led more by vague notions of what the university sector now badges as 'employability'. Zohar, as noted above, chose a degree in business management above his passion and talent for art because 'as you get older, you become less stupid' (2012). He studied at UEL because 'it's the one I got into. I applied for Greenwich, didn't get there. I applied for Middlesex, didn't get in there, applied for UEL, and I got stuck there'. He completed his degree and enrolled for a master's degree in system management, but left after a year, with a diploma: he said, 'I had had enough.'

Mohammed, as mentioned above, fell into studying Law at Kingston on the advice of one of his tutors on his access course, and because he enjoyed the 'mooting' sessions it included. Having failed to take his A-levels twice, he enrolled as a mature student, completing a Foundation Course, which he described as 'the hardest thing I've done in my life'. He recalled, 'My mum was laughing at me. She was like, you know, she thought I was going to be about fifty by the time I graduated. My dad was quite happy, but my mum's like "why don't you just open a business or look out for stuff [a job]". And I was like, I'm better than that' (2012).

Shakiel, sadly, gave up his passion for sports and sports science and settled for a degree in computer science, which he loathed. He told me in 2012 that problems at home with his father meant, as the only son, he felt unable to move away to study sports science, a problem compounded by the lack of family support: 'family members … people that have gone to university, everyone, you know, raised an eyebrow … So I ended up getting into computing. Computer Science. Worst decision I ever made.' The course turned out to be very different from his expectations:

> I guess everyone has their own expectations of a subject and computer science for me was, you know, building a computer, building a TV, that kind of stuff … Something a bit more hands on, maybe more creative, you know, but it wasn't … I didn't think for a second it was going to be sitting there and writing codes … Three hours of code to get the ruddy screen to change colour and I was, like, 'what a waste of time'.

Shakiel persevered: 'And I thought well, you know, it will probably get better … It's going to get better, it's going to get better and by the time I realized it's only going to get worse, I'd already gone through a year, and then, you know, I didn't know what to do, really.' Because his closest friends, Khalid and Mehraj, had not gone to university, and the couple of members of his peer group who did 'were different people', Shakiel was unsure where to turn: 'That's what I was saying – if I had someone … I could have spoken to, to guide you or even give you a bit of advice, it would have helped a bit. But, you know, looking back, I don't think I did.' His family meanwhile pressured him into staying on: 'They knew I hated it. They saw how stressed I was … [but] you know, they were "you just have to try and get through it". I think it was probably more pressure. They just wanted you to do it.' He summarized his experience succinctly and, even a decade later, with some vehemence: 'I hated university.'

Others echoed a feeling of alienation from their university life. Even Hanif, who was perhaps the most focused on his chosen profession, and a very positive, friendly and sunny person by nature, described his degree as 'like the worst three years'. The campus he attended at Kingston was primarily for law students, and Hanif recalled,

> I just found law students really – they're really competitive, quite selfish and … also at that time I think I was becoming more focused on like religion and that formed a big part. Because what the whole of uni life was like, it didn't appeal to me, you know, in terms of what most of my friends there were doing, and what they would get up to. It was all about drinking and so … I always kept my distance from that. So in the first year I went, but the second and third year I was like a ghost.
>
> (2012)

His older brother, Shahin, had a similar experience at Middlesex: 'at university it was all really competitive – you know, past exam papers, people would hide them in the library because they didn't want other students to look at them' (2012). He, like Hanif, made relatively few friends at university: 'there's a couple of guys from the law school that I, yeah, I'd spend – like some Friday nights we'd go out … but it wasn't …. I didn't make close friends at university.' Even Mohammed, who insisted 'I've got loads of good friends from university that I stay in touch even until with today' (2012), noted that, as a mature student, his perspective was different from his university peers:

> You saw the immaturity through and through and, you know, obviously I socialised with a lot of people … but I knew that I was there for a reason … And I just found compared to the eighteen-year-olds who were at uni at that time I was a lot, lot more focused and that helped me through quite a lot.

Apart from Mohammed, none of the young men made close friends at university, and spent most of their time with their friends from school and the Estate. Shakiel commented,

> I couldn't relate to anyone. But it's not to say I had a boring time in university. I had a good time outside the university, you know. I used

to attend university, do my stuff and then as soon as, you know, ding ding, it was over, I was off. I had stuff to do, I had friends to meet and we'd be doing stuff.

(2012)

Even Mohammed told me that most of his spare time was spent with his friends from the Estate: 'we still made time for each other. I mean, we went through a phase when Friday or Saturday night, no matter what, you'd at least come out, whether for a meal, or just sit on Abbey Street, or wherever it was' (2012). When not in lectures, Hanif studied in a university library closer to home, or was at work, and his free time was spent with this same group. He recalled his Stoneleigh friends being very supportive of his studies:

Even when I passed my degree, I can remember they all got me this really big card. I've still got it at home somewhere, and you know [they] had written all these really nice messages inside … And they were really proud and they all took me out to dinner to celebrate and everything.

(2012)

… And Moving Out

The ties to home – of family and friendship – remained surprisingly strong through the early post-school years, through college and university. As Hanif suggests, above, this was partly around the importance of the friendships made at school, which provided a sense of security and continuity through a period of change and uncertainty, the pressures of competing expectations (of self, family, community) and the larger world into which they now entered, outside the boundaries of the Estate. As will be explored in Chapter 5, these ties were to prove resilient and, in some cases, fragile and attenuated as the gap between school and work, friendship and family lengthened. However, it is also important to recognize the ways in which these experiences of college, of university and the futures they promised (or denied) were also indelibly shaped by more mundane, material concerns.

This is perhaps most apparent in the overlap between education and employment: all of my participants took on paid part-time employment alongside college and university lives. As will be explored in the next chapter, the impetus for this was a mixture of financial support for their families, to cover the costs of their university education, and a more personal need to bankroll their own transformation into independent men, with the material trappings of success – car, clothes, social life. Most were acutely aware that they did not have the financial capital to devote themselves entirely to studying. Mohammed explained:

> It's like a full-time job, your studies and stuff. People that have focus from their parents, you will see this is all they focus on, and work and other stuff is not a key concern for them. Whilst with us, we were trying to still buy all the designer wear, and trying to work part-time shifts here and there, and then still get to college and then still finish the coursework and revise for exams.
>
> (2012)

I cannot remember any of the young men working during their school years, when their time was divided between family, school, youth project and friends. For Mohammed, and his friends, the shift from school marked a significant break in this pattern. He continued, 'In fairness, I didn't have any responsibilities to earn for my family, but there was kind of an expectation that, you know, you're going to college now, you should be self-sufficient.' During college, the young men worked in a range of part-time jobs – retail, fast food (though not the reviled 'Indian restaurant' sector) and play- and youth-work. This work was selected primarily because it fitted around college or university schedules and was never considered more than temporary, for most at least. While this balancing act was taken for granted, and embraced in a forthrightly utilitarian manner – what Shakiel summed up as being 'just money' – it undoubtedly altered their experience of college and university life. Shahin, for example, described his schedule during his A-levels:

> I decided to do the A-levels intensive, because I think I was working about twenty hours a week .... That's twelve and a half at the play

centre – so that's two and a half hours every afternoon, from 3.30 to 6.00, and then I would leave the play centre and go to my youth project from 6.00 to 9.00. And so I'd be at college in the day, but maybe two or three days a week … So when I got home at 9.00, I'd eat and then from 10 to about 1 o'clock, go through my college work. Yeah, it was possible, but it's just – you had to be organized. And it was nice to have the money at the same time.

(2012)

He maintained the same schedule through university, though he did, he told me, drop his Saturday job at River Island and reduce his playwork hours during his third year. He contrasted this with the experience of his girlfriend Emma (whom he later married), who had attended a Russell Group university:

It was all very routine, so it wasn't like – like Emma's experience at university, which is completely the opposite of mine. Mine was sort of, yeah, 9–2 lectures at university, and then drive to work. I worked three days – six hours – and then maybe some weekends. So six hours every Monday, Wednesday and Friday … and then it might have been an hour hanging around the Stoneleigh Estate or something … And then coming home to study, because you've got seminars to prepare for the following day.

He reflected, 'I remember talking to you at the time and I think it, you know, because I was living at home and working and then … it seemed to me like it was like a job. Going to university was like a job …'

Next …

When I began writing this chapter (May–June 2021), I had initially imagined that the transition from school through college and university would be a shortish subsection or two, which would provide a quick recap on the original project and a narrative hop, skip and jump to the future pathways into work. Several weeks and 8000 words and counting later, I realized that this period was actually crucial to understanding what happened next in the lives of 'the Asian gang'.

College and university (where it happened) represented a crucial transition phase for the young men, reflecting both continuity and change, solidarity and, later, fragmentation. While I lamented, on their behalf, the loss of the liminal, transformative space of college and university as a 'rite of passage', and the more prosaic, workaday experience that post-compulsory education in the early twenty-first century represented for working-class, ethnic minority young men, I also realize now that this transition relied on a space of security within which change and separation could occur. Abbey Road, the Stoneleigh Estate, the SAYO project, even Thomas More School, provided a web of connections – even a safety net – which were to shape these choices (for good and ill), and both constrain and enable their next steps. College and university, and the links to home, family and friends, provided both a familiar foundation and a space from which to launch their future lives and careers. It was also a time and place when the trials and possibilities of adulthood would start to fracture these bonds and to break new pathways – often unplanned and unexpected, sometimes bad, occasionally bizarre – that would impact all aspects of their lives. The following chapter explores what happened next.

Work

Renaissance Man, Bengali Style

I first met Silver in the early months of my arrival on the Estate in 1994, when he was the senior playworker at the neighbouring Stoneleigh Estate Play Association (SEPA). In his early twenties, a slightly built Bengali young man with a round, always-smiling face, Silver had been a member of the first incarnation of the SAYO project, and rejoined the project as a youth worker in 1996. The eldest son in one of the first Bangladeshi families to arrive in the area, Silver had lived on the Stoneleigh Estate since he was two, and he attended the local primary and later Thomas More secondary school. Silver started work with the local playservice and youth service at the age of sixteen – 'I had a big mouth so I was out upfront as a worker', he recalled in 2012. He became a senior playworker at the age of eighteen, and the following year attended university in East London, one of the first Bengali young men from the area to enter higher education. When he joined SAYO in 1996, he was still centre manager at SEPA, and also completing a Master's degree in Public Service Management at South Bank University.

When the SAYO project closed, Silver moved to a sports project in a South London football club, where he was involved in the early years of the 'Kick It Out' campaign. At the age of twenty-five, he was employed to head up integrated youth services in a north London borough, working with 'high risk' young people:

> The idea [was] that a young person could come under one roof and get multiple needs met … So for eight years I spent developing those projects, building those up, working with different organisational cultures, different types of professions.

By the time he left, the project (which was still running) had twenty-two full-time staff, seven of which were young people who had entered as project users. Taking a sabbatical year from his role, Silver set up a training company focused on youth work development. Drawing on earlier connections from the Stoneleigh Estate, including Zohar and Yasmin, Silver's company trained youth workers and mentors. He recalled:

> The money thing wasn't an issue. So I just did it. People had no choice but to employ me because they didn't even have to pay me. I just made a clear decision that I wasn't going to price myself out of the market. So £100 a day, fine, £200 a day, fine, oh nothing, fine, if I like the work I'll do it.

After meeting with a national sports organization, Silver was employed to do some action research in South Africa – expenses only, he informed me – and he returned there several times, paid, to deliver youth work training and consultation. He later set up his own NGO in South Africa to develop youth leadership programmes and established a 'gifted and talented' scheme. He told me that in 2011 the programme had a full-time director and a budget of over £100,000. His training company had also established strong links with national sports organizations and foundations, which had led to work in Africa, Asia and South America. He laughed, 'I spent a lot of time in the last year travelling.'

Alongside, and interwoven with, this extraordinary career trajectory, Silver had a number of more conventional entrepreneurial business interests. He had bought his first house to rent while we were working together at the SAYO project – and I was, in fact, his first tenant. When he worked with the South London football project, he set up an events management company, which provided security for carnivals, *melas* and football events, and employed a number of young people from the Stoneleigh Estate. He recalled, 'It was very powerful at twenty-three going round with a bid that says this is my company, I'm a director.' Silver handed over control to his business partner in 2003:

I ran that for two years, but it was a weekend thing … and it got too big to a point where I had to make a decision to stay with my career or run the company … I realized I couldn't go down the road of full-time employment because it wouldn't tick enough of my boxes.

While working in north London, Silver opened a restaurant in the south London suburbs with three friends from the Estate – the Shapla. He recalled that he had worked as a waiter at the National Theatre when at school, and he had continued working in restaurants even when working at SEPA. Unlike some of the younger Bengalis, who eschewed restaurant work, for Silver owning a restaurant was a long-established ambition:

It's really funny, in my NRA at sixteen I wrote about my pleasures of working in the National Theatre and what it had given me in terms of skills set, and I said who knows, one day I'll open my own restaurant … So this opportunity came and I was blessed to be around a really motivated group of friends from the Stoneleigh and outside.

He reflected, 'I was twenty-five and it was a big risk. I think part of it was about we didn't care if we were going to fail – we were just fearless.' Later he added, 'We didn't have a clue.' Though he was mainly a silent partner, his youth work subsidized the money he needed to borrow for his share of the business. Five years later, the group opened a second business in Kent, and they had opened a third 'flagship' restaurant just six months before our interview. Less traditionally, the Shapla group had also just launched a charitable foundation, involving Zohar, Shahin and others from the 'older lot' on the Estate, to work in Bangladesh to promote social change through sport, bringing together the two strands of Silver's work life. With initial funding provided by the restaurants, Silver had already made two trips to Bangladesh in its first year and the Foundation was supporting seven projects in Sylhet:

We fund an orphanage, a girls' only project around skilling up girls in sewing and becoming employable in terms of the sewing factories. We work with tea gardens with the young women there. There's a disability project, there's a primary school that we're funding. There's a cricket project and there's a football project.

******

Silver's career can hardly be said to be typical – of his peer group, area or ethnic community – and still less should he be viewed through the lens of the 'role model', which is a slippery position for anyone, especially from a disadvantaged ethnic minority community, expected to shoulder the 'burden of representation' (Hall 1992). Silver himself was acutely aware of breaking new ground in education and employment, and was widely respected by the young men from the SAYO project, but very few followed directly in his wake. While he embodied a sense of possibilities, some preferred to envision a life outside of the Stoneleigh Estate and a career spent in service to others, while others (especially the older lot, who were closer to his age) often dismissed Silver and his friends for escaping, or avoiding, the violent conflicts that scarred their teenage years, and later lives.

Nevertheless, his trajectory captures some key elements that resonate more broadly with the experiences of 'the Asian gang' as they left education and entered the workforce. In particular, it captures the moment of flux – the sense of expanded horizons and seemingly infinite possibilities with which the young men faced their futures. As noted in the previous chapter, Silver's peer group were some of the first Bangladeshi young men from the area to even imagine going to university, and this opened up new opportunities, and new uncertainties. These educational shifts developed in parallel with new employment experiences for many of the Bangladeshi young men on the Estate. For Silver, these opportunities instilled a strong ethos of community service, of 'giving back', and of collective responsibility: 'Suddenly all around me these fantastic young people who were doing really great stuff and I felt a huge responsibility to continue to do the best I can do for them as well as for me, because I'm opening those doors. It's an integral part of who I am', he told me.

At the same time, there is a strong drive for more material measures of success – money, cars, status – combined with a restless, almost-hustling mentality that Silver described simply as 'business':

> I'd always done business, Claire … even at school I was doing stuff to survive. I think the economics of our circumstances, situation, means that you're extremely creative about anything and everything to make a bit of money … We were all raised in poverty, you know; there was not a judgement attached to it. It was a fact and there wasn't money around. Our parents couldn't give us the things we wanted and aspired to, so we had to find ways to get them … So business was always in me … It was just in me from young to make 2p from 1p.

For Silver, as a schoolboy, this had meant 'buying and selling things to kids, buying and selling stolen goods. Just doing things, making stuff … It wasn't because I was bad or evil or because I was antisocial; it was about survival'. This sense of ambivalence – the blurring of opportunity and precarity, of change and fragility, of ambition and necessity, of the licit and illicit – is one that haunts many of the young men from the SAYO project as they entered a shifting and uncertain workplace, in a changing employment landscape. For Silver and the 'older lot' in particular, these routes were often opaque: an irreversible break from the jobs their fathers did, for sure, but also a shift from the options open even to their older brothers. As Silver himself commented, 'The ones who are older than me, their pathway was really defined by the economics of needing to go and get a job to put food on the table.' In turn, and as in education, the experiences of his generation paved the way for their younger brothers who seemed not to share some of the anxieties of their older brothers.

Indeed, it was this sense of change that brought me back to 'the Asian gang' in the first place, and it was the 'older lot' who particularly piqued my curiosity because of the diverse career pathways they had taken. Sitting at the table at Zohar's wedding with a solicitor, a brace of bus drivers, a publican/restauranteur, a limousine driver, a call centre worker, a takeaway owner, a manager of an unemployment centre/

sandwich franchise owner, my interest was very much on the ties between this increasingly occupationally and socially diverse group of friends. Around the table, only one, Shahin, had a university degree, though a few had been to college (with varying levels of success) and a couple had been in prison; some were financially and occupationally successful, while others were bumping along the margins of the gig economy. Zohar himself, seated at the wedding top table, had just started his youth organization with Silver. At the time, and even until now, it was these differences that intrigued me – how the ties of friendship and community had attenuated and transformed over the previous fifteen years. These dimensions will be considered in the next chapter. However, re-reading Silver's interview, ten years on from the time it was conducted, I was struck less by what differentiated them than what brought them, and held them, together – or rather the *where* and *when* – and how this had shaped, and continue to shape, their present and future. As Silver explained:

> That area, and the uniqueness and specifics of that area, good and bad, formed who I am today, no two ways about it. From my childhood development to my transition for my professional development. I got everything I needed from that Estate and that area.

Silver described his personal ethos as leaving 'footprints and legacies' – making a positive and sustainable change to the lives of those he worked with. However, this image also conjures for me the ways in which the shared histories of the 'Asian gang' and the Stoneleigh Estate were to imprint, energize and curtail the ambitions of the young men, and how their adult lives continuously circled back to that foundational place and time, physically and imaginatively.

This chapter, then, picks up the story from the time that 'the Asian gang' left college and entered the workforce, and follows their journeys across the subsequent decade-plus. The focus in this chapter is broadened to explore the lives and choices of some of the 'older lot' who did not feature directly in the earlier book, though they were present in its background. This is in part because they occupy and exemplify some of the shifting terrain around employment for Bangladeshi men in the early 2000s, but also to illuminate the often narrow margins between success and failure, and the 'business' that underpins both. For a few, this spelled disaster, for a few others remarkable success: for most, something in-between – a way to pay the bills, build a life, raise a family. As with their fathers before them, these are a pioneer generation.

Bangladeshi Men at Work: Continuity and Change

As discussed in Chapter 3, the fathers of the young men from the SAYO project had followed a typical trajectory for Bangladeshi migrants who had arrived in the 1960s and 1970s, and who had worked in steel mills or textiles and leatherworking, and retired early due to redundancy or poor health. A couple of the younger fathers, such as Humzah's, had worked in the catering sector, though not in the 'Indian' restaurant trade which grew through the 1980s in response to increasing unemployment in the industrial and textile sectors where many Bangladeshis were employed (Alexander et al 2016, Kalra 1999). Despite these shifts, and the resilience and resourcefulness with which these communities and individuals adapted to a changing and hostile environment, the picture of employment for these post-industrial cast-offs, and their British-born and -raised descendants, has remained both depressing and strangely static.

As Clark and Drinkwater show (2007), levels of employment for Bangladeshi men from 1991 to 2001 (the period which spans my first period of fieldwork) rose from 45 per cent to 52 per cent, while levels of self-employment rose slightly from 10 per cent to 12 per cent. Interestingly, rates of self-employment for UK-born Bangladeshi men shrank across this period from 15.2 per cent to 11.2 per cent, suggesting entry into the mainstream labour market for the second generation. Self-employment data across the period shows the overwhelming importance of the catering trade, although by 2001 transport and finance sectors had increased significantly.

Nevertheless, the situation for British Bangladeshis remains hard, despite increasing educational achievements across the same period (Alexander & Shankley 2020). Kapadia et al (2015) note that while unemployment rates from 1991 to 2011 dropped (from 26 per cent to 11 per cent) for younger Bangladeshi men (aged 25–49), this was balanced by the increase in part-time work – increasing eleven-fold. By 2011 over one-third (35 per cent) of Bangladeshi working men were employed part-time. Data from the Office for National Statistics show that even in 2019, Bangladeshi men are twice as likely to be unemployed than white British men, suffer longer periods of unemployment and have the lowest mean weekly wages (£386) compared to white British men (£651), Pakistani men (£507) and Indian men (£720) (Clark & Shankley 2020: 132). Levels of employment for 25–49-year-olds (the category that includes my participants) still lagged behind the national average (65 per cent compared to 85 per cent).

However, it is not just the numbers but the kind and quality of work. Data from 2018 highlights occupational inequality by sector, with Pakistanis/Bangladeshis underrepresented across all of the higher managerial categories and overrepresented in sales and customer service, process, plant and machine operatives and elementary (unskilled/semi-skilled) occupations. These proportions and occupational sectors have remained largely consistent since 2004.[1] A recent study by the Institute for Fiscal Studies noted that in 2019, 11 per cent of Bangladeshi men were employed in hospitality and catering, and 17 per cent in road transportation (compared to 2 per cent and 5 per cent overall), and had the lowest median hourly wage of all groups (£9.90 compared to £14 for white British men). The authors note 'an "unexplained" employment penalty still remains for racialized groups' (Mirza & Warwick 2022: 51). Others raise the possibility of both an 'ethnic' and a 'Muslim' penalty in the mainstream labour market (Muslim Council of Britain 2015, Li & Heath 2020).

There is comparatively little work that explores these broad patterns at a deeper, more qualitative level, or which examines the diverse choices, positions and experiences that these categories encompass, and obscure. While there has been research and policy concern around the labour market experiences of Pakistani and Bangladeshi women (Dale et al 2002, Salway 2007, Dale & Ahmed 2011), comparatively little has focused on men. A notable exception is work by Sarah Salway which examines the labour market experiences of Bangladeshi young men in East London, and which points to exclusion from mainstream labour markets coupled with 'strong forces of inclusion within the Bangladeshi community' and a 'heavy dependency on intra-ethnic networks' (2008: 1128). Salway's findings resonate in part with the experiences of my participants – particularly the lack of knowledge about education and employment opportunities outside of their immediate experience, and the distaste for the restaurant trade that dominated it. However, her account fails to capture the diversity of work that these young men pursued, the processes through which these paths were negotiated and the changes over time. It fails, too, to consider the different ways in which 'community' may be understood or enacted en route. In what follows, I trace some of these journeys, embracing a broad spectrum of what 'work' might be, and following the interwoven pathways that were painstakingly, and sometimes painfully, carved.

However, I start in the Stoneleigh Estate in the mid-1990s.

Entry Points

As discussed in Chapter 3, most of the young men from the Stoneleigh Estate started college, though comparatively few finished it. At the same time, all started work alongside their studies, most usually in part-time, temporary jobs in the retail and service sector. These early forays into the labour market are significant in terms of shaping both their future careers (in some cases by highlighting what they did *not* want to do) and their broader aspirations around money, status and individual potential. They also highlighted tensions between these individual ambitions and other responsibilities, particularly in relation to family position and expectations.

As Mohammed noted previously, leaving school was seen by the young men and their families as an entry into adulthood: the time to become at least financially self-reliant and, in some cases, to contribute to the family income. Humzah, for example, had worked for McDonald's and Tescos for short periods of time, and on leaving college, in the storerooms at Argos. 'I just needed the money that time, you know, just like, give me a job anywhere, whatever I could find that time', he told me in 2012. For Humzah, as the eldest son in a family of seven children, the pressure to support the family was intense:

> I mean mine's quite a big family isn't it, and mum and dad not working as well, their lives getting tricky, so whatever you can get. I was feeling it as well, I'm supposed to help; it's that time.

His younger brother, Ifti, similarly felt enormous parental pressure to bring in money, and on leaving school (and while theoretically attending college), he worked three jobs: shelfstacking in Sainsburys, McDonald's and mini-cabbing. Mustafa, who was Silver's peer group and a couple of years older than Humzah, left school with no GCSEs and then flunked out of an apprenticeship in motor mechanics. 'I thought, everybody's got cars, but that was the wrong choice. Done that, didn't like it', he informed me solemnly in 2012. 'I done a service on a car, half way to France, the wheel came off. The man said to me, "This is not for you".' His mother insisted Mustafa found work:

> She kicked me out of bed and she said 'this ain't a hotel, you know' …
> I had to find work and bring the money home to her, that's it. So I've been working since. I worked in printing places, factories, anything, offices, anything that I thought could give me some money. Anything just to get my mum off my back, basically.

In these cases, the familial pressure to earn did curtail other ambitions. In others, a balance was achieved between financial responsibilities and career choice, though as Shahin's study/work schedule suggested (see Chapter 3), this could be gruelling. This pressure was exacerbated for those who were the eldest sons. Khalid commented of his older brother, Shahin, 'in Bengali families it's like the oldest son has to look after the whole of the family by working and all that, study whatever. He's got more pressure on him because he's the oldest' (1996). Shahin himself, however, said he worked mainly to support himself and that his mother 'if she could have it her way, it would have been just study' (2012). Shakiel, the only son in his family, also told me that the money he earned from working in a local clothes store partly 'contributed towards the house and everything but … I saved a lot. I wanted to buy a car' (2012). He continued:

Money, even now, it makes you, you know, it gives you a bit more independence, doesn't it? You feel a bit more comfortable, a bit more secure, and obviously when you're young, you know, you want to do stuff.

For others, like Zohar, while there was no obvious financial pressure (he had older siblings who were working), his parents also had a strong expectation that he would work alongside his studies. He recalled that his mother, in particular, who had worked from home as a seamstress, was a particular influence:

She's a believer in work. I think that's why we've all got the work ethic in our family. It's like you have to work. She said, 'As a woman then, I worked and now I'm still working. You lot can work so don't tell me there's no work out there. It doesn't matter what it is, you learn something and you learn the trade, and you learn how to be what the work is'.

(2012)

For the little ones, most of whom had older siblings, the pressures seemed less, and although they all worked through college, this was mainly for their personal use and enjoyment. Hanif, Jamal, Sayeed and Mohammed all worked multiple jobs through this period, including at various McDonald's restaurants in the West End. Hanif recalled, 'I was doing playwork at the time, but I needed some extra money, you know, because we was going on holiday somewhere – I think to Magaluf or something stupid like that' (2012). The friends applied together and were allocated to the same restaurants:

> So me and Ismat would work in the same McDonalds, and Jamal and Sayeed and Layaak were in the same McDonalds. And Sayeed and I were the only ones that hated going to work, and so there was once that I clocked in and Sayeed had come to my store and said, 'Oh, Hanif, I'm not going to work'. So I said, 'Ok wait for me' and I clocked out ... and I just walked out and no one knew if I was there ... So, yes, I wasn't there for long.

Sayeed agreed, stating, 'I didn't have no commitment. I was lacking in commitment really bad ... I used to go into work, sign in, then I'd think, "Oh, I hate this job", walk straight back out' (2012). Jamal, in contrast (and in contrast to his approach to studying), took work much more seriously, and through college had two jobs – at McDonald's and at Dickins and Jones in Oxford Circus. He told me:

> Even when I was at college I was doing part-time work ... And I just thought to myself, do you know what, I prefer working, and I prefer the money I'm getting ... Because obviously, you know, I never grew up in a very wealthy family, so like my mum and dad couldn't afford to give me x amount of money per week, so when I was earning it for myself, I felt, you know, independent .... I saw the rewards of it immediately, whereas with college and stuff I didn't.
>
> (2012)

He worked shifts at McDonald's during the week and then Dickens and Jones at weekends: when he left college, he increased his time to four days at Dickins and Jones. He enjoyed Dickens and Jones because of the discount on clothes, but also because of the buzz of the West End, which was a far cry from the Stoneleigh Estate: 'At that time, Oxford Circus, well, you know it was the main thing. Everyone would go shopping there so working there was great in that sense.'

Mohammed similarly worked through college with multiple jobs: 'I worked in McDonald's for a little bit, then I worked in Selfridges. I was even doing deliveries for [Sher Khan's restaurant] after I passed my driving test, in the evening' (2012). Like Jamal, he enjoyed having the money – 'When I started university I had a BMW ... seven or eight years ago, literally I was just going out and buying anything and everything I wanted' – and working in the city centre, but the monotony of the work also focused his ambitions elsewhere:

> I quickly realized that I was a lot brighter than the people that are working there for years and years, and I was like, this cannot be all of my life ... I just knew there was a bigger world out there.

Breaking In

As Mohammed indicates, the entry into the workplace was an insight both into life outside the Stoneleigh Estate and an aspirational future beyond even the glamour of West End retail. However, while, as the labour market picture above suggests, young British Bangladeshis are increasingly entering into the 'Sales and Customer Service' industry, it is also true that for the young men from 'the Asian gang' project, these jobs were viewed in through a highly utilitarian lens – as a means rather than an end in themselves. None of the young men I knew remained in retail or customer services for more than a few, early, years at the most. This suggests that the labour market, at least for these young men, was more open, more mobile and more transitory than the 'big picture' suggests, at least at an individual level.

Big pictures aside, there was a more local feature of the employment landscape of the Stoneleigh Estate during the early 2000s that was to have a more significant transformative impact: the opening up of playwork and youth work across the Borough. As discussed above, Silver was one of the first individuals from the Estate to enter this arena. However, several of the older lot were also recruited as volunteer workers, including S. Ahmed, Shahin and Humzah (who laughingly moaned, 'I used to do voluntary youth work from quite young and didn't even get paid for it, bloody hell' (2012)).

Building on this early work, Majid, the Council Youth Officer who recruited Yasmin to the SAYO project, initiated a drive to diversify the playservice, and recruited a number of 'the older lot', including Humzah, Shahin, Zohar and S. Ahmed. Later Khalid and Shakiel were also recruited, along with a number of other Asian (and non-Asian) young men (and women) from the Estate. Humzah recalled, 'There was quite a lot of us got into it first … There was like lots of Asian faces there, lots – it was like we all knew each other. It was quite funny.' For Shahin and Zohar, who were at college and then university, the short hours and relatively good pay fitted well around their studies, and both graduated to youth work. Shahin, in fact, was briefly employed as a youth worker at the SAYO project, and he, Zohar, S. Ahmed and Humzah joined its first Management Committee.

Both Shahin and Humzah moved away from this work after several years. For Humzah, the part-time work was not sufficient for his needs and obligations:

> I enjoyed it. I was just, at the time I didn't realise, it was actually good money, but I thought it wasn't enough … After I left, I thought oh my God, I was doing less hours, I was getting more, but at the time I thought I could get more, so I remember I went to the restaurants and stuff.
>
> (2012)

After a couple of years of disrupted study and indecision, Shahin decided to pursue a career in law:

> There was a time when I was thinking, Oh, you know, should I just think about youth work as a full time career? But no … youth work's a noble profession [but] … I want to try something like a bit more challenging and then having experienced, you know, all the problems with the law … [And I thought] you know, am I going to just have all these part time jobs or actually pursue a career?
>
> (2012)

For Zohar, however, the entry into playwork, and then youth work, was to change his life. His family were already well known for their community work – his older sister and her husband had run the local

Bengali Saturday School for many years. Zohar himself had started volunteer youth work, with Shahin and Humzah, from the age of sixteen and was inspired by Majid:

> He had come around and he tried to empower the Bangladeshi community by saying you need to be part of the system, you need to get involved ... He would come down and talk to us, and talk to the Council and so he expelled that myth of 'they don't want to get involved' ... It was kind of fun and that's now I got into it.
>
> (2012)

Zohar continued work with the playservice through his university studies, and it became more significant than his earlier imagined career in banking:

> I used to always help people, give back to people. I was part of that to do something, and yes, that's the kind of stuff, and I loved it. When I started working at playservice I loved it ... I don't really want to do anything else.

He dropped out of his Master's course in System Management at Birkbeck College, and went to work at Kickstart, a crime prevention youth scheme. He took on a playcentre project in Tower Hamlets: 'It was new. I'd never worked in a Bangladeshi community like that before in my life ... It was a learning curve, I can tell you', he recalled. Alongside the playwork, he was involved with youth inclusion projects in the borough, working with a number of 'hardcore trouble makers in the area', Bengali, white and Black: 'I told my mum and dad that I've got a full time job. They said they weren't too happy. I think they wanted me to do something better than that', he reflected. He shaved his trademark floppy hairstyle and took on a streetwise persona:

> The kids talked to me very well, funnily enough, because one, when they saw me outside, because I had my head shaven and ... they didn't even know at the time that I was Bengali ... They thought I was this kind of coolie kind of West Indian guy, and then I started talking to them in my broken Bengali ... I think that actually helped me ... because I had this whole South London accent, they were fascinated that I was from South London.

When the project closed due to funding cuts, Zohar returned to his home borough and worked on a neighbouring estate to the Stoneleigh, developing his management and strategic skills:

> I became more and more passionate for me to work with them [the young people] and the communities, and that's when I really knew. I put my stamp on it and said, 'This is the work I'm going to do, work with, in the community', and that was when I was like, started thinking, my brain was straight.

When a colleague from the Kickstart programme set up a national charity doing youth inclusion through sport, Zohar and Silver were key partners. When we spoke in 2012, the charity had been running for five years and employed seventeen full-time staff, and Zohar had just taken over a communication and development role. He and Silver had also just established the Shapla Foundation discussed above. Of this new venture, Zohar said,

> We do so much of this here, and we've got this, we have the skills, why can't we set something up in Bangladesh? … you go out there and you see that, and you want to progress and make sure that you help, what your forefather had done and everyone else had done, so it's all that … I think obviously it touches our hearts, being Bangladeshi, [seeing] young people struggling out there.

Following in the footsteps of the older lot, a number of the younger members of the project took up playwork, though mainly for short periods. Like Humzah, Shakiel left to look for more money – in his case, through mini-cabbing – while Hanif, Mohammed and Jamal all did playwork through college ('it was just something that got me through' Mohammed told me). However, few considered the work as long term: Jamal told me, emphatically, 'I really hated it, really, really hated it … that two and a half hours was like almost nine hours to me' (2012). Hanif did playwork through college and university – 'you know, the timing was good. It was only a few hours and then while you're there, it was relatively easy' (2012) – but left when he started his LPC and began work as a paralegal.

Only one, Hanif's brother Khalid, settled on playwork as a longer-term option. Having dropped out of college and after a brief stint at McDonald's ('I think I got three pay packets and that was it, I left', he recalled in 2012), he started summer playwork, with Shakiel, at his old primary school: 'So that was weird and nice, and I so loved that summer holiday ... So when the term time [work] started ... I went for an interview.' He worked at a local primary school for over ten years, and later progressed to being a Centre Manager. He told me, 'Maybe me not being academically good, working at the playcentre, I felt like I was the person that was able to be more free and deliver what I'm doing'. A sweet-natured and caring young man, for a long time Khalid seemed to have found his place in the playservice and completed his NVQ levels 1 and 2 at the weekend. He took on lunchtime playwork in a number of schools around the borough, and later worked full-time as a classroom assistant in a local primary school.

Despite a promotion to Centre Manager, Khalid left playwork due to problems with co-workers and a sense of stagnation in his role:

> I was the best playworker there, but there was a part of me missing still, to be complete ... I just didn't want to be just a good playworker ... I was just comfortable, I never looked, and sometimes you've got to move, haven't you? Sometimes you have to go and take opportunities, look out for opportunities and take them. I just sometimes was a bit slow in identifying opportunities.

Khalid worked for several months in TK Maxx and then for five years in a high-end Chinese restaurant in Mayfair, and when I interviewed him in 2012, he was working for the NHS as a healthcare assistant, and had just started training to become a nurse.

While most of the young men moved on from playwork and youth work in the Borough, Sher Khan, typically, bucked this trend. A decade older than the project participants, Sher Khan had joined the SAYO project initially as a volunteer. He grew up on a neighbouring, mainly white, Estate, and he and his older brother co-owned a successful local restaurant, under the nearby railway arches. The restaurant was opened by his father, a former kitchen porter at a local hospital. When we spoke in 2012, the restaurant had been established for over twenty-five years. Sher Khan worked with SAYO for four years, combining the youth work with his restaurant job. 'It was like doing that in the day time and then juggling it with the restaurant in the night time, which wasn't easy at the best of times, but if I weren't enjoying it and getting self-satisfaction, I don't think I would have done it', he reflected. Unlike the younger men, Sher Khan had a substantial income from his business, so for him youth work was solely about self-development. When the project closed, he worked with Silver in North London, then with Zohar in East London, qualified as a youth worker and mentor, and moved into behaviour support work in schools across the Borough. He told me:

> Today, I'm working in schools and I'm working with young offenders, I'm working with behaviour support, and … a lot of people know me for that … I've changed careers, so I took a step back on the restaurant side of things and I've sort of gone full blown [on the youth work] … it's all sort of fallen into place really nicely, like a puzzle. And it weren't hard work neither.

When we spoke, he had just started working with Zohar, bringing him back full circle to the Stoneleigh Estate.

It is, of course, important not to overstate the significance of this time and place. There were many young men, I suspect, who left the Stoneleigh and never looked back; others who had a very different connection to the Estate and their peers, and pursued different paths into work; others still for whom these early years after school and college were simply a way to make money on their way elsewhere. I do not know what happened to subsequent generations of young people, Bengali and otherwise, for whom these opportunities vanished along with the youth work in the area. Nevertheless, these entry points do reflect a changing landscape of employment opportunities and challenges for these young men in the early 2000s, and a sense of expanded horizons. 'Breaking in' to new spheres of employment, either spatially or professionally, reshaped the ways in which Bangladeshi

young men were seen by others, and the way they saw themselves. As
Sher Khan reflected:

> Growing up on the Stoneleigh, it weren't easy to be yourself, you
> know? … A lot of them weren't sure where to go, or what to do with
> themselves and a lot of their parents were coming through the restaurant
> trade, and they're all chefs, waiters, but it was time to make change. It
> was time for change for the whole Asian community, for young people
> to break into other fields, and I think we've done that now.

Breaking Out

Breaking out of the Stoneleigh, and into other professions, areas or
forms of employment, was not straightforward, and was met with
chequered success among those who attempted it. This was the case even
for those who stayed within more 'traditional' forms of employment,
as will be discussed in the next section, but for those who broke new
ground, the path was often convoluted and strewn with obstacles. Some
never made it. Others – the comparative few – did, through a mixture
of talent, determination, hard work and, usually, a shred of serendipity.

Shahin is perhaps the most successful of the young men I met through
'the Asian gang' project, in terms of education, career and, possibly,
financial position. An articulate, strikingly handsome and ambitious
young man, even aged seventeen when I first met him, Shahin was, and
is, characterized by a curiosity and restlessness which drove his career,
but which also seemed at points, from the outside at least, to verge on
recklessness. As noted earlier, Shahin took some time before deciding
on a career in law. After a number of false starts, a turning point was the
events after his attack in Hammersmith, and particularly when Mustafa
went to prison (see Chapter 5). Seeing the events unfold with the police
and courts fascinated him, but he also recognized the vulnerability of
his own position:

> My life could easily have gone in a different direction … And then,
> obviously, after Mustafa going to prison, you think, okay maybe this

is, like, a shock to the system, you know. Could have been many more people ended up in prison, and you know, maybe it's the time to do a U-turn.

Shahin completed his Law degree at Middlesex University and then his Legal Practice Course (LPC), and having done work experience in both a solicitor's and a barrister's chambers during his degree decided to become a solicitor. He was clear-sighted about his ambitions and the limitations of his degree, given the inherent biases of the legal profession against post-1992 universities: 'There's nothing wrong with having ambition, but I think at the same time you need to be realistic', he told me. He noted that on his LPC course, 'there were sixteen of us, and of the sixteen of us, four didn't have training contracts, and we all went to new universities'. There was an intersecting element of racial inequality too: Shahin reflected, 'Not many black and Asian people had training contracts, so you do the LPC, taking the risk without a job.' He covered his expenses through working and using his student loan money to buy and trade shares – Tesco, Vodaphone 'and a few other companies' – getting advice from a Chinese former schoolfriend, Paul, who worked in an administrative role for the *Financial Times*.

What struck me at the time, and again when speaking to him in 2012, was the level of strategic planning that underpinned all Shahin's decisions. He worked through his LPC as a paralegal to gain experience, determined not to follow the conventional route into High Street criminal law. He laughed:

> In fact, if I went down the criminal route, I could probably have been a very successful criminal lawyer. I mean, half of [our area], as the clients were ready made … I think I just wanted to avoid [it] because everybody assumes … that it's only criminal law or the High Street type.[2] But nobody would think about corporate law or employment law … and I just thought … I should aim for something different.

Shahin was particularly drawn to employment law: 'One of the lecturers, she was a trade union lawyer and I've always had sympathy with the trade union movement … I wanted to act for the individual.' He applied for training contracts while studying: 'I think I probably made about 200 to 300 applications … when I was going for interviews, I probably had about twenty-five.' He started work as a paralegal in a city law firm specializing in personal injury and then moved to another firm in South-West London to pursue employment law. He eventually got a training contract with a small high street firm in West London, where he helped them develop their personal injury department, and volunteered at the Islington Law Centre to develop his experience of employment law. He reflected:

> I was always thinking, Oh my CV has to look better than somebody, another person that's applying … I just think you need to have … an endpoint, where you want to be. Maybe not too far ahead, but make sure that you set yourself targets, but realistic.

When he qualified, Shahin obtained a position at a well-known firm in Central London, specializing in personal injury. He explained:

> What I liked about the firm was … they met that desire, you know, being on the community side but wanting to be a successful lawyer and make lots of money as well, at the same time.

He worked at the firm for three years and left to focus more on employment law, moved briefly to a trade union firm in East London (for two weeks) and then moved to a larger, branded firm specializing in employment law, where his younger brother, Hanif, was already working. He worked there for three years, rose to become a deputy team manager, overseeing the work of eight lawyers. Always in a rush careerwise, he told me, 'It was just such a large firm and then I thought, oh, to move up is going to take years'. He moved to a small firm in Mayfair, which worked mainly for employers: 'I thought, "I've got six years' experience of acting for individuals. Let's see what it's like on the other side."' The firm was relatively new, and Shahin was attracted to learning more about how businesses were established:

> It would be quite a good way of raising the firm's profile and raising my profile at the same time. And because it was smaller you could be more creative … there's a lot more autonomy … I just saw it as experience and yeah, it was good.

He resigned suddenly a year later and decided to start his own firm – something that both his mother and I were convinced was doomed to failure. The firm's name would be a combination of his and his wife's surnames, to lessen any perceived stigma of an Asian Muslim brand. He commented:

> This is how bad the profession is, or it's society. When I was thinking about the name, I was thinking, in my mind, should I actually use my surname? I mean that actually crossed my mind … The market I'm focused on is different, so it's not the high street, and not many of the city-type firms have an Asian name … And then you've got all this negative [stuff] about Islam.

Shahin developed a stylish website and took on an expensive sounding address in Docklands to mitigate this possible stereotyping, and already had ambitious plans for expanding using consultants and remote working. When I interviewed him in the summer of 2012, he was waiting on professional indemnity insurance and was about to launch. He laughed, 'The idea is that hopefully I can retire before I'm fifty.'

As with Silver, Shahin's career illuminates some important tensions (or balances), between ambition and constraint, self and others, money and 'being on the community side', where you come from and where you imagine yourself going, and what it takes to get there. Unlike many of his friends and peers, Shahin was extraordinarily strategic and tenacious in his career development, moving jobs frequently, doing unpaid work to accumulate the necessary experience, identifying opportunities and gaps where he could use his own background and experiences to his advantage, taking what sometimes seemed like foolhardy risks, but always with a back-up plan. I would often tease him that he seemed determined to do everything the hard way though, on reflection, I am not sure there *was* another way. He told me:

> I've always just thought, you know, you can't sit back. You need to, if you want something, you need to go out for it, and it's not [just] going to come.

Shahin's account is littered with the people who supported him and opened up opportunities along the way – first and foremost his mother, but also the youth project, university lecturers, partners in the many law firms he worked in. It is striking that he rarely dwelt on the obstacles or barriers, whether racial, religious or classed, except as things to be negotiated or overcome or, indeed, turned to his advantage. And, as with Silver and Zohar, the Stoneleigh Estate remained a foundational place:

> My values are still the same ... you can't forget where you've come from and you know; if you've grown up in a council estate then I think you should be open about it rather than try to create something that's not the truth. Because I think it's good. It helps, and it's made me better, it's helped me work hard, twice as hard, because, you know, there's all these pressures and ... the labour market could be a lot more transparent. But I think, you know, being Asian you have to work twice as hard, a bit like women as well, and in this age, being Muslim as well.

It is interesting to compare Shahin's career with that of his younger brother, Hanif. As discussed previously, Hanif had settled on a career in law while at school, partly because of his father but also because, I think, he enjoyed arguing with people. A very different personality from his older brother, Hanif is a gentle and unassuming person, with a diffidence that hides a deep moral sense grounded in a strong religious ethic. He does share both of his brothers' good looks and charm, and a warmth that is very endearing to those around him. Like Shahin, Hanif qualified with an upper second-class degree in law from a post-1992 university, but could not afford to immediately take his LPC. He obtained work as a paralegal for a firm specializing in mental health law – 'a real eye-opener', he told me in 2012 – and used the year to apply for funding.

> I knew I wasn't going to earn enough there to save up to do the course and so ... what I then started doing was looking for funding ... I didn't know where I was going to get the money from to make the application, put the £250 deposit down ... we, mum didn't have the money ... So I went to the library, looked up the Charity Commission book and then looked through so many different charities that would provide funding for that kind of thing.

Hanif obtained funding from the Law Society (£4000) and the Sir John Cass Foundation (£2000) and the rest was from smaller charities:

> I raised the full £8000, so I didn't pay a penny for the LPC. And, you know, I was really grateful for that. And I was able to do the course, but otherwise I wouldn't have known how I would have ever – I probably wouldn't have ever done it because I would have probably gone on to work and then never gone back into it.

He applied for training contracts (what seemed like hundreds from my memory of the time): 'It took me nine months, which was quite disheartening because most you wouldn't get a response from ... but having seen Shahin go through the same process, I knew what I was up against', he told me. He got a training contract at a large City Centre firm specializing in personal injury and employment law and was kept on, later specializing in employment law. When I interviewed him in 2012, seven years later, he was still there and he stayed until he joined his brother's firm in 2016. When I commented on the very different trajectory he had chosen from Shahin's, he reflected:

> In the round I've always been happy with everything at work and the work that we do. You know, it's morally, it's working with the trades unions ... so from that point of view, that's really important to me as well.

When I asked him about Shahin's new venture, he laughed, 'So Emma thought he's going through a mid-life crisis ... But you know, it's going to be risky. So I think if you feel it's right, you know? And I think he'll make it a success'.

For Mohammed, a career in law proved less desirable. Having completed his law degree, Mohammed started paralegal work at a high street firm in Essex, but 'I quickly realized that I didn't want to become a solicitor' (2012). He told me, 'I felt that it was overglamorous, underpaid drastically' and the work – 'a lot of human rights stuff' – was challenging: 'it was meeting a lot of vulnerable people. I just didn't find that comfortable'. Worried about paying for his LPC and in a rush to be earning bigger money, he returned to do a part-time master's degree in corporate governance. He explained:

I've always been quite commercial … I was always into how to make money and buying and selling, and stuff like that – obviously not on a big scale … Car stereos, or whatever I can get hold of, or sometimes to buy stuff from the internet, spyware, and then sell it to my mates, or at uni, or laptops, just stupid, stupid things.

Mohammed started work as a compliance analyst for an insurance company in south-west London while doing his master's, and then as a legal and compliance officer for an insurance firm in Surrey. With the birth of his first child, he decided the commute was too far and set up a consultancy that worked for a number of city-based insurance companies, advising on risk and compliance. He told me proudly, 'What I do at the moment is so niche … because it's such as small sector. It's quite a big money making sector … we're talking like million pound, billion pound cargo insurance.' He closed his company and took salaried work for a City insurer after the financial market collapsed: 'I felt that like when the market collapsed and stuff, I couldn't get work for a bit. I thought sod that … I'll just get a job and it will be a little bit easier.' The firm had offices worldwide and Mohammed had to liaise with these branches, and travel widely. However, he also felt that his career was constrained by his religious beliefs and his family life:

I can expedite my career a lot more if I went out drinking with all the guys and stuff, but it's not something I've ever been interested in, and I'm quite happy to either work late on a Friday night or come home and spend time with my family. I think those are the limitations for me, but … it's just how I choose to live my life.

Interestingly, and in contrast to his peers, Mohammed was cagey about his background in the workplace, clearly feeling it was more a liability than asset:

If someone said to me, where are you from, I'd never say I'm from somewhere I'm not. But I think, like, you just realise that people in that field are not people that I would meet in my day to day life … I'm exceptionally proud of where I'm from and what I've done and what I've achieved, you know, personally for me … [but] the people that I sit with and stuff, and the people that I have to advise, they have to take my advice.

For Mohammed, perhaps more than the other young men I knew (with the exception of M, discussed below), the trappings of material success were a main driving force – a feeling exacerbated, perhaps, by his position as the eldest son. Rightly proud of his achievements, his ability to support his parents was particularly important: 'I think my dad's really proud of me. I look after my dad quite a lot, I give him a lot of cash and stuff so he can kind of look after himself.' Nevertheless, for Mohammed, there were clear tensions between family and community, and work, which he largely addressed by compartmentalizing his life. It is revealing that Mohammed had moved away from his old friends in recent years – something that will be explored in the next chapter. He described the differences between 'home' and 'work' as sometimes feeling 'like a case of schizophrenia'. Tellingly, he told me that while his parents were proud of his success, they did not understand what he actually did:

> I don't even bother talking about my work. No one understands what I do. They just think I just go to work in a suit and come back in a suit … that's enough for them, you know.

The same was true of his friends. Hanif laughed:

> Did you ever watch 'Friends'? No one really knew what Chandler did. Do you remember? It was like that with Mohammed. He got his job. I swear to you, even up until now I still don't know what Mohammed does.
>
> (2012)

As discussed in Chapter 3, Jamal had a difficult, and unconventional, route through education in his pursuit of an 'office job'. Having dropped out of college and given up playwork, he told me:

> Then, I hit a brick wall. I was unemployed for a little while and living on benefits. It was just the worst time of my life, you know. I just couldn't do nothing. State benefits don't give you peanuts. So then I applied for jobs.

Jamal's first post-college work was in a Nat West bank branch in North West London. The work was obtained through an agency, which restricted his time there to a year. At the end, he was interviewed for a permanent role, but was not hired: 'They interviewed me and they asked me what my expectation was in terms of salary, and had I known what they were interviewing me for, I probably would have lowered it a bit' (2012). Jamal had been covering for an assistant manager on maternity leave, so asked for a similar level of remuneration, not realizing they were recruiting for a more junior cashiering role: 'I think they frowned upon that', he reflected.

After the bank, Jamal obtained a job as assistant manager for William Hill bookmakers in East London, which had a large number of Bangladeshi customers. Echoing Zohar's comments above about the difference between East London and the Stoneleigh Bangladeshis, Jamal told me:

> It really opened up my eyes to the East, how Asian culture is in East London, you know, because when you're growing up you don't see the hidden stuff that goes on on the streets … When I was working there, there were people like in my father's peer group that I was smoking with.

At the time, I recall, this job was a source of some tension with his more religious friends, Hanif and Sayeed, although they were supportive of his need to earn money. He himself was ambivalent:

> It's a sin, and all of that stuff, but at the time, I just needed to get a job. I really just needed to get a job and that's what I was doing. And also the fact that I wasn't publicly promoting betting, you know, I felt that was ok for me. But looking back at it now, obviously me putting up posters and all of that is promoting it in a sense, so …

Sayeed, who was in the interview, interjected:

> I knew he'd been waiting like two years or something like for a job … and he was finding it hard. I could see in his face he was like going through depression … So when he did get this job, I didn't want to make him feel like 'Islam tells you not to do this, don't go for it' … I said to him, 'look once you're in the job, look for another job, so you can get out of that job'.

Jamal stayed for five years (until 2008), eventually moving on a new post in a bank. He explained:

> I just decided, you know, this is not my life. I can't live in the underbelly of society, you know, because the gambling, the whole, everything associated with that is very negative and very slimy.

An additional factor was that he had started looking for a bride and was concerned that his employment might count against him. He said, 'My mum was like finding that she was going to a dead end everywhere, so you know, I had to change my job very quick' (see Chapter 6). Jamal started working for Barclays Bank as a cashier and had since moved up to be a personal adviser. In 2012, he was working in a branch not far from the Stoneleigh Estate. This came with its own challenges and worries:

> I was like, oh shit … it's quite dangerous … a lot of school people might still be walking up and down there … I don't want them to know where I work … It's like, if someone knows you, they feel like you're going to give them more stuff … like in terms of charges, they think 'come on man, just get rid of that charge' … But then I went there … and it's been a positive move in that sense [and] … it's only a stone's throw away from my house.

Recently married, he told me, 'My ultimate aim is to become like a branch manager, and then probably move on to fraud investigations or something like that'.

For others of his peers from the Stoneleigh Estate, the schoolboy ambition of an 'office job' was to prove more elusive. Shakiel himself, having completed his hated degree in Computer Science, first started work in procurement for the NHS, a post he obtained through an employment agency. Although he said his degree helped him get the job, it was of little relevance to the work itself: 'All you did there was you, basically, you used catalogues' (2012). While he liked the people, he left within the year: 'It wasn't well paid because it was through an agency.' He moved to work for RBS, again through an employment agency, in the human resources department in North London. He recalled:

I think it was whilst working with them when I, kind of, decided that wearing a suit and getting up in the morning and going to the office, sitting in a room in front of a computer, was not what I want to do.

When his department relocated to Manchester, Shakiel took redundancy. Having decided office work was not for him, he tried to open a takeaway with family, which later fell through, and returned to mini-cabbing, something he had previously done to support himself through university. I pick up his story in the next section.

The Re-Invention of Tradition

Although I met Jadil in the 1990s when I was working at the SAYO project, I do not recall ever holding a conversation with him until, probably, Zohar's wedding in 2010. A quiet and shy moon-faced young man, a year or two older than Shahin and Humzah, Jadil rarely came to the youth club and was always in the background of group events (most usually providing the transport). When I did see him he would rarely speak directly to me, or look me in the eye, though he always seemed to be smiling or laughing with his friends. Mainly he seemed to be working, all the time, in his family restaurant, where, it was rumoured, the older lot were often to be found hanging out after hours. Jadil was the youngest of a family of four children, and the only boy, and grew up on the Stoneleigh Estate. He left school with no qualifications and started working from the age of twelve in restaurants owned by his extended family: 'I wanted my own money. I wanted to learn the restaurant trade … all my uncles used to do it … I used to go to their restaurants and help out', he told me in 2011. When he left school at fifteen, and having problems at home (his father was disappointed that Jadil had 'messed up school and everything'), he moved to East Sussex to work in a restaurant owned by his brother-in-law, where he stayed for eighteen months. Life outside London was a shock to the young Jadil: 'I didn't realise it was going to be like that … I'd just look out of the windows. Just work really, and that's about it, just wander round the town'. He returned to London just before he turned seventeen, and opened up his own restaurant in partnership with his father. He bought the business for £30,000: 'Someone already went bankrupt. Well, about six people went bankrupt ... [but] I just wanted my own place'. He recalled, 'As soon as I went in there it started going up every week. I started working hard. I was working long hours, like thirteen, fourteen hours a day and it started improving every week.' He had eight staff and was learning on the job:

> I knew most of the trade, and then my father brang [*sic*] in the main head chef. So I knew front of house and he knew the kitchen and then I went into the kitchen to learn everything for myself. So I done another six months in the kitchen.

Jadil kept the restaurant for a decade and sold it to his sister, who, in 2011, was still running it successfully. He told me he sold the business for £50,000 and with the profit took a year off 'going out with friends, girlfriends, just enjoying myself'. He then opened an off-licence on Abbey Road on the Stoneleigh, 'but I didn't like it ... You sit on the till and then you have to deal with a lot of kids stealing and everyone complains about the prices', he nutshelled. He also received a visit from a group from East London Mosque, who disapproved of him selling alcohol. He shrugged, 'I just told them to go away because it's my business place and I don't want to discuss anything.' A year and a half later, he compounded his offence by selling the shop and taking on a pub on a rapidly gentrifying high street nearby. Jadil saw this as an opportunity to return to the restaurant trade too: 'I thought I could make the restaurant upstairs and I could learn the new trade downstairs.' Despite some teething problems, 'it was hard, to tell you the truth, to start with because I ran it down first. I lost business ... there was a lot more stuff involved'; when I interviewed him in 2011 the business employed sixteen staff and had an annual turnover of £1.2 million (30 per cent food, 70 per cent drink, he estimated). He told me, 'It's a good amount for a pub ... we've got a really good late night trade ... City and office people. We're packed every night.' Jadil said that he was now 'taking it easy', coming in around eight in the evening and closing up at about five in the morning. He was using his 'spare time' to build a chicken coop for his children, but was also venturing into the property business. He had purchased four houses in London, which he rented out, and was also investing in Bangladesh, where he had built a 'mansion' for his parents and, when we spoke, was waiting for permission to start construction on thirty-three apartments in Chittagong City.

In many ways, Jadil most closely fits the 'traditional' career route for young British Bangladeshi men – at least, until he does not. Around 60 per cent of Bangladeshi men are employed in the hotel and catering industry, with over a quarter employed as chefs, cooks or waiters. The 'Indian' restaurant sector is dominated by Bangladeshi Muslims (about 80 per cent of 'Indian' restaurants and takeaways are Bangladeshi owned), and comprises over 10,000 businesses, employing around 80,000 people (Alexander et al 2020). In 2010, just before I did my interviews, the Indian restaurant and takeaway sector was one of the fastest growing food retail sectors in the UK, and in 2020 was worth an estimated £3.5 billion annually.

The history of the sector is a mixed one: on the one hand, it points to the resilience and adaptability of Bangladeshi migrants and their descendants who were forced out of the steel and textile factories during the 1970s. On the other, high levels of self-employment, even where businesses thrived in this notoriously precarious sector, was an indication of the racism that blocked avenues to mainstream employment, while employees faced long hours, poor pay and working conditions and racial hostility, which to render the work increasingly unpopular. By the 2000s, many young British-born Bangladeshis felt that the restaurants were a workplace of last resort, reserved for school dropouts, the newly arrived or illegal immigrants (Salway 2008, Alexander 2013) – a sentiment reflected by several of the young men from the SAYO project.

Nevertheless, the picture requires nuance: while working in restaurants was generally eschewed (what Jamal referred to in 1996 as 'slave labour'), owning a restaurant or takeaway business was considered more favourably (with restaurants the more prestigious option). For employees, there was a clear hierarchy between trained chefs, who were greatly desired, well paid and could ensure the success or failure of a business, front of house staff (managers and then waiters) and then kitchen workers. In addition, all the young men recognized that for their fathers and older brothers restaurant work was often the only option to feed their families, and they were respected in this endeavour. For the young men too, the work had its advantages – like Jadil, several travelled outside of London to work in family businesses or through extended-community networks. For Jadil and Silver, restaurants offered an opportunity to learn new skills and gain valuable work experience. For Silver too, the restaurants were a link to the history of the British Bangladeshi community, while for Jadil, the link was a more personal connection to his family, particularly his uncles, and a chance to reconnect with his father. For those who opened their own businesses, it was a chance to work for oneself, provide secure employment for family (and sometimes friends) and, of course, to make money.

A number of the young men passed through this sector, and several opened their own businesses – most usually takeaways, and often for only short periods of time, with mixed success. As with Jadil or Sher Khan, these were opened with family and sometimes, as with Silver, with friends. The latter were more likely to be short-lived and, occasionally, tumultuous. Humzah, for example, bought into a takeaway business in Surrey owned by Samir (who was loosely attached to the 'older lot' and a cousin of Shahin's) and his brother. He had a 25 per cent stake, which cost him about £8,000, which his father borrowed on his behalf. He recalled,

> I just wanted to do my own business … but it's very hard work and it was far away … I used to pay off [the loan] every week so that way I used to get less [money] … it's never good to do it like that. It's good to do it on your own.
>
> (2012)

Humzah worked taking the orders and delivering the food, and the business increased its weekly turnover from around £3,500 to £5,000.

However, over time, tensions grew over the workload and the profit sharing: 'It's easy doing business with people, but when money's involved, it's very tricky, it's not the same. You make loads of friends and stuff but it gets tricky, very green-eyed monsters and stuff', he explained. After two years, the takeaway was sold: 'I came out with about double the money I put in, so that's fair', and Humzah opened another takeaway with Mustafa and his 'cousin-brother', this time in Kent. His share cost around £15,000: 'Basically it's a three-way partnership, but me and Mustafa were the main ones running everything. He was like a silent partner, you know. [But] you still have to give him the share, isn't it, at the end of the week.' However, Mustafa proved a temperamental partner and boss. Humzah laughed:

> Like he was beating up people, he'd beaten up the chef ... he got a pan and banged the chef on his head ... We got busy, we got really busy that time, we couldn't handle it. There was three of them in [the kitchen], they panicked ... And Mustafa scared the crap out of them ... It was hilarious.

The takeaway went downhill when the beleaguered chef left, so Humzah sold his share in the business: 'I gave fifteen, I got fifteen [thousand pounds] back, so I didn't want to make profit off him or anything', he told me. The mixing of business and friendship for Humzah was

> Good, but it's very tricky. I'd say, stay away from business when it comes – money, friends and stuff, it's very tricky ... with a friend it's very hard to sometimes say when you don't want to hurt the guy's feelings .... With family it's alright, you can say things and get away with it.

Family, though, could also prove difficult. With the money he received from his takeaway, Humzah's family opened another takeaway with his father and brother, Ifti, in South London. However, this business failed – something for which Humzah blamed his father: 'Most of my money got wasted on that ... He spammed the place up.' Ifti told me a slightly different version: 'I gave it to my brother and that to look for it and find it, and they kind of picked a wrong one, because it needed a lot of work basically' (2012). With Ifti and his father both taking wages ('He just sat there', Humzah scowled, of his father), as well as the costs of the chef and delivery driver, the costs were unsustainable. Humzah worked briefly in the business with his father and brother – taking over from the chef, whom he sacked – but then went on an extended trip to Bangladesh to sort out some problems with land the family owned there. He told me, 'I got bored. I was doing that [takeaway work] … non-stop about four, five years … I wanted a break from it.'

Nevertheless, the lure of the restaurant/takeaway sector was powerful, particularly for many of the older lot, faced with limited employment prospects. In particular, the idea of working for oneself was often expressed as a key attraction – perhaps more even than the idea of making large amounts of money. For Mustafa, who had recently left prison, opening his own business gave him a chance to work and earn money in what would have been an otherwise difficult transition, but also gave him space to be himself, away from the stresses of more formal employment. He told me, 'I had to get a job. I had to work. So I thought I'd work for myself, I can pray whenever, I'm my own boss' (2012). Big Hanif similarly told me: 'I always wanted to be free … I wanted to make money to buy myself a house' (2012). Having arrived late in the UK, aged fourteen, Big Hanif had spent most of his time at Thomas More School learning English as a Second Language, and later qualified with a BTEC at a local further education college. He had opened up his first takeaway business in Surrey in the late 1990s, with a friend's cousin. They sold the business a few years later, bought another one: 'We sold that one a few years later, we made some profit, we opened up another one.' In 2004, he said, 'We realized the takeaway business was kind of shrinking, there were too many because the competition was too much, so I thought, I'm going to try something different.'

As Humzah's experience makes clear, the 'freedom' attached to self-employment came with a hefty downside of precarity, fraught relationships and hard work, which might account for the fact that most of the young men moved out of the sector. Even those for whom the businesses were a success, such as Jadil, Silver or Sher Khan, looked to balance this with other interests, for personal success or financial stability, in a fast-changing consumer environment. Where for Big Hanif his withdrawal was a strategic assessment of the viability of the business, others saw it as a chance to make quick money and others still simply tired of the work, particularly when family commitments became more important. As Mustafa told me, 'I gave it up because it was too much stress' (2012).

Nevertheless, the restaurant and takeaway sector did function as a kind of safety net, a place to fall back on when all else failed. It is noticeable how many of the young men worked in restaurants and takeaways at points in their lives, and for the older ones, at least, it was there as a refuge. Interestingly, then, this precarity meant that the door was always open for them to leave, but also to return. In some ways, this is a twenty-first-century version of the kinds of work that their fathers might have done in the textile mills in the 1960s, which facilitated the circular migration that allowed them to return home to South Asia at regular intervals (Alexander et al 2016). A similar function was served by mini-cabbing, a trade which has been dominated by South Asian Muslims (see Kalra 1999, Sarkar 2019), and other more recently arrived immigrant groups, excluded from the mainstream labour market. A number of the young men had worked as minicab drivers at some point in their lives – for example, Mohammed and Shakiel while working through college, Big Hanif, between his takeaway businesses and Ifti when he first dropped out of college.

As noted above, Shakiel returned to mini-cabbing when his work at RBS ended and his attempt at opening a takeaway business fell through. He commented:

> I've known the people at that mini-cabbing company for a long time, so. And mini-cabbing, you can come in and out for as often as you like. So I've jumped in and out of there many times. Whenever I'd come out of a job, you know, I went straight back there.
>
> (2012)

He later put this work on a firmer footing when he moved to Addison Lee,[3] a large national company, for three years, and then to a rival firm Lewis Day for a further three years. He explained, 'Because you're self-employed … how much work they give you and what quality of work they give you depends on how much you're around, and once I started getting rubbish, I moved again.' Despite the downsides of precarious self-employment, Shakiel appreciated the flexibility of the work: '[It gives] a bit more freedom. And also, because I've always stayed at home and, you know, my mum's all over me … so if you're out late it was a good cover.' While increasing restrictions on mini-cabbing – licensing and biannual MOTs, amongst other things – and the insecurity of long-term self-employed status had become 'a bit of chore', Shakiel had plans to do 'The Knowledge' and become a black cab driver: 'I've just enrolled with them to do taxi knowledge. So I'm going to give that a go. It's like a degree course. It takes three bloody years.' Nevertheless, he had longer-term plans to 'own a business' (though he did not specify of what kind).

It is also true, of course, that in these days of zero contract and gig economies, there are new forms of marginalized work opening up, reinventing the traditional spaces of poorly paid and precarious employment where minority ethnic and urban working-class young people are concentrated. As already discussed, the fast-food sector and supermarket backstages (warehousing, shelf stacking) were places of work familiar to most of the young men I knew. Though they preceded the era of Amazon, Uber and Deliveroo, the new pit stops for the racialized reserve army of labour, several of the young men did pass through the noughties equivalent, often in the gaps between more 'traditional' work. Humzah, for example, worked in a number of contract security jobs, in Bristol, Bluewater Shopping Centre and Oxford Street: 'They used to send me to a bloody lingerie shop – bloody hell. I was a security guard in La Senza … it was flipping hilarious', he recalled (2012). His longest period of employment was working maintenance for an arcade on the South Bank, which he did for four years. After not-working in McDonald's and not-finishing college, Sayeed worked briefly as a salesman for Npower, on commission only: 'I was quite good at it, but … you had to pay for your own fare, and they took me out to Stevenage … and I couldn't pay for it. They didn't give no money to you; they said, whatever you make, you can pay for that', he told me in 2012. He did stints as a delivery driver for a high-end catering company (but gave it up because he discovered they were delivering alcohol), in a laundry ('it was an easy job, man, [but] they paid just a little bit') and then for Canon Hygiene, collecting sanitary units (which only lasted a few days). The latter two jobs were obtained through his older brother Salman, who was similarly stuck in a call centre, security staff, delivery driver treadmill. 'In between, I was basically just loafing about, claiming job seekers allowance', Sayeed told me.

After his father died, Sayeed decided it was time to settle down. The youngest child, and the only one still unmarried and at home with his mother, he told me, 'I thought to myself, I've got to do something. And I remember my dad saying, before he passed away, he was going "why don't you get a job as a bus driver?" and that stuck to me'. He applied and started in 2004, and was still bus driving when we spoke in 2012, 'the thing is, it's alright money, it's good money … because I'm only doing three days now and I get near enough twenty-one grand'. He continued, 'I didn't really care about the job … I don't really care about money, because money's not the main thing, but money's a means that you have to do to support your family … As long as you can survive, that's all that matters'.

Several of the older Bangladeshi men from the Estate were already working as bus drivers, which may be where Sayeed's father got the idea. Big Hanif took up bus driving when his takeaway business closed. Like Sayeed, he spoke of this as a turning point: 'Everybody wanted to move on, make something of themselves, that's what it was', Big Hanif reflected in 2012. 'I was looking for a job and there was this interesting bus driver job, and I thought … I haven't done this before so I applied for it … and since then I'm still doing it.' In fact, Big Hanif was often the bus driver on my journey home from work at the LSE and would always take care to drop me at the end of my street. Mustafa had also started work as a bus driver when his takeaway business with Humzah closed. Like Big Hanif, he was inspired by the example of other peers from the Stoneleigh, and indeed by Big Hanif himself: 'People said it's good money … They were all saying, "go and do bus driving, try it". And I just went in there … I wouldn't have thought of it [otherwise] … it never occurred to me to drive a bus' (2012). In 2012, he had been driving for five years – he told me, with some relish: 'I like driving buses. I drive the bus very fast, very fast … people are shocked … sometimes I drive the bus, people fall over.'

Three issues are worth highlighting here: first, the opening up of new avenues of mainstream employment, which are outside of 'traditional' arenas. Second, the ways in which these avenues are facilitated by relationships rooted in school, friendship, family and estate, and become self-replicating (a new tradition, in fact). Third, that none of the young men who had gone into bus driving intended to stay long term. Indeed, Sayeed, Mustafa and Big Hanif all intended to look for their own businesses – at the time of his interview in 2012, Big Hanif was already looking at an opportunity to open a grocery store, and Mustafa had his eye on a takeaway business in Kent – suggesting a balancing between the 'old' and the 'new' ways of working. Again, there is an important trade-off between the safety of a regular wage versus the safety of the known, the fears of breaking new ground and working for someone else versus the independence of even precarious self-employment. For most, as with their friends and peers, there was an attempt to maintain the best of both worlds. As Mustafa told me:

> I'll keep one foot in the bus driving …. That's the plan. I'm trying to look for a [takeaway] property … I like working for myself because when you work for other people, very rarely they appreciate you … To them you're just another number …. If there's anything after bus driving, it's going to be that.

Crossing the Line

For all of the young men from the Stoneleigh, regardless of their career path, there is a shared experience of what I think of as 'hustling' – a mobility, partially enforced, partially chosen, in which 'getting by' and 'getting on' are blurred and where failure is an always too-proximate possibility. The margins between success and failure are often narrow and slippery, and my participants moved between precarious employment and self-employment, stepping up, down and sideways in a labour market snakes and ladders (with more snakes than ladders), with a mixture of strategy, tenacity and blind luck that Silver described simply as 'doing business'. While for most, this entailed temporary flirtations with what we might now call the 'gig economy' before finding more stable employment, and for a few a more settled existence on the shadow margins of self-employment, others crossed the line to illicit activities. For some, this was a temporary residence, which had no or minimal consequences – this varied from Silver and Mohammed buying and selling dodgy computers in their teenage years to Jadil, who told me that he dealt drugs from his pub in the early days when his business was struggling:

> I was just doing what I can on my own … I was desperate, because when I took this business over … it cost me nearly 200 grand … I was struggling where I didn't know the pub trade and I lost a lot of custom … and then I just thought anything goes now.
>
> (2011)

Drawing on contacts from school and neighbourhood – 'All my mates were involved, so I had the links through them', he explained, though clarified that these connections were not Bengalis ('blacks, Columbians … proper sources') – Jadil dealt marijuana and cocaine for two years until his pub business stabilized and he decided to apply for a late licence. He reflected, 'It was very risky, but I didn't understand at the time … I'm more strict now. Like anything that would affect my business, I don't allow it.'

For others, the consequences were more serious. Several of the older lot dabbled in drugs, as users and dealers, in their early twenties, with disastrous results. Shortly after Jadil bought his bar, S Ahmed, Salman and Liaquot started dealing drugs and would use the bar as a base – something to which Jadil initially turned a blind eye. He told me, 'They used to come here and they used to do their rotas and cash up and everything. I didn't want to get involved.' As Jadil's description suggests, the idea of dealing as a 'business', with employees, rotas and accounts, was one which appealed to the group, and suggests the porous boundaries between licit and illicit enterprises and ambitions (see Venkatesh 2009). At one point, while studying for his Higher National Certificate in Computing at a local university, Big Hanif was 'employed' by the group as a driver. At the time Shahin told me, with some amusement, that Big Hanif was paid a fixed nightly wage and a 'fried chicken dinner'. We worked out that he would actually have earned more per hour stacking shelves at a supermarket. Reluctant to talk about this period in his life, Big Hanif simply told me, 'Because of my streetwise things, I got into a lot of trouble at home, with police, everything' (2012). At the same time, the blending of friendship and business proved difficult and treacherous – which Big Hanif described as 'troubled times'. Inexperienced and dealing in unfamiliar territory in East London, S Ahmed and Liaquot were very soon caught by an undercover female police officer. S Ahmed skipped bail and fled to Bangladesh for an extended period, and went to prison when he returned several years later (sometime after the interviews in 2011/12).

Two of the young men I knew from the Stoneleigh Estate, Ifti and M, were more successful in their career choice, at least in the short term. Ifti told me he started dealing while at college, and as a way of compensating for his lack of academic success:

> Money's such a big thing in life and the way I saw the thing is before I get to a certain age I just want to get rich and settled. Because I knew my grade wasn't [good] … so I knew that I needed to recover in some way.

> (2012)

Ifti had split away from the 'little ones' soon after leaving school and spent most of his time with a group from a neighbouring estate, including a slightly older Mauritian man, Avi. He told me that he, Avi and Enam were approached in a nightclub by some 'Algerian and Moroccan' dealers and asked to deal for them. 'We thought about that at first, because we didn't know if it was risky, but then we had nothing to lose at that time. And so we thought we'd go ahead', he explained. Having watched S Ahmed and the others ('I think we learned from their mistakes', he told me), Ifti recruited other people – 'Asian, Chinese, White, Black' – to sell for him, using networks from the area: 'Certain people that was in problem, needed things, or they were struggling, so we gave them an option and a way of making money.' He explained,

> Basically, you get your custom, you build your custom and you have your line. I might give you the phone and there'll be people calling. And I've given you specific instruction of where they're meant to go, or a place ... you introduce him, you'll come first and tell us. We'll see who it is, and if we don't like him, we won't serve him. It's as simple as that ... We were making our piece; we were making a lot of money.

Ifti claimed that at its peak, the group were making 'thirty, forty grand max' a week: 'We divided it between us, like after expenses and, you know, pick up and everything.' At the same time, he was working three legitimate jobs – in Sainsburys, McDonald's and mini-cabbing – which provided some cover for his illicit earnings and kept him away from the face-to-face dealing that landed S Ahmed and the others in trouble, 'because I was working, I was hardly in the field. I didn't have to go in the field. I was on top'.

I was a frequent visitor to Ifti's family around that time, and remember that Ifti was rarely around and kept odd hours, which were 'covered' by his mini-cabbing work. I also recall that he often gave large amounts of money, in cash, to his parents, who never suspected where it came from, or never asked. The money was partly used to fund the takeaway business with his father, discussed above. He was also supporting his Turkish-Cypriot girlfriend (and later wife), Ana, who was pregnant and had been forced to leave home. Ifti was dividing his time between the family home and a rented flat, and leading, effectively, a double life (see Chapter 6). Later Ifti and Ana married, and their son Kerim was born: 'So I forgot about all the trading and everything.'

Feeling increasingly under pressure due to family conflicts, Ifti moved out from home and then split up from Ana. He told me, 'Life kind of stuck and [went] mad at that time … Everything just went mad. Basically it was family. I lost my family, my wife and kids.' He moved to East London 'and I got into this shit more. I went into like proper gangster land. I was living hard'. He started dealing again, in a new area and away from 'my trustworthy soldiers', and started drinking and taking drugs.

Ifti's account of this time in his interview in 2012 is confused and mired in self-justification and anger towards the many people he felt let him down. In relation to work, it seems that his new attempt at drug dealing was badly compromised by his increasing addiction, and by working in unfamiliar territory with unknown people. He himself blamed his drug problems on new 'workers' who, he claimed, spiked his drinks with cocaine and heroin. Whatever the reality, it is clear that Ifti soon got out of his depth, and he and Avi were both injured in violent conflict with other dealers. He told me:

> As I say, shit happens, isn't it? That's what happens when you're in that game and it's a life and death situation, isn't it? Some people can kill you for it. Some people will do madness for it. It's crazy … That's why you need soldiers, trustworthy soldiers. You can't do it alone.

He re-entered 'the game' but his addiction grew, and he eventually turned to his brother for support: 'I stayed home for a month, fixed up, and then I went back to the selling and I was doing good.' During this time Ifti went to prison for three months (of a six months sentence, for a fight with a bouncer), and shortly after he was released he reconciled with Ana, and restarted dealing, but in a lower-profile way: 'I was still in the game. I was making money but I wasn't too big … it was me and I had nine workers and a few other people.' He was later stopped by the police in a random stop and search: 'They searched me and found my money and my phone was ringing off the hook and they were putting one, two together.' He was remanded in custody. Identified by one of his workers, a young woman, who turned police witness, Ifti was found guilty of supplying illegal drugs and sentenced to five years in Brixton prison (where he shared a cell with M for some time). He was released in 2010, about eighteen months before the interview and at that time was living back with Ana, who had two more children with him, and trying to go straight: 'I came out and it's just basically going back on my feet, living a normal life and just being happy', he assured me. He told me he was considering mini-cabbing or bus driving as a career.

M's story echoes much of Ifti's, though on a larger scale. Although not born on the Stoneleigh Estate, M had cousins who lived there, and he had known the Stoneleigh Bengali boys for many years. Around the same age as Khalid and Shakiel, M actually spent time on the fringes of the older group, and he was often around the Thomas More School and the SAYO project. A very small, slight young man (even by Bengali standards), a talented footballer, with a cheeky grin and a twinkle in his eyes, he was frequently the quiet instigator of mischief in the club, and outside. While I liked him, and he was a great favourite of Yasmin's, M always seemed to me to be reckless with himself and careless of those around him. I particularly remember one Eid, when he was around sixteen years old, when he crashed a rental car full of the little ones into a lamppost on Abbey Street, breaking Sayeed's arm in the process. He was, like Ifti, unquashable, amoral and charming, with surprising moments of generosity and sweetness, but also with the capacity for extreme rage and violence. Jadil once commented to Shahin, 'Being with M is like being with a ticking time bomb'. When I interviewed him in 2012, M was several months into a twenty-year sentence, in a maximum security prison, though he was characteristically optimistic that this would be reduced. We talked for a couple of hours and I was surprised (and occasionally alarmed) by the frankness of his interview; less so, perhaps, by the heroic narrative he carved for himself. Before we started recording, he boasted, 'I've sold more drugs than you could fit in this room. I've made more money than most people see in a lifetime'. When I returned home that evening, he called me from a phone he had hidden in his cell to check that I had got back safely.

The youngest child, and 'the black sheep of the family', M had a difficult relationship with his father and was often in trouble at school for fighting. Street smart, but an unreliable student, he started work in a family restaurant aged fourteen, and for a short while worked there full time when he left school: 'I thought, I've got family businesses, let me help my brother, we'll be alright … I don't really need to study.' At sixteen, M opened his own restaurant, but after a falling out with his older brother over ownership, he left the business:

> That's when I thought, do you know what, fuck this, I can make money. And that's when I started doing a bit of drugs. I thought … I've got to make money, isn't it Claire? … I thought only short term.

After a short period in Feltham prison, related to the events after the attack on Shahin (see Chapter 5), M started work as a courier for a forensics laboratory. He also started using marijuana and dealing to his friends:

> I met some other guy and I used to buy skunk off him. Slowly, slowly I used to give others a cut, because he give it to me for a very good price. That's how I started off. I used to do that as a friendly favour, like. Other people were paying £140 for an ounce of skunk then; he used to give it to me for £100. So I used to think, that's a pretty decent price, £40 difference … so I used to go to friends, 'here you go, give me whatever, £120 or something' … I didn't want to sell it … but then I realised, hold on a minute, I can make money out of this.

From there, M started selling heroin and then, through a chance encounter with a former schoolfriend, he started dealing on a bigger scale: 'I was making two grand every week … next minute, I had thirty grand, forty grand, within four or five weeks … I was making thirty grand, like, every week, for a good year and a half.' 'My thing was [like] clockwork, Claire', he assured me. Indeed, it was M's very high-profile success – the new expensive cars and cash – that led S Ahmed and others to try their luck in dealing. M was caught by police with a kilo of cannabis in 2002 ('I had another cocaine … in my boot but they never found that and I dropped that in the police station', he told me), but he jumped bail.

He was caught in 2004, and served several months in prison. When he came out, he moved to East London with his wife and two daughters and resumed his business: 'The people I used to deal with were coming to me from Manchester, even Birmingham. I was international.' At its peak, he claimed to be shifting 200 kilos of heroin a week.

M told me he stopped dealing drugs in around 2006/7: 'I used to look in the mirror, I used to think, who the heck am I? I never used to like myself … like I never had no morals in a way because I was selling a lot of drugs, and it's like the devil was on me.' He invested his money in a nightclub and a luxury car rental company: 'Everyone that I used to sell drugs to before, I started renting cars to them for a good price.' However, he was on the police radar:

> There's no physical bank evidence to show my money … It's because they know me from previous, my lifestyle … with the big cars, and then how's this guy gone from a council estate in [South London] to living in Essex … ? They've seen my passport, they've seen I've travelled to Turkey … [for] two, three days, come back, that's common … I go to Holland all the time. I've got a lot of big mates in Holland … certain people I've worked with.

It also proved hard for him to leave behind his former contacts:

> My motto was, I don't want to do nothing else. I just want to invest the money, do it up, make it good. I wanted to get everyone in and then sell out and make money, all change. That's what I wanted to do and that's how I got done.

He insisted, 'I came out of prison, Claire, I'm in here now because of *not* going back in the game.' According to M, a former contact wanted him to move drugs through M's networks, and set him up with a group from Cyprus who wanted to shift a large amount of heroin (with a street value of over three million pounds). In a narrative that sounds like something from a Guy Richie movie, the partner wanted to steal the drugs and split the profit, and M refused:

> So then I had an argument with him about this because he's telling me to rob them, and I don't want to rob them … I'm a business man,

> I've got a company to run … I said I can pass you on to them because they're still doing what they're doing, and that's it. But just keep me out of it, you get me?

While the events that followed are not entirely clear, it seems the partner was picked up by SOCA (the Serious Organised Crime Agency) and betrayed M to save himself:

> That one guy, he's a player … so when the shit hit the fan for them, he's done a deal with SOCA telling them 'I'll give you the main guy if you let me go'. So that's what he's done, he's set me up. But now SOCA's realised that I wasn't involved in none of that, but still they're thinking 'but we've got him for some previous things he's done', you get me?

While it is tempting to be sceptical of M's conspiratorial account – it is a long way from the Stoneleigh Estate to multi-million-pound international drug deals – the sentence does seem to confirm the scale and seriousness of M's activities. He protested, 'My sentence is twenty years. It's ridiculous. The guidelines for what they trialled me on is fourteen years maximum, top end, so I should have got a ten, twelve, but look how they stung me with a twenty, Claire.'

M's petition to have his sentence reduced was later refused.

Meanwhile, Elsewhere …

While this chapter has traced the myriad pathways of 'the Asian gang' out of the Stoneleigh Estate, what has been particularly interesting for me has been what they have shared, and retained through this journey. As noted in Chapter 3, the Estate, and the shared histories it encompasses, provided a place of safety (and constraint), as the young men ventured out beyond its physical and imaginary confines. Work, even more than college and university, drew the young men into the wider world and into new, often uncomfortable places – the choices they made would have implications for friendship and family, for the men they aspired and would grow to be. Work represents the spine of this study, in that it holds and frames the future of 'the Asian gang', but it is also shaped by other intimate relationships – friendship, marriage, religion – which will be explored in the following chapters.

In trying to weave a narrative out of their individual stories, to examine a whole that emerges as more than its individually fascinating constituent parts, I am particularly struck by an absence and a recurrent presence. First, by the absence of any explicit account of racism and racial exclusion. There are several possible reasons for this: most likely, I suspect, that racism and racial discrimination are, for these men, like water for fish – so much part of their lives that it is simply taken for granted, rendered unremarkable. Not naming it does not, of course, lessen its impact. It is there most explicitly when Shahin chose his new firm's name or when Mohammed decided not to go out for Friday night drinks. It is there in the structural racism (inflected by classism) in the granting of training contracts or the proliferation of zero hour contracts and agency work. Though not discussed, it would certainly be there in the routinized everyday and often violent racial abuse encountered by restaurant workers and taxi drivers and bus drivers and shopkeepers. In most cases, the young men ignored it, worked around it or found other employment. For some, working in multi-ethnic environments – playwork, youth work or the drug trade – racism played less of a direct role. Others chose work in 'traditional' environments, like the restaurant trade, where they avoided the more insidious forms of structural racism and labour market exclusion and where direct racism was kept front of house. Or perhaps I simply never asked the question directly.

What is apparent is that 'work' for these young men was an increasingly diverse experience, with new paths being broken and old ones reinvented, both from without and within. This is not to deny the overall patterns of disadvantage, exclusion and struggle that 'the Asian gang' encountered every day, in multiple spaces and across decades but to acknowledge their agency, resilience and creativity, within and against those constraints. A key factor in this was the Stoneleigh Estate itself, which not only formed their ambitions but has remained, twenty-five years on, a source of return, connection and renewal.

When writing this chapter (August–September 2021), and wanting to check on a few details, I dropped a note to Zohar asking for Silver's email address. Zohar told me that Silver was, in fact, back doing some training for the youth charity that Zohar now co-directed, in the borough they had both grown up in (which included the Stoneleigh Estate). When I commented that 'we never seem to escape the Stoneleigh' (email, 24 August 2021), Zohar responded, 'It's so hard to leave the Stoneleigh; it has some mystical attachment lol' (email, 26 August 2021). He laughed 'It's funny, we have a Stoneleigh Estate WhatsApp group and a few of them have mentioned they have started to read the first book' (email, 24 August 2021).

Shortly after, Shahin wrote to tell me that Jadil had recently opened a new restaurant in South London, with himself as chef and Humzah as front of house manager. He continued, 'If you're in London at all in the near future, let me know and we can try grab a bite to eat … we could check out his cooking skills' (email 26 August 2021). Speaking to Humzah by phone shortly afterwards, to mark (a little belatedly) our shared birthday, he told me about the new restaurant and said that Shahin and his brothers, Zohar, Mustafa and the others, had been down to eat, to support the new business. Mystical or not, the attachment between the Stoneleigh denizens remains strong, twenty-five years on from the first project.

In the next chapter, I explore these friendships further.

Friends

Retrospective: 1996

When I first met 'the little ones' in the SAYO project in the summer of 1995, they were between thirteen and fourteen years old. My photos of the time show them clustered together on a slightly battered old sofa positioned along one wall of the youth club, or perched precariously on the adjacent window ledge. Hanif, Mohammed and Enam have their hands across their chins, in the time-honoured position of super-cool teenage boys everywhere, while Sayeed and Jamal lounge against the wall, arms crossed and hands in pockets respectively, adopting a nonchalant unsmiling stare. Faruk, a year younger than the others, but already a head taller, flourishes a half-eaten chocolate bar as he lounges across his friends on the sofa. Faruk, in my memory, is always eating. Ifti, wearing baseball cap and dark denim jacket, sits alone in the background, on a table across the room. Shafiq sprawls on another sofa, feet on a table in front of him, affecting a 'gangsta' pose, of which he was very fond. Ismat does not appear in the pictures for some time, though I recall him being there. Like Faruk, he is tall, especially for a Bengali, but he often seemed more on the edge of things. This may partly have been because he went to a different school than the others, or perhaps because he was always more reserved, more watchful and less trusting than his friends.

The little ones formed the heart of my earlier 'Asian Gang' study, and the first book mainly focused on the experiences of this tight-knit group of friends across two years of the SAYO project. With the exception of Faruk and Shafiq, who were in the year below, this period coincided with their final two years at school. At that time (1995–7), the young men formed a relatively cohesive and distinctive group, bounded by a series of overlapping, or in most cases 'nesting', ties of ethnicity/religion (Bangladeshi/Muslim), neighbourhood (the Stoneleigh Estate), school (Thomas More) and youth club (SAYO). With the exception of Hanif and Jamal, the friends had all grown up as part of the small Bangladeshi community on the Stoneleigh Estate, and had attended the same primary school, next to the Thomas More School. All, except Ismat, attended Thomas More School, and had become close in Year 9 (the year before they joined the youth project). And, of course, all attended the SAYO project, and while they were not the only young people who attended, they were the consistent core of the project and its activities. In the club, in school and on the Stoneleigh, the group had a strong presence, which led to them being labelled by the school administration and police as 'a gang'. This image was in part consolidated by the fights that dominated their final year in school (and outside) – though they themselves always insisted that they were 'just a group of boys hanging around together' (Sayeed 1996). Although they were by no means the only Bangladeshi young men of their age on the Estate, their own sense of distinctiveness was underpinned by the view from the local community, the school administration and the police that this particular group were 'bad'. 'Good' Bengali boys, Mohammed informed me, were defined by 'dressing up neatly … no smoking, staying on your own a lot or with a few friends, and not playing out, staying home a lot' (1996). And, as Jamal commented, there was always 'the hair thing' (1996).

Despite, or perhaps because of, this general vilification, the core membership of the group itself remained relatively consistent across what turned out to be five years of fieldwork. While individuals within the group had other friends (including non-Bengalis) from primary school, home or classmates, these were never part of the group-proper, and outside of home and class, the group spent all of their time together. As Ifti told me, 'When we go to lessons, yeah, that's the only time we split up' (1996). While at times the numbers swelled to include more peripatetic individuals, such as Layaak, and at one period expanded to include a number of Bengali young men from the neighbouring Amersham Estate (see 2000, Chapter 5), these affiliations tended to be temporary and fragile.

For the core group, their friendship was centred on two – in some ways opposing, in some ways interchangeable – elements: fighting and fun. As noted in the original study, fighting served to demarcate the boundaries of belonging: to weld a sense of loyalty to the group in the face of external threats. Mohammed told me at the time, 'We are all Bengalis, and then if there is any sort of fights or anything, you know that there's all these people behind you. It's like protection, innit?' (1996). Inextricably linked to this 'protection' was the idea of trust and loyalty: Ifti insisted, '[I] can trust them ... they will back me up' (1996). Given the what-seemed-like-constant violence during their mid-teen years, it was easy to see how necessary this trust-protection dyad was – or was felt to be. As Ismat commented: 'I'd say they're good friends to back you up ... *It's important because there's a lot of trouble coming along back and forth, so it is important.* Everyone keeps look out for each other's back' (1996, my emphasis).

Of course, being part of this very visible, voluble and adventurous group was often itself a provocation to 'trouble', especially with their peers in school and outside. It is true too that they would often seek out conflict themselves, as a way of marking their collective presence, to strengthen their identity, to defend against perceived slights or simply for the fun of it. Nevertheless, the ever-presence of racism and the violence that accompanied, and scarred (literally and imaginatively) their teenage years means that the need for 'back-up' should not be underestimated and, often, could not be denied.

Looking back, though, I realize how much of my focus at the time was centred on these more 'extreme' moments, and the way these encounters shaped the dynamic of the group in its interaction with others – opponents, older brothers, parents, the police and school authorities, the community. Rereading these original interviews now, what strikes me more is the importance of these friendships 'at rest', in the more mundane interstices between fights, and in the long periods of simply hanging out, having fun or doing nothing much – what Jamal captured as 'doing stuff' (1996). Mohammed elaborated, insightfully, 'When we are in a group, we think we are protecting each other ... normally, it's just like you are sitting together outside, maybe just playing cards or chatting' (1996). Trust remained a key feature, even in these quieter moments: Mohammed defined his expectations of his friends as 'I expect them to be loyal, not cheat, stick up for each other' (1996), while Hanif echoed, 'It's like you can trust them and that, and it's like you know they won't backstab you' (1996). Jamal's definition of friendship was, typically, endearingly eclectic: 'It's like we have a lot in common – we have the same taste in clothes and stuff, like the same taste in girls, in cakes, stuff like that' (1996). Ifti nutshelled, 'Friends are friends; they're good to talk to' (1996).

Earlier in his 1996 interview, Ifti insisted that 'we're all the same, all ways'. The idea of sameness, and of 'being equal' within the group, was something that many of the little ones insisted upon. However, even in these earlier days there were, if not tensions, at least a recognition of internal differences – of personality, outlook, ambition. Interestingly in terms of what was to follow, there was a clear core to the group, comprising Hanif, Jamal, Ifti and Sayeed – each of whom told me that the others were the people they trusted most. Tellingly, this quartet were the individuals most usually seen as the heart of 'the gang' by the school administration, with Ifti characterized as the 'ring leader', Hanif as 'the mouth' and Sayeed as 'the hitman' (Ifti 1996). Jamal, a quieter and more critical fourth, pointed to divisions even within this core:

> I can relate to Hanif better, but with Sayeed and them, I can relate to them to a certain point where they go their way and I go my way and that's what separates us ... Nothing disagreement, it's that they have different views on things like work and education, stuff like that.
>
> (1996)

These differences were particularly apparent in the moments when the group were not fighting, and simply spending time together, particularly in the run up to leaving school:

> We used to do quite fun things, you know, we used to go places, do things, but now it's getting a bit dead. Like everyone wants to stay round lazing around – *that is when you can tell what they are going to do in the future you know* ... And like some of them are strapped for cash, that's one thing. *But it don't really bother me.*
>
> (my emphasis)

Implicit in Jamal's observation are distinctions focused on family status, on future aspirations (or the lack of them) and on (in reality, slight) economic differences. To some extent these are rooted in minor, but highly salient, differences between local Bangladeshi families, around what might be broadly characterized as a caste-class-respectability nexus, which had implications not only for financial prospects, education and employment but also for marriage. These minor distinctions often proved a faultline for disapproving parents in terms of 'good' and 'bad' Bengali boys, and desirable or undesirable friends (which were known but largely ignored by the young men themselves). However, of more significance is Jamal's final insistence that 'it don't really bother me' – the determination to sustain the friendships in spite of these differences. Some of these differences were already apparent in the futures they imagined for themselves prior to leaving school, and were to become more visible as they passed through college and university into employment. When I asked Jamal in 1996 if he thought his aspirations might cause tensions with his friends, he told me:

> I don't know, I have different hope to them ... I want to stay in contact with them [friends], as much as possible. I also want what my parents want – that's getting a good job and all that. ... *It's quite incompatible, but I try my best to stay in contact with both things.*
>
> (my emphasis)

However, what is important, and poignant, is Jamal's emotional commitment to the group and the obvious distress with which he wrestled with the possibility of change and separation:

> I would want to be successful, but if that means putting them down then like it's a different matter. I would want to be successful for myself but I wouldn't want to say, 'Yeah, I'm successful, but you're dumb and you're a layabout.' I wouldn't want to rub it in like that. If I was to be successful and they wasn't, just like a loafer, I wouldn't want to rub it in; I'd still be equal with them.

As they faced leaving school and entering into the wider world, several expressed both uncertainty about the future of these friendships and determination to retain them. Mohammed, for example, insisted that the trials of the previous year in particular had cemented their bonds: 'I think now everyone's coming more close together, like now we're getting mature, now we know what's going on' (1996). Hanif was, typically, more circumspect: 'Everyone says they're going to stay together, but anything could happen' (1996).

Hanif's caution perhaps reflects seeing the experiences of his older brothers in the transition from school and Estate. During his time at school, Shahin had been part of a large group of Bangladeshi young men – once jokingly self-tagged as the 'Bengali Bad Boys' – who had been involved in a lot of fights locally and had established something of a reputation for themselves. Humzah, Ifti's older brother, told me at the time, 'There used to be a lot of us – there used to be fifteen, sixteen, seventeen of us … we were much closer, we were always twenty-four hours together' (1996). The group, he recalled, were 'into fights and drugs'. When they left school, the group splintered, leaving a core of only five or six, and by the time of my research, had merged with some older individuals, including S Ahmed and Zohar. This older group, which included Big Hanif, Jadil and Mustafa, had in turn been part of a larger cohort who had been some of the first to fight back against the violent racists who attacked the Stoneleigh Bangladeshi community (see below). During my fieldwork and as they grew through college and into work, the shared activities of this group changed. As Shahin reflected at the time:

> When we was young … it was really just messing about outside, trying to create hazards … Now we just go out to some far places, and looking for girls as well. Now and again, you might go raving or whatever.
>
> (1996)

Nevertheless, a sense of loss at these changes was palpable, even in these early days. Humzah reflected, sadly, 'We had a lot of fun times, and jolly times, like the good times … now, what's happening is, everyone's changed. Before it was different … we used to have more fun … it started getting boring afterwards' (1996). Most recognized this change as inevitable. Shahin commented, 'It's just like a phase, do you know what I mean? … Like the groups come up and they go' (1996). Zohar mused of the 'youngers', 'that's how we used to be, like that, close and we stick together' (1996), while Humzah prophesied, 'I can tell you this – give it another three or four years, they're all going to split up. Cos we were like that one time' (1996).

As it turned out Humzah was both right *and* wrong. Looking back now, twenty-five years on, and with the benefit of hindsight, it is easy to read the differing personalities and tensions in these early moments that were to play out across the following years and fracture this group, especially in the early post-school years. Yet this would be to do a disservice to the strength of these friendships at the time, and to the enduring, if changing, nature of these teenage ties into, and through, adulthood. Indeed, as discussed in Chapter 1, one of the last times I saw the little ones together was Hanif's wedding in 2009. The friends (minus Ifti and Faruk) were in his wedding party, escorting him to the dais, along with his brothers and uncles, dressed in matching pale gold *sherwanis* and cream pyjamas.

These moments of collective presence – of solidarity, of duty, of care and of affection – are at once an affirmation and a conjuration of these long-standing bonds, and the shared history that grounds them. They map, at a given moment, the contours of these alliances, tracing the shifts and fractures across time, while insisting on their timeless and enduring nature. They are a testament to friendship, and its fragility. While weddings were one site for these configurations – and one of the few public places that were accessible to me, as a non-Muslim woman – there were others, of course. Some marked equally momentous lifestages, such as funerals, increasing in number across the decades. More significant, perhaps, are the mundane connections – Friday prayers at the Abbey Road Mosque, the biannual cycles of Eid celebrations, or the continuing tradition of football and cricket matches at Gaol Park during the summer.

This chapter explores these friendships in the period from 1996 to 2012, examining the place of these important relationships as 'the gang' transitioned into adulthood, and beyond. The overall picture that emerges, as with other overlapping spheres (of education, work, family and religion) is one of continuity and contradiction – of a loosening of ties, but also of their enduring significance over decades: of fracture and reconciliation, of friction, understanding and forgiveness, of resilience, constraint and the fear of loss. Of love. And fun. And 'doing stuff'.

Off-stage

While *The Asian Gang* focused primarily on the 'public life' of these young men as it played out across the youth club, the school playground and the streets of the Stoneleigh Estate in the mid- to late 1990s, this only constituted a very partial view of their lives at that time. Although the youth club was an important space – and seemed at times to consume the whole of my life and those of the other workers – it was only one, spatially and temporally contained, backdrop in the wider canvas of the Stoneleigh Estate. Certainly, and obviously, most of their lives happened elsewhere – at home, in the classroom (or at college or work for the older lot), on the corner of Abbey Street next to the 'Nigerian phone box', or 'offstage' in the more private places and moments where they 'hung out'. As noted in Chapter 2, at the time most of the young men lived on or near the Stoneleigh Estate, which was itself a red-brick panopticon of community surveillance and control. Finding a place away from the gaze of peers, family and community was a necessity, and an open secret – widely known but rarely mentioned outside of the groups, and with little mixing across the different spaces, reflecting the relatively rigid social boundaries of the different age-cohorts.

While I was aware of these places during my fieldwork, I was never invited to them and they were rarely mentioned during our interviews in 1996. I did not fully appreciate their importance until I revisited the Estate in 2011–12 and re-interviewed the young men, several of whom recalled these spaces – and their younger selves in them – with a mixture of affection and embarrassment. For the little ones, this 'plot' (as Ifti called it in his interview in 1996) was an abandoned garage under the railway arches that edged the Stoneleigh Estate. The only one to mention it at the time, Ifti told me, 'We used to bunk school, kotch in there, play karam, play snooker … [it] saved us to get out of trouble that's why we used to do that.' In 2012, Hanif recalled,

> It was near the train tracks … we used to have, you know, crates in there with cardboard on top for seating areas, or sometimes someone like Ifti would find a sofa somewhere and he'd pull it into the garage … We used to have a lock on it and everything … I never knew whose garages they were but no one ever questioned us about it and we'd be there until all hours.

The 'rat house' (as Hanif evocatively described it) was a place for a larger group of Bengali young men from the Estate than those who attended the SAYO project, and even included young men from the nearby Amersham Estate. The garages were a place of retreat and safety:

Hanif: We had it secured … and we even had all like supplies of
    weapons there, so if someone kicks off …
Claire: when you say weapons?
Hanif: Well, we had broken into the school gym [on] one of our
    nights in, when the youth club was open and we nicked the
    hockey sticks that the school had. So we had the whole Thomas

> More supply of hockey sticks in our garage … and whenever
> something would happen, it was easy access. And they were used
> quite a few times, actually [*laughs*].

More usually, though, it was a place for hanging out and spending time
with young women, out of the sight of peers, older brothers and the
wider community:

> [We'd] just sit, talk, smoke, and we'd also then be joined by some of the
> girls that we were associated with at the time … [*laughs*]. So there'd be
> lots of people and I'm surprised no one ever really, you know, called
> the police … No one seemed to bother really. Occasionally at night-
> time we'd have the police pass through and they'd come and ask what
> we were up to … [But] apart from that it was as if you had the licence
> to do whatever you want.

It was this space too that became the backdrop for tensions within the
group, especially in the final year of school. Hanif told me that as time
went on, and the end of school loomed, the group abandoned the garages:

> It probably tailed off towards the end of the fifth year in secondary
> school, I think. Because I can't remember having it when we were in
> college …. Because that's when we all sort of broke away.

While the shift to college and work, and away from the estate,
provided a natural break, internal tensions were apparent even before
the end of school. Jamal articulated this as a difference between the
Stoneleigh young men and those, like himself and Hanif, from outside
the Estate:

> The Stoneleigh people, like if you look at them, they all have a similar
> mentality, and if you look you will see Sayeed who's quite different
> from that. So for me and Hanif, establishing ourselves as a friend with
> Sayeed was very easy because he thought along different lines, whereas
> they kind of all had similar opinions and similar outlook on things.
>
> (2012)

When I pushed him to elaborate, he temporized, 'just general, you
know, school, college, you know, marriage, money, clothes, girlfriends'.

When I suggested that the Stoneleigh Bengalis could be seen as 'more traditional', he insisted, 'It's not just traditional, they just had more different views ... I don't know how to explain it to be honest with you'.

Jamal's struggle to explain the difference is revealing. Certainly the differences could not be clearly articulated as a 'Stoneleigh/non-Stoneleigh' divide, since Sayeed himself was born and brought up on the Stoneleigh, and the 'similar mentality' seemed to include those from the Amersham group as well as Ifti, whose family had moved from the Stoneleigh several years before. Sayeed himself shared many similar views around marriage and family to the 'Stoneleigh people' and by his own admission was neither academic nor particularly ambitious around work and his future. Sayeed, who did a joint interview with Jamal, elaborated:

> To be honest with you, it was more like a status thing ... they wanted to establish their name ... I've always felt that they want to show to people, you know, I've got this, I've got that ... It's different [for us], it's not for show – it's for personal reasons ... but there are a lot of people that used to do it for show and status.
>
> (2012)

The unease expressed by Jamal and Sayeed seems rather to originate in some long-standing personal antipathies and a worry that the ongoing association would tie them into behaviours and choices that they were determined to leave behind. For Sayeed, who had become much more overtly religious, this was a moral divide:

> Sayeed: The thing is, even back in those days, with me, when you become friends you care for each other, you know, no matter how bad or good, you know? But when people go through bad times, you see the real things come out of them. And they had a lot of evil mentality, you know, to your own friends, and you would think why would you do that for?
> Jamal: There was a lot of fighting, you know – like Enam was someone that, he felt, you know, he could just beat up anyone for anything and we felt that this is not what we need ...
> Sayeed: It's like bullying.

Even in the first study, many of the young men were critical of Enam, who was generally felt to be 'untrustworthy'. The conflict with Ifti was perhaps more of a surprise, given his centrality to the core group until this time. Hanif recalled:

> I think it would have been the summer that we left school ... You could see as we were growing up there seemed to be a difference in outlook on things and priorities and things like that ... So the core group would have been myself, Jamal and Sayeed. So we were very close and I suppose Ifti had always saw himself with us, but then he moved away because he was doing other things himself ... Ifti chose to sort of move away but then blamed me, Jamal and Sayeed as if we sort of betrayed him.
>
> (2012)

Mohammed commented:

> Obviously everyone's got a different personality, even at school, or whatever stage in your life, but I think those materialized a lot more after we left school. You know you quickly realize, for example, Jamal, Hanif, myself and to some degree Sayeed, we knew that we wanted to go to college in some shape or form, whilst with Ifti it probably wasn't a focus for him at all.
>
> (2012)

He continued:

> I think it was just different people had different values in life. Different people wanted to achieve different things. Like if you want to go to shop A and I want to go to shop B, we can't travel on the same path, you know, at some point we'll have to part. And it was one of those, like, they want to do this, okay, I've not got an interest in that, so it's not worth me coming along for the ride.

This was compounded by other 'lifestyle' choices, especially around drug use:

> I think the thing with Ifti and a few others specifically, from what I recollect, they got involved in drugs and stuff, like heavy drug use ... For me personally it was never an interest; I just took a dislike to

that. For me, fun was, you know, going out with my friends, having a laugh, not being stoned out of my head to sit on some street corner, kind of thing. And that's what it started to get down to.

The reality was, perhaps, less clear-cut, since most of the little ones had dabbled in drugs, and Jamal and Sayeed both admitted being regular cannabis users in the years around leaving school and into college:

Jamal: I put my hand up, I was one of the ones that really did rely on it. Not rely on it as in like it was a thing, but I really enjoyed it.
Sayeed: You're not the only one, there's pretty much everyone enjoyed it … [but] you could see that stuff took people off the path straightaway. Whatever path that was, it took them away.

(2012)

By the end of the summer of 1997, Mohammed told me, 'The group proper became numbered to single figures and then I think it just got smaller and smaller from there on' (2012).

These tensions were played out through a series of minor arguments and scuffles in the summer after leaving school. Ifti told me, 'Like when school finished, we didn't break up, but then you can see with the brawling and with the silliness and with all the stupidness going on … everyone went and done their things' (2012). One event precipitated a very public falling out, which was to divide the little ones irreparably. Over that summer, Ismat had started dating a young woman from the Estate, Farah. A bright, attractive and sparky mixed-race young woman, I knew Farah a little from her work as a playworker at the SEPA adventure playground. Farah was ambitious and intelligent, a talented dancer but also quiet and kind. She had known most of the young men for many years, and was friends with a number of them, particularly Hanif, Jamal and Ifti. Sayeed described her to me as 'a girl that, you know, she was open to pretty much everyone – not sexually, I'm not saying that – but she was good to everyone' (2012).

It had been clear to me since I met her that Farah had an enormous crush on Hanif, so I was a little surprised when she hooked up with Ismat. My surprise was echoed by the others in the group: Jamal recalled, 'She was more close to me and Hanif, you know, and then obviously she liked Sayeed as well. And then she went out with Ismat … which was really bizarre' (2012). My suspicion at the time was that she was trying to make Hanif jealous, though he seemed largely oblivious to this, a view echoed by Jamal: 'She couldn't stand him [Ismat] but it was more to do with, I think to get Hanif jealous because she really liked Hanif … that was her ploy, but it didn't work you know.' He continued, 'Hanif, sexually, can be very, what do you mean, locked on like – he can control himself, so if he was feeling any jealousy, he was probably suffering very minimal.'

According to Jamal and Sayeed, Farah was unhappy with Ismat, but unsure how to break up with him:

> Sayeed: Thing is, she would tell me every so often 'I regret it', and I
>   would say that 'you're stupid, you know … you're not only fooling
>   him, Ismat, you've fooled yourself, basically'. And she was going,
>   'Yes, how do I get out of it then?'
> Jamal: And then one thing led to another, escalated and then …

The 'another' thing was, actually, several sexual encounters involving Farah with Hanif, Jamal and Sayeed, and, on one occasion, Ifti. This seems not to have involved full penetrative sex but what my generation would have euphemistically referred to as 'heavy petting'. Hanif explained that during the holidays, the group used to 'all hang around Farah's house in the daytime when her parents was at work' (2012). Hanif was obviously embarrassed to tell me more directly, explaining – or not – 'I don't know, it was, I don't know really, it was all quite – I can't remember exactly what happened'. Jamal and Sayeed were a little more forthcoming, but still evasive:

> Jamal: you see the problem, okay, if we're being very candid and being
>   very honest, whatever me, Hanif and Sayeed did with Farah, it
>   wasn't – at the time we was young, obviously, and we wasn't, we
>   wasn't very, er, thing.
> Sayeed: We were stupid.
> Jamal: Yes, stupid, it was immature and stupid, but it wasn't done in
>   a sinister way, or in a bad way, it was just, we were having fun sort
>   of thing.

(2012)

Ifti, by contrast, who even fifteen years later seemed outraged by the events, was more explicit:

> So what happened there was this day … I was being stupid with Farah … so along with me, Hanif joined in, Jamal joined in, Sayeed joined in, so they were all kissing her up. Do you know what I'm saying? They were hicking her, everything.
>
> (2012)

According to Ifti, after this first occasion, the group felt guilty and, on his instigation, confessed to Ismat:

> We told Ismat. I pulled him up and I said, 'Look, I need to get something off my chest', and so I told him. But when I told him, they weren't happy that I told. So then when I told they came along and said it too … So afterwards Ismat was really upset about it … It wasn't the guilt, it was the fact that we had done it behind his back. And he said, 'You could've done it openly, like'. And then he cried. And that made it worser. He said, 'You lots all my friends, my only friends.'

Despite assurances to Ismat that this was a one-off, a few days later, there was a repeat – this time without Ifti. Ifti continued:

> Then after, like everything died down, and we cleared it up … Then what happened was, a few days after, they done it again with Farah. Hanif, Jamal and all of them were doing it. But I wasn't involved this time, so I didn't feel bad. But I knew about it.

Ifti's account blends a sense of betrayal of Ismat and, for reasons that are less clear, himself. Partly, it seemed, he felt that Hanif, Jamal and Sayeed had interfered in his relationship with Farah: 'They came between me, friendship and that girl', he complained. Hanif commented, 'I think it was more a case that Ifti thought that he would like to have been involved in some of this. You know, some of the stuff we did. I'm not proud of it, but I think he would like to have. I think it was more that' (2012). Perhaps more significantly, Ifti felt that the others had betrayed the wider group by allowing a girl to come between them. He insisted, 'Girls shouldn't thingy you – girls come and go at that age, you know' (2012). Whatever his reasons, Ifti confronted them, told Ismat and then left the group – hoping that others would follow him:

> So that pissed me off basically. After everything we've done, or I've done for them … that's where you lots fucked everything up, and I thought, you know what, enough is enough of that … That was the fooling. I turned my back on everybody.

While the others agreed that they had behaved badly towards Ismat (and Farah, though largely as an afterthought), Ismat himself seems to have sided with Hanif, Jamal and Sayeed. Jamal commented, a little defensively:

> After everything that's happened, he still couldn't get the person that was the victim, which was Ismat, on his side … Ismat's a very complex character. He's very locked-up … He knew everything that was going on but yet he would act as if nothing happened, and then when it came to light he came out with this whole, you know, victim sort of thing.
>
> Sayeed: That's understandable, okay, he hasn't got anything to do with it and you know what we've done to him … [but] we didn't do nothing seriously bad or nothing like that …
>
> (2012)

They continued:

> Jamal: It is probably one of the biggest things we regret as friends, you know. We do regret it a lot … but like you [Sayeed] were saying, it's just this young mentality, and stupidity more than anything else. It was just one thing led to another and that's what it was. It was never done in a malicious way to hurt anybody.
>
> Sayeed: The thing is we did confess to Ismat, and we said to him what we've done, we're really sorry, you know, you've got the right to leave, you've got the right to hit us and things like that … and he accepted it and he said, 'No I want to be with you lot'.

Hanif agreed:

> You know, we was open and we spoke to him about it, you know apologized. And you know, of course he was upset, understandably. And that was that.
>
> (2012)

I was not able to ascertain what Ismat himself thought, because he refused a second interview – though I do wonder if it was partly this incident that made him reluctant to talk to me. And of course Farah herself remains something of a cipher, a catalyst for events, acted upon, rather than acting – at least in these accounts, and mine. I do know that she and Ismat broke up and the group stopped speaking to her shortly afterwards, although Hanif told me that he had met up with her later, after leaving university: 'Yes, I was in contact with her again for a period, actually, although we never really discussed what went on.' When I interviewed the young men in 2012, Farah had been married for several years and was working as a streetdance instructor.

While this incident does shed some light on the trials and tribulations of the teenage sex/love lives of 'the Asian gang' – and goes some way to explaining why very few of the young men developed independent romantic relationships during their teenage years – it is significant here for two reasons. First, it highlights clearly the strongly held shared norms around trust and loyalty within the group dynamics, and the ease with which these are transgressed, shattered and rebuilt. It speaks to the fragility of friendship bonds formed across years, and to their resilience, which was to continue to position these friendships as some of the most crucial relationships across the following decades. Second, and more immediately, it splintered the 'little ones' permanently, with a clear division between Hanif, Jamal, Sayeed, Ismat and Mohammed (along with some others), on the one hand, and Ifti, Enam and Faruk, on the other. Only one of the young men, Shafiq, moved between the two splinter groups with any success, and was regarded by both with a degree of scepticism, if not distrust. I pick up this story below.

Origin Stories

In contrast to the little ones, the older lot were an altogether more motley crew. Although, like their younger brothers, the groups had splintered in the years after leaving school, unlike the former, who had remained a relatively stable and cohesive unit, the older lot had reconfigured in a loose network, which spanned at least three age cohorts and two distinct groups. The first of these groups, which included Khalid and Shakiel, remained small and relatively stable – in large part, I think, because Khalid's presence (as the middle brother between Shahin and Hanif) made it impossible for much social interaction with the other two groups, due to the hierarchical boundaries of 'respect' between brothers (see 2000, Chapter 6).

The group met in Thomas More School – where, Khalid told me in 1996, he had a fight with Mehraj (Shakiel's cousin and later a close friend) on his first day – but unlike the older and younger groups mainly seemed to avoid wider conflicts in school, or outside. Shakiel recalled in 2012:

> Within our group there was always, like, a wonderful tight unit – say me, Mehraj, Khalid, Ashraf [Faruk's older brother]. We've all, you know, we've always been hanging around, even from when we was in school. We didn't have mobile phones then, so they'd come out underneath the house and whistle up, and you'd look out the window and go out. We used to hang around even then, you know, and like, when the youth club was open, at the youth club, you know. We used to find things to do.

Unlike their younger and older 'brothers', this middle group did not have a fixed place of their own on the estate:

> Claire: Did you have a place you used to go?
> Shakiel: The Adventure [playground]. Where else? Well, actually, you know, before we had cars, we used to find a little spot somewhere. But then after, when you got your cars, the car was a place to kotch, you know. You had a stereo there, you had a heater, if it worked and, you know, you'd drive around. But yes, we used to hang around … clubbing … We used to smoke pot, do that kind of stuff.

The core remained relatively consistent through the immediate after-school and college years, though there were more occasional members, such as Big Hanif's brother Sadiq, whom I knew, but at a distance. There was some movement between more occasional members of this group and the older lot (though not between this group and the little ones). M., for example, who was the same age as Khalid and Shakiel, actually spent most of his time with Shahin and the older group. For others, mixing was more constrained. As Khalid explained:

> It's just we were never mates together, like going on a mates' night out, purely because of me and my brother. Same reason for Shakiel and all of my mates with all of my brother's mates – they were all a year apart. The only barrier was [the one] I put between all of my mates and them lot. Because they never went out with them lot either, because of me. So that carried through up to this day, and it's just the way it is now.
>
> (2012)

The older lot-proper, at the time of the first study, was comprised of three age-groups: Shahin and Humzah (and including Liaquot and Salman), who had been at Thomas More School together; Zohar, Jadil and S. Ahmed, who were a year or two older; and an third group, which included Mustafa and Big Hanif. The latter group were three or four years older and were only a year or two younger than Silver. Although they were rarely in the youth project, I often saw them around the Estate, and they were a significant part of Shahin and Humzah's circle at the time. Indeed over the following fifteen years, they would become pivotal to the friendship group as it transformed into a looser, but still important, social matrix.

For the older lot, the shared history of growing up in the red brick blocks of the Stoneleigh Estate was foundational. Jadil, who had been on the Estate from the age of one, told me, 'Adam [Ismat's older brother] used to live on my block, Silver and that, they were on the opposite block, Mustafa was opposite me, Zohar was just down the road. Everyone was on the Estate really' (2011). As a child, he reflected, 'it was really good on the Stoneleigh, yes, I enjoyed it a lot. Because it was an estate, there was always something to do. I'd play on the football pitch, and play in the sheds … most of my younger friends were from the Stoneleigh'. Nevertheless, racist abuse was a common part of their growing up, and their teenage years were scarred by violence (2000, chapter 4). Mustafa described his experience:

> In the '80s, when we were about ten we got a lot of racial hostility, verbally. It wasn't physical, but it was verbal ... from younger kids, from the same age group as us and older as well ... [From] about fifteen to about thirty, if you're in that age group, you would be experiencing a lot of racial violence. And we did experience a lot of racial problems ... People wanted to, you know, do physical harm to you because of the colour of your skin.
>
> (2012)

As a teenager, Mustafa was part of the first group of local Bengali young men who took on the racists, many of whom came from the neighbouring Amersham estate:

> I wasn't a timid person. I knew I had to stand up for myself. And there was likeminded people like me, as well. We knew how to stand up for ourselves ... If you were coming from the same age group as me, then it would be – then we were able to confront it and tackle it and face it down.

Big Hanif similarly told me that when he arrived as a teenager on the Estate in the late 1980s: 'Even though I came new, I wouldn't take that [racism] ... You know there was a lot of trouble like that around here. It was from that angle I came to meet Shahin and them lot' (2012). He recalled one particular incident, in the early 1990s, when he was about twenty years old:

> One day they [Shahin and others] approached me and said they was having a problem and they needed us to go somewhere ... Something [had] happened round here – I think with S. Ahmed and them lot, that S. Ahmed's mother got attacked or robbed, or something. And it was through that incident that I hang around with them.

Other Bengali young men on the Estate were less keen to defend their community:

> Some of my friends that I used to hang around with, they said, 'Oh no, forget it, they're just troublemakers'. And I was like, 'Well, they might

be trouble makers, but they are our local brothers … we need to stick up for them.'

There is little doubt that the fightback against racist violence had a dramatic impact on the lives of Bangladeshi families on the Stoneleigh Estate, and especially the young men. Silver, for example, had told me in 1996:

One of the fundamental problems [growing up] was racism … Things are different now because they're quite established in terms of people knowing now generally not to mess around with the kids from the Stoneleigh Estate, the Bengali kids.

The successes on the Estate also shaped the interactions in school, where Shahin and Humzah were in their third year, and took the lead in defending the Bengali young men: 'I can tell you hundreds', Humzah told me in 1996, 'but forget it … There were fights and fights and fights … suddenly everyone started to get guts'. As Big Hanif suggests, it was this sense of shared struggle and safety that united the young men across age groups, and welded a sense of common identity and loyalty that was to underpin their interactions for decades. In the shorter term, too, it provided the foundation for the idea of 'the Asian gang' locally, which the young men both rejected and embraced, creating first the tongue-in-cheek tag, the 'BBB … Bengali Bad Boys' (Humzah 1996) and then the involvement of some in local 'Triad' groups (see 2000, chapter 4).

At some point, then, the fighting became less about self-defence, and more about fun – although perhaps the two were always partly interchangeable. M. for example, told me that, although he was 'technically' part of Khalid and Shakiel's peer group, he preferred 'hanging about' with Shahin and Humzah:

Because the others were more quiet like, you know, they're not all into the fighting and that. And I used to be one of them people who didn't mind having a scuff … I used to find it a bit of an adrenaline rush to go and have a little scuff [laughs]'.

(2012)

Humzah similarly told me that as the group got older (in the early post-school and college years) the fighting became more about maintaining this semi-mythical reputation – what he referred to as 'a bit of a hype':

> [We] used to take drugs. Go to raves. Have fights in raves. Meet girls. Have more fights and then come out. It was really just fights. It was more of a rep thing. I think we were building up a rep ... We were making quite a name for ourselves ... It became a bit of hype.
>
> (2012)

Zohar, who even as a teenager was strongly opposed to the fighting and maintained a careful semi-detachment from much of the group, commented:

> I was distanced, even then, because that was the thing. Even then, I was thinking what is the point? ... It was always a defence thing, isn't it? ... There was always protecting your group, protecting your reputation ... [But] it's a different kind of protection because then it was protecting because of racism, and now they're protecting because it's a group, and then this person had a fight. I just never got it, why they'd done that. Even I laugh at them now ... There was no need for it. It didn't resolve an issue; it created more issues as a result of it.
>
> (2012)

'I wasn't really hard-core with them in that days', he told me. 'I wouldn't fight.' Interestingly, when I saw Zohar recently (October 2021) for dinner, his overriding memory of that time was of the racism that all of the young men faced, and he seemed to have slightly changed his view of the fighting and his friends' actions.

However, as Zohar insisted in 2012, the friendships were always about more than fighting: 'It was kind of, because you played football together, you had your bikes together, everyone knew everyone.' In their school and college years, the group would spend most of their time in 'the shed' (which was to become the template for the little ones' garage 'plot'), a former communal laundry room on the first floor of one of the blocks of flats, which had been turned into storage rooms and then largely abandoned. Zohar recalled:

That used to be like a magnet in our teen, college years … It brought in people that I'd never even seen before … That's how everyone knew everyone.

Humzah similarly told me:

We used to have a plot on the first floor, basically a shed. We made that into a living room with electricity, furniture, tape recorders. We used to always hang out there all day until 12 o'clock … So we were always together.

(2012)

Zohar laughed:

Everything you could bring, we found round the area was saved, like from a bloody cabinet to a door lock. We've got a lock on the door; you have to knock to get in. It's all silly. We were all scared because everyone was like doing a bit of stupidness in there … all the curiosity things that you do as a teenager. And then a few of the dads found out, they'd come knocking on there. If there was a knock … suddenly there'd be a sudden silence when you hear a different knock … They already knew we was in there because we were smoking away and it's all going out the door!

(2012)

Looking back from the vantage point of 2012, the older lot seemed to view those years with a mixture of nostalgic fondness, laughter and embarrassment over the vagaries of their youth. However, the internal dynamics of this loose collectivity were dramatically impacted by one particular event from outside the group, and outside of the Estate – the attack on Shahin at Hammersmith College in 1995. In 2012, Humzah reflected, 'After the Shahin fight, after Hammersmith when he got rushed, that affected us, the group, a lot.'

As discussed in the first book, in October 1995 Shahin was attacked just outside Hammersmith College by a group of around a dozen young men, mainly of Pakistani and Bangladeshi origin, and was severely beaten with baseball bats and iron bars, leading to several days in hospital. The incident was sparked by an escalating series of minor conflicts with another Bengali young man, Rahul (who, Mustafa told me later, had once lived on the Stoneleigh Estate), over Shahin's then-girlfriend, which led to a fight between the two young men at Streatham Mela. At the time, Shahin described it as 'over nothing, just nothing, you know … it's just that when we used to look at each other, you know, we just used to screw each other and we just had a fight … and like I hit him. I hit him over the head with a bottle' (1996). Rahul returned with his friends about four weeks later and attacked Shahin, M and another young man: 'They chased me out of the college and they caught me like, and I got whacked in the head with a baseball bat, and then they just battered me on the floor.'

The attack caused shock and then fury amongst Shahin's friends. In the days and weeks that followed, the Stoneleigh group travelled to Hammersmith seeking revenge on Rahul's group, leading to a series of attacks. Humzah told me in 2012:

> The day he [Shahin] got rushed, we went into the Hammersmith College that day. I was really pissed off. We went to the college, we started dragging people out … Salman was even headbutting some people. We were going crazy to be honest.

The retaliation continued over several weeks: 'We used to drive to Hammersmith every day at night … we used to park in front of the guy's house and all that rubbish, and throwing petrol bombs and all that. It was exhausting.' When I asked Humzah what he felt, seventeen years after these events, he paused, but still insisted, 'As long as you are fighting for the right reason, it was good'. When I pushed him, 'So you thought those reasons were good reasons to fight?' he responded, 'Well, our reason was that our friend got beaten up, so that's like a good reason'.

The group dynamics of this incident and the response have been discussed elsewhere: however, what is of particular interest here is the impact on the 'older lot' in the later months and years in terms of friendship. Humzah noted the ongoing conflict caused friction between the friends: 'We were all pissed off to retaliate, as in do something. Everyone wasn't organized, ready enough, quick enough. So that done a lot of friction in the group.' Most significantly, despite their best and repeated efforts, they were never able to confront Rahul himself. The ongoing skirmishes were to culminate over a year later in a complex 'sting' led by Mustafa. Mustafa described the plan:

> We went a few times in the area looking for them. Where the spots where they hung around, we went there and we smashed those places up. And then one day we discovered he [Rahul] wanted to sell a BMW. I decided, well I'm going to go and buy that BMW then and then once I lure him, we'll give him a kicking and that will be the end.
>
> (2012)

When I asked how they had found out about the car sale, Humzah told me, 'He had a certain type of car ... and everyone was joking, watching *Auto Trader* ... What a coincidence, oh my God' (2012). Mustafa continued:

> I phoned up and it was him. He didn't know me, he'd never seen me, he didn't recognize me, so I went and decided to play along with the idea and test drive it. Test drive it to a point where they were already there waiting, and we gave him one. And that's what happened and we got caught.

Humzah, who was not present for this incident – 'I was supposed to come. They went early, seven or eight in the morning, I can't wake up that early', he recalled ruefully – recounted what happened in more detail. Having driven Rahul to the rendezvous point, it seems he spotted the car containing a number of the other Stoneleigh young men, including Liaquot, Salman, M and Gareth, a long-standing African-Caribbean friend of Shahin's, who was the only non-Bengali present. Shahin himself was not there. Rahul panicked, tried to exit the car, and Mustafa hit him with a hammer he had strapped to his wrist and forearm, hidden under his shirt. Rahul was pulled from the car and beaten, and the police were called. M. told me:

> What happened was, we all got caught ... they took my fingerprints and let me go, they gave me bail. So obviously, I jumped bail now – so everyone jumped bail apart from Mustafa.
>
> (2012)

Eventually only Mustafa and Gareth were prosecuted, with the others called as witnesses against their friends. When the case came to court, Mustafa insisted that he alone was responsible:

> What happened was I decided to take the full responsibility. I decided, 'I'll tell you what, whatever happens, happens, they had nothing to do with it'. I saved all of them. In my statements, I didn't grass anybody up. I said they weren't there, they were just around. I jumped into their car. Gareth ... [I said] I thought he didn't know, I misled him into just checking the vehicle over. He was found not guilty. And then I was found guilty and I was sentenced.
>
> (2012)

Having always been curious about why Mustafa had chosen to do this, and having heard a number of theories posited over the years, I asked him directly. He responded simply, 'I did it because I wanted to save my friends.' When I pushed him further, he elaborated:

> They could have all jeopardized their careers ... And I thought to myself, what the hell, ah, let me just save them. I can't grass them up. It's not something you should do, you know. Just save them. Whoever escapes, good for them.

After a short pause, he continued, 'To tell the truth, I didn't expect it to be such a heavy sentence'. Mustafa was sentenced to six years, and served three. He reflected:

> It was a heavy sentence. I thought I'd get about two years, do about twelve months and come out. The sentence was shocking. I didn't expect the sentence. It's probably because I didn't plead guilty. I pleaded not guilty to the charges.

The shock of Mustafa's sentence was to prove crucial too to the rest of the group. It seemed, indeed, to mark the end of a period of teenage innocence, where actions had been, to that point, largely without consequences. Humzah, who had been 'back home' in Bangladesh during the trial, commented:

> I felt sad for him that time. It affected the group as well a bit ... He didn't do the fighting and he took the blame for everyone. He took

it on his chin. It's very hard to do that. You saw later on none of the others could have done it. They didn't do it. They just ratted each other out ... They just got away with it.

(2012)

For Shahin, the events were life-changing. In 2012, he described the whole series of events as 'just pretty juvenile, you know, you look at that type [of conflict], or whatever, girls, it's just really silly'. Distantly related to Mustafa, Shahin felt both profoundly grateful to him for his act of selflessness, describing him as 'a loyal person ... not the type to ... grass on other people that might have been involved or anything like that', and determined not to repeat his mistakes: 'Mustafa went down ... It could easily have been me.' It was around this time Shahin settled on a career choice, in law, and moved away from spending much time with the majority of the Stoneleigh group. The shed was abandoned and the group became more fragmented, and more distanced – an occasional constellation of individual relationships rather than a definable collective entity. Mustafa himself was imprisoned in Wormwood Scrubs and devoted his time to learning more about Islam. He emerged three years later, as Shahin described him, 'a changed man'. Mustafa described this to me in 2012 as a 'blessing': 'To tell you the truth, on my heart, sincerely, I don't regret one single second of prison.'

The Muslim Archery Club

For the little ones, the 'big split' of the summer of 1997 was to prove permanent. The division between the two groups was reinforced spatially by different choices of college, with Hanif, Jamal, Sayeed, Ismat and Mohammed moving to Kingsway College, and Ifti to Southwark. Shafiq and Faruk were both still in school, but seemed to have largely dropped off the radar for some time. While there were overtures made by Ifti towards the others – particularly when Hanif and Jamal ran into trouble with the Drummond Street boys at Kingsway College – these were rebuffed. Ifti recalled:

> I seen them because we made up – well, we didn't make up, but you know. There was a time I remember, when Jamal and Hanif got attacked … and I heard about it and we came. We came to help them, and we wasn't even friends at that time. And the first thing they said, 'Ah, come on, we don't want no trouble. Don't thingy it. Don't do anything for it' … So I thought, you know what? We shouldn't even thingy bother, we shouldn't even have bothered or anything, but I thought we did it for old [times] sake.
>
> (2012)

For Ifti, this was still painful, even fifteen years later: 'You grow up to be all loyal, you know, all that talk, and then suddenly you realize all these people just chatted shit', he told me. Ifti's friendship circle shrank to himself, Enam and his Mauritian friend Avi, who were all involved in dealing drugs together, with Shafiq and Faruk as more occasional companions. Ifti told me:

> We hanged about, but everyone was doing their things. Shafik was doing his things, but he used to come and [be] social … We never used to involve him that much, you know, because of the things we know, because he's a bit here and there, so we kept him in-between. I mean, Avi and Enam was really into core things, with working, you know, and earning money.

Hanif told me that there had been attempts to smooth over these past conflicts several years later:

> I think I was doing my LPC at the time and they came around and said, 'Oh, you know, Hanif, why don't we sort this out?' So then I got everyone together, we tried to speak and it was just [pauses] – it's been so many years.
>
> (2012)

For Hanif, the different choices of the two groups made reconnection, if not reconciliation, impossible, despite their shared history. This seems not to have been a particular moral objection to Ifti's lifestyle per se but was articulated as a 'different path':

> There's no animosity any more. We see each other and we used to speak, but people have just moved in different directions ... our lives had taken different paths by then. So obviously what maybe brings you together when you're young, those factors no longer remain, and so you're looking, and there's really nothing there, to be honest.

Ifti similarly told me,

> Last time we saw them was last Eid day, and we spoke and said hi and bye. We do speak, it's not like thing, we do speak, but I haven't seen them in a long time.
>
> (2012)

The exception to this settlement was Shafiq. Always a rather mercurial figure (or what Hanif described as 'just a drama queen'), Shafiq initially allied himself with Ifti and Enam – in part, I think, because he was dating Farah's younger sister at the time. He had certainly been close to Ifti during the difficult months leading up to his wedding to Ana, and we had both been at Ifti's registry office wedding in 2000, along with Faruk. However, as Ifti commented, he was 'a bit here and there', and was regarded by both 'sides' with caution. Hanif told me that Shafiq appeared at his door one morning, several years after the initial split,

> And I come out and we're speaking, and then he was saying he's really sorry for everything that's gone on, and you know, he felt that he was in the wrong ... And so then I did speak to everyone and yes, so then he came back.
>
> (2012)

I had been hoping to speak to Shafiq to learn more about this period, and how and why he manoeuvred between the two groups, but, as in 1996, he turned down my request for an interview. It is revealing that Shafiq approached Hanif in the first instance, perhaps because Hanif was more forgiving in nature than some of his friends, and also the moral centre of the group. Jamal and Sayeed were more sceptical,

> Jamal: Shafiq is someone who would never tell you everything, you know, and so,
> Sayeed: You have to put the pieces together …
> Jamal: And someone like Shafiq, as much as he is part of our group now, me personally, I never see Shafiq as a close friend, never … I don't trust him fully because I think certain things he does is very still of the same old mentality … So I keep my business away from him, but yes, I am mates with him, but I'm not a close mate to him.
>
> (2012)

These minor bumps aside, the Kingsway contingent remained close in college and outside, and this continued through university and/or the entry into work. It seems from the interviews that they made very few friends outside of the Stoneleigh group and much of their free time was spent together – as well as time when they should have been working or studying. Jamal and Sayeed told me:

> Jamal: I mean lunchtimes and break times we'd always be together
> Claire: Did you make other friends?
> Jamal: Yes. No, we definitely broke out and, you know, made other friends, but not so much that they were close to be that, like we are.
> Sayeed: I mean, there was a core already established and that core wouldn't break … So, I mean, there were additional friends that these lot knew … [but] they'd just be for lunchtime breaks sort of thing, then just go your way.

The Stoneleigh Estate remained a key part of these friendships – having given up the garage, they would often meet at the Adventure playground:

> Because it was enclosed, so we'd just sit in there after college. Everyone's got their bags and everything … And then we'd just go home.
>
> (Hanif, 2012)

As time went on, Hanif recalled,

> We'd still come out and hang about, really, or go somewhere to eat, maybe, or catch a film or something. But generally it would just be coming out and just hanging out somewhere and just chatting and catching up, really.

He maintained that even as their study and work lives diverged, the group shared the same values and were understanding and supportive of each other's ambitions:

> I think it helped that we had moved on from the bigger group ... The group that remained, even though they probably had no aspirations academically, you know, their outlook on life generally was still sound ... Everyone wanted to make something of themselves. It didn't have to be academically – just even getting a job, you know, settling down and maybe having more of an inclination religiously as well. Whereas the other group, everything was still, you know, the so-called high life of sex, drugs and rock 'n' roll.
>
> (2012)

Mohammed echoed:

> So everyone [was] already fixated on how they were going to, kind of, take their life forward. I think everyone was supportive, no one was, kind of, looking down on one another – like you're not doing this, or you're not doing that, and I think that was quite a nice thing ... It wasn't anything out of the ordinary [but] it still felt that everyone was still there.
>
> (2012)

These small acts of care, of kindness and of understanding mark out these friendships across the following decade and a half – at once mundane, generally unspoken and often invisible, but crucial in cementing, and transforming, the bonds formed through school. As their lives increasingly diverged, Hanif told me the friends had a WhatsApp group, which allowed them to keep in contact on a daily basis (and would later play a role in a rift within the group, explored below). As the demands of work grew, the time that the little ones spent together became more attenuated, and so maintaining these connections became more deliberate. Perhaps because most of the young men in the group were in consistent and relatively well-paying work, these planned activities became quite adventurous. Building on their early experience in the SAYO project, when they went on a holiday to Tunisia, the group went on a number of vacations together – to Granada in Spain, Egypt, Morocco and Turkey. And, in an early excursion, to Magaluf, though Sayeed commented, 'Magaluf was the only different trip than the rest … because that was like a normal Western [holiday], you know … boys out sort of thing' (2012). He elaborated:

> Drugs, alcohol, whatever or not. From that, after that time, it switched dramatically. We don't actually go to holiday because of that. We actually go for sightseeing. Sightseeing and, you know, history and things like that. It's more enjoyable.

When I interviewed them in 2012, they were planning a return trip to Morocco that September. Hanif told me that they particularly liked Granada: 'That was almost like our retreat, so every summer we'd go there, and we knew some of the people there … We'd go to the same place and you build up relationships among the locals there.' For Hanif, a primary attraction was the connection with Islamic history:

> There's one part within Granada they call the Arab quarter, so it's like all the Moroccans … and the brand of Islam there is like a really soft philosophical, more Sufi trend, and you can sort of feel that as well, and it's just a really pleasant atmosphere.

When I asked him if this was important for the group as a whole, he hedged:

> Yes. I mean, *I've* always been really interested in Islamic history and I'd usually arrange the trip because no one else would, you know, be bothered to do it. But then I'd ask everyone if they wanted to go and everyone would be up for it … And then when we'd go there, I would have to sort out the itinerary for everyone and sort out where we're going sort of thing, but everyone's always been interested as well.

When I asked him later who shared his interests, he responded, 'Sayeed certainly does. Jamal does. Lateef does. And then some of the others, they do and then they don't'.

The group also did activities closer to home. Hanif explained, 'We either go to someone's house or we'd go to eat or the other thing is we'd meet at religious events ... Like lectures or talks, and those sorts of things, really. Or we go football.' Two summers before, 2010, a large group had travelled for a weekend to Scotland to go salmon fishing. Hanif laughed:

> We bought some rods. Because Shafiq has been a few times to Dover, and so he sort of sold the idea to everyone. So me, Sayeed, Lateef, Shafiq, we went down to Dover one morning, like six in the morning or something. We all brought our rods and everyone really, really enjoyed it, even though we caught nothing. We caught nothing for like twelve hours.

He continued:

> So we thought we'd go to Scotland for a fishing weekend, a long weekend. We drove there. It took us like eight hours to drive there and we never did go fishing .... Because it was really, really bad weather that weekend ... So while we were there we just went out, you know, climbed a few mountains.

Having spent several – often sleepless – weekends away with the little ones when they were at the youth club, I was curious for more details. Hanif elaborated:

> We sort of tried to work as a system so that someone would go out and do shopping ... Shafiq took it upon himself to be the chef for the whole event. He was always happily making something in the kitchen ... And then someone took their computer with them ... Because it was the World Cup at the time, [so] we all did World Cup tournaments, we chose different teams and we had different rounds, and it got to a final, and that's still contested up to today.

He reflected, 'So it was nice to get away. And at that time ... some of us had just got married, so it was nice to sort of get away and just share experiences really.'

As it turned out, the Not-Salmon Fishing in Scotland was the last time the little ones went away together, as the commitments of work and married life, and children, intervened. Hanif told me, 'No one really sees each other that much anymore … everyone's just more busy now'. Jamal similarly commented, 'To be honest with you, lately, in the last two, three years, [there's] nothing, because everyone just does their own thing now' (2012). Sayeed continued,

> Even the ones that aren't married, they've got family, you know … so I mean it's a bit difficult then. But not only that, even if you are the one, when you do make your time and everyone's together, then people blow out sort of thing … You shouldn't really think badly – it could be a genuine reason, it could be a fake reason, who knows, but this is the situation. But it's nothing compared to what it used to [be].

As time went on, the boundaries of the group ebbed and flowed. When I interviewed them in 2012, Shafiq had largely disappeared: 'But he does that', Hanif commented. Ismat too had also 'vanished': 'You know, he's just by himself all the time … he's quite weird, I think' (Hanif). Within these broader changes, Hanif, Jamal and Sayeed remained a close-knit and loyal triumvirate, at the heart of the group. Jamal insisted:

> We don't care about the materialistic things of each other; all we care about is the friendship. You know, the honesty in the friendship and the support we get in each, that's what we were at, that's why you see people like me, Sayeed, Hanif, so close. Because no matter what we go through, we've all been through very hard times, depression and, you know, mad thoughts in our mind, things like that.
>
> (2012)

Sayeed agreed:

> The way me, Jamal and Hanif are, the rest of the group were not like that. I mean, one way, they're not open to each other, they hold things.

Hanif told me:

> Me, Sayeed and Jamal has – we've always felt able to trust one another and I think trust is key … We've always had that there and know that

that person would always have your back, not just from [pauses]. When you're younger, 'have your back' it always meant just in the physical sense, if a fight broke out – but [now] just, you know, genuine in all respects.

(2012)

Hanif and Jamal had been very close all through school – perhaps because of their initial shared 'outsider' status amongst the Stoneleigh Bengalis, and their love of Peter Andre and hair gel – but it was only in the period after school that Sayeed became part of this inner group (which I came to think of as 'the three Musketeers'). Very different from the educationally ambitious Hanif and materially minded Jamal, Sayeed was, as Jamal described him (and Sayeed agreed), 'not, you know, so much committed to work'. His family were more 'traditional' and, as will be discussed more in Chapter 6, Sayeed had an early arranged marriage to a cousin in Bangladesh. Nevertheless, after his father died, and Sayeed became more interested in Islam, he and Hanif had become very close, with Jamal a not-particularly-spiritual but inseparable third element. The connection between the three friends had a dynamic that was connected to, but also separate from, the broader group, particularly around Sayeed and Hanif's interest in Muslim history and culture.

My favourite of their shared activities was what I came to think of as 'the Muslim Archery Club' – a centre for field archery on the outskirts of London. Run by a Libyan-Malaysian Muslim, Hanif had first found the club and gone with Sayeed and Ismat for a couple of weekends. He, Sayeed and Jamal had picked it up again about two years before the interview, and would go every Sunday. When I first heard about it from Hanif at that time and I asked him why he was interested, he told me, with mock solemnity, 'Well you know, Claire, it is every Englishman's duty to practice his archery. It is still a law of the land'. When we spoke in 2012, he was more earnest: 'I think I was reading about … the Ottoman Empire and the Ottomans were known as one of the best archers … so that got me interested in archery again.' He continued, 'We do field archery, so it's outside … we do the traditional archery, so it's the old bows.' For Hanif, the sport was 'really fun and it's … quite therapeutic because the focus that's involved'. The three friends had even gone so far as to buy their own matching longbows – though I tried not to imagine what would happen if they had ever been stopped by the police and found to have bows and arrows in the boot of their car.

The religious element was particularly important: Sayeed insisted, 'It's an Islamic archery club.' He told me, 'Not only do we do it because we like it, [it is an] Islamic Sunnah, our Prophet used to do it … I think it was more to do with religion than anything' (2012). Jamal continued, 'Yes, it's more that sense that, you know, one of the things that you have to do as a Muslim is, obviously, to be able to defend your faith, to be able to defend your family.' When I asked what made it Islamic, they explained,

> Sayeed: Because he's following in the Prophet's footsteps. The way he used to …
> Jamal: … hold the bow …
> Sayeed: I mean there's a lot of history, there's Hadith – you know the Prophet's books and sayings on archery. So what he used to do and how you should spend your time on it. The best way of shooting, how you've to shoot it. For every arrow that you shoot and you get the target you get rewarded for it … So it's not just for fun … He [the owner] done it on that basis because he's a Muslim, and he's doing what the Prophet would have done, basically. That's what he's trying to teach.

Interestingly, Hanif was more cautious:

> Most archery clubs don't do traditional archery, so this was one of the ones that did traditional. And [hesitates], and I think also because of, you know, the prophet did it. And it's not to say, oh that's why you should … but yes, it certainly played a part in the interest in the initial stages.
>
> (2012)

His caution seems to have arisen from a concern around possible misinterpretation by others:

People here think archery, Muslims, and they think, oh you know. But they're really, again, more like a Sufi type of Islam, so it's really, you know, mild-mannered, soft. It's not hard radical. They're not like that.

I will return to the role of religion in shaping these relationships in Chapter 7. However, it is worth emphasizing that religiosity was not a cause of friction within the group – indeed, the opposite could be said to be true, underpinning both a sense of shared identity and a tolerance for the different places that individuals occupied on their spiritual journey. While in the years leading up to my interviews in 2012, and more so later, the circle of friends dispersed, or what Mohammed called 'diluted', this was generally accepted as an inevitable part of getting older, as marriage and family, and work, intervened. On only one occasion did these intrusions become a source of overt division – this time with Mohammed. The rift was comparatively recent – sometime between Hanif's wedding and the interviews in 2012 – and was still a sore point in the interviews:

> Jamal: Don't talk to us about Mohammed.
> Claire: Okay, talk to me about Mohammed.
> Sayeed: It's a different mentality, isn't it? …
> Jamal: Mohammed is, we, you probably don't know, that but we've not spoken to Mohammed as a group – well, me, Hanif, Sayeed and Lateef, have not spoken to Mohammed for almost a year and a half, two years.

The argument arose from a discussion in which Mohammed had confided in Lateef about a new job and his salary – claimed to be £70,000 per annum. Lateef had, apparently innocently, shared this news with the group via WhatsApp. Jamal and Sayeed explained:

> Jamal: Seventy grand, yes. So, OK, that's fair enough, you earn what you earn, if you do your job, whatever. Anyway, we took it as an opportunity to cuss him, so we did … It's a group text, and no one's hiding anything, everyone's cussing openly to his face, you know, but he took it personally.

Sayeed: And to be honest with you Claire, there had been times when
I've dissed him, like cussed him more serious than that, but he's
taken it as a joke.

Jamal: Yes, but this one got to him, because of the fact that we feel
that he was lying … So basically he made a decision to leave the
group and he didn't inform anyone

Sayeed: [He] didn't respond to calls, didn't respond to texts or
anything

Jamal: He wouldn't come out to discuss it.

To some extent, these tensions with Mohammed had been of long
standing: even in the first project, a number of the little ones had
described him as 'political', which seemed to be shorthand for his more
marginal attachment to the group and a perceived tendency to be
underhand and manipulative in getting his own way. Jamal and Sayeed's
annoyance in 2012 seems too to reflect their long held assertion in the
'equality' of the group internally and a belief that Mohammed had
challenged this internal norm by introducing external status markers,
such as education, job and money. Hanif explained what he referred to
as 'the whole Mohammed issue' in relation to his own position in the
group, and the web of negotiations and silences that this entailed:

No one's ever asked me, 'How much do you earn?' I've never said
to them, 'This is how much I earn', or made it an issue or boasted or
anything. So my work's always been my work, and my friends have
always been my friends. And the way I've related to them when I was,
you know, thirteen or fourteen, I related to them in the same way, you
know. And so I've never changed … no matter where life's taken me.

(2012)

Perhaps most serious and most unforgiveable was that Mohammed
had seemingly betrayed the long history of friendship borne and
sustained through almost two decades on the Stoneleigh. Echoing,
with unconscious irony, Ifti's earlier sentiments about his split from his
former school friends, Jamal and Sayeed told me:

Sayeed: I confronted him once, though … and he just blamed me,
said like he had no interest, that I'm doing what I'm doing. I'm like

'Mohammed, how can you do that, I've known you all my life and you walk away like ...

Jamal: ... Nothing's happened'. So that shows the character that he is. Someone who grew up with someone, you can't leave that person over something they say ... How can he, over something so stupid and insignificant as his salary, yes, decide to leave the group? So, what we realized is he never held us as friends in the first place. For him to do something so easily as that ... it offends me ... To be honest, if I ever see Mohammed, I would want to punch him in his face, or I would give him my mind.

(2012)

Hanif expressed his feelings of hurt over the incident in a similar vein:

For some reason, his so-called status, or what he thinks about himself is so important that he felt it necessary to cut away his friends ... Especially when you've known someone for like fifteen, twenty years, and just to throw it away over seemingly something so, you know, so petty. There's obviously more to it in his mind, and it's obviously the fact that he never really did see you as a friend, even though he used your friendship, you know. So I was quite hurt by that.

(2012)

Mohammed himself was reluctant to discuss the argument with me. He told me, 'I haven't seen them for a while, but we had a small disagreement', but insisted, 'like we still speak to each other and stuff' (2012). Although he avoided telling me the details, his account of the fallout was quite different: '[It was] just a private dispute, it was nothing big. It was just like a misunderstanding between a number of people but, you know, we carried on ... I still see them in the Mosque.' Citing the pressures of work and married life, he insisted, 'It's not that I don't want to see them, I just don't get the chance, unfortunately'.

Straight Outta Stoneleigh

After the events of 1995/6, and Mustafa's imprisonment, the older lot seemed to disperse and their lives moved off the Stoneleigh Estate itself, and largely out of sight. Having abandoned 'the shed', a smaller subset reconvened in the basement of Jadil's restaurant. In 1996, Shahin had described it to me as 'a little club': 'We'd go there at ten or eleven[pm] you know, because in the basement there's like a little club there. You know, sit there, talk, smoke, there's a bar there as well so you can drink'. The core group included Jadil, Liaquot, S Ahmed and Salman, with M, Humzah, Big Hanif and Shahin as more occasional visitors. Humzah told me,

> Whenever everyone was working, we used to meet up in restaurants and stuff. Mainly it was in [Jadil's] restaurant. Afterwards people made it a habit. That wasn't me ... I never used to like being there every second of every minute. I didn't mind going there once in a while.
>
> (2012)

When I asked what they did there, he continued:

> Everything. Drinking, smoking, talking, eating. It was nice – sort of our little club. It was just that club mentality. The way we were at the youth club.

Jadil similarly told me, 'We used to hang round after work ... they used to hang out. We used to have a room at the back so we just let everyone hang round there' (2011). When I asked if this interfered with his business, he shrugged: 'It was just one of those things, because I enjoyed my mates' company. Maybe it did at the time, but I didn't realize it then'. Of course, Jadil himself was only then in his late teens, and, he told me, 'I used to only sleep for about two hours a day, yes, because we used to go clubbing every night'. As with 'the shed' previously, the basement provided a safe space, away from the eyes of the Stoneleigh community, for the older lot to socialize together and try new things, which seemed increasingly to centre on drug use. Humzah told me there was 'a lot of drug use there ... Everything. First it started from marijuana, weed and all that stuff, to crack, cocaine. They weren't into heroin and stuff' (2012). Jadil, however, told me the young men tried 'Everything. Heroin. Crack ... Cocaine. Everyone was on crack that time ... Oh my God, that crap lasted for about three years' (2011). He continued later, 'We'd get together at the restaurant after we close, close the curtains, have a session.'

While for most, this was a temporary phase, for others – notably S Ahmed and Salman – drug use became a serious problem. Jadil continued:

> S Ahmed and Salman never could kick the habit of crack .... I remember that it was in the restaurant where we first – where they first made me try some ... And they haven't really kicked the habit. Yes, they're still on that same thing.

Humzah confessed:

> I've tried everything, that's it ... I didn't like that crack sort of thing. You can't eat, you can't sleep. What's the point of having all that stuff? ... I really can't have that heroin, it's just ridiculous. There's no point ... It was a fun thing, dare thing for us and finally one Eid day, there was so many of us, and we were like, 'Come on then, let's see. Oh, it's rubbish'.
>
> (2012)

At that point, he recalled, the group 'started thinning out ... Everyone got married, work. It just thinned out totally'. However, he insisted this was a natural shift: 'We didn't fall out. There were no big arguments or this, or that, no.'

Zohar and Shahin in particular made conscious decisions to distance themselves from the other friends, particularly as, for some, their drug use shifted into dealing. Zohar told me that although he knew about what S Ahmed and Liaquot (and separately, M) were doing – 'I think it was just a hype. At the end of the day they saw quick money' (2012), he commented – he kept a clear distance: 'I was well away from all that, but I said to them, "Don't come next to me, man".' He continued:

> I showed them, not explicitly, but I showed that in my ways, because me and Shahin kept away from them. One, Shahin was studying to be a solicitor, he could not get involved in that, and I was working with young people, so I couldn't afford to get in any kind of trouble, in that kind of state.

Nevertheless, Zohar demonstrated a strong affection for his more wayward friends, whom he jokingly referred to as 'cats'. Of M he laughed, 'M was always a little terror, so he's a cat. A lot of the cats have grown up to what they would be ... M was always wild and outspoken ... He's a nice guy. He's got nothing but love ... I don't judge him.' For Zohar, who was always more on the margins of the group anyway, this distancing seemed an easy decision. For Shahin, the choice was equally clear, but less easy to follow through, particularly since he was close friends with M who had been part of the post-Hammersmith incident alongside Mustafa. He was acutely aware of the potential pitfalls of maintaining his wider friendship circle as he developed his career in law. In typical plan-ahead Shahin-style, he told me, 'Because obviously, you can't have a conviction. That's something that, you know, I remember looking into.' He articulated this partly as a difference in lifestyle choices:

> I won't mention any names, but some guys, you know, were still doing the same thing as they were doing when we were sixteen. And you know, like you say, 'Look at what you're doing, you're wasting your life'. And, you know, some got into dealing and then spent some time in prison.

There was also a strong moral objection to those who moved into dealing drugs:

> I just think they shouldn't have ... Yeah, if you're an occasional user of drugs, that's obviously a personal decision you make, which is fine. But you know, to start dealing, and to even younger people from your community, I just thought, Oh that's really low. You could be dealing drugs to like your younger brothers or people younger than them ... And it wasn't something that was quiet. It was all quite, you know, sort of promoted and everybody knew they were doing it and it was just really silly.

For Shahin, 'community' here is a rather loose term, which encapsulates the Stoneleigh, the Bangladeshi community and younger people in general, but also suggests a betrayal of the respect/responsibility associated with the role of older brothers. Shahin stopped seeing most of his Stoneleigh friends regularly in his early twenties, though a complete break was difficult:

> I would still go out with them on Eid or something … so you'd sort of catch up and see what everybody's been up to. Or, I think the Mosque's quite good – if you go on a Friday, then everybody would normally be around … And everybody talks, and you know, my brothers were mates with people that were still living in the area.

I recall many (possibly nagging) conversations with Shahin across the years around how to balance these ongoing relationships with his emerging law career, and particularly about the dangers of his friendship with M. Even after M went to prison, the two friends were in contact over the phone, and he was one of the first people that M contacted on his release in 2021. M told me that, early on at least, Shahin would occasionally accompany him and others from the Stoneleigh older lot on club nights out in the West End but that 'one good thing about Shahin, he always stuck to his study; he never left that. That's a good thing. This is why he is where he is now' (2012). He insisted, 'I always used to encourage him.' Shahin himself was more circumspect:

> I remember being out with him once, I just said, 'Oh look, if you want I'll come out if you're doing something legit … I don't want to get involved with this stuff because that's too much to lose … ' [So] if I went out with him it was always we would just go and play snooker somewhere … I always made sure that it was just us, and none of his other mates around. So I wouldn't see.
>
> (2012)

As was discussed in my earlier study, 'not-seeing' or 'not-knowing' was a key part of navigating both familial and friendship relationships. 'Not-telling' was also important – Shahin told me that M 'kept that [his business] quiet from me, like, he wouldn't boast … he never discussed all that with me'. Most likely, Shahin reflected, 'He might think he would get an ear bashing'. He had, however, given M advice on moving into legitimate business and, when his court case was looming, recommended some barristers – both of which fell on deaf ears. 'Not-listening', then, seems also to have been a recurrent feature of these relationships.

Jadil similarly confessed that increasingly he had avoided his old friends, apart from Zohar and Shahin. He told me, 'I don't want to hang around with risky people now, because I've been close to going to jail a couple of times myself, and anything risky I'm trying to keep away from' (2011). He particularly avoided M:

> I used to be scared of hanging around with M, to get in his car. He's too risky …. He used to come and see me now and then, but if he asked me to come and meet them somewhere, I'd just make up a story or something and not go.

Nevertheless, Jadil clearly felt a strong connection to his friends: he told me, 'I do feel a sense of loyalty. I do have some kind of loyalty to my friends. They have it to me as well.' This was to lead him into some poor business choices (as with the early restaurant basement 'club'). For example, as noted in Chapter 4, he had turned a blind eye to S Ahmed and Liaquot dealing drugs from his pub, and later, when S Ahmed had returned from Bangladesh and after his prison sentence, he employed him as a barman, alongside Humzah, who was employed as a general factotum-cum-bouncer. This loyalty was to turn sour when S Ahmed, still addicted to heroin, stole from him and was, reluctantly, fired. And, as mentioned previously, even this year (2021), Jadil had still chosen to employ Humzah and Salman in his new restaurant.

As discussed in the previous chapter, the mixing of friendship and work was often a volatile mix, which provided both a sense of security and trust, and a source of tension. These tensions were particularly stark in the illicit world of drug dealing, when the ties of loyalty were strained and, in some cases, broken. For example, when S Ahmed and Liaquot decided to start dealing drugs, they relied first and foremost on their immediate friends: Big Hanif and Salman were 'employed' as drivers, and Jadil's pub was a base where they would meet to cash up. As Shahin commented, above, the activities were widely known amongst the older lot, and the other young men on the Stoneleigh. Humzah told me, 'Bloody M was making loads of money that time, wasn't he? He was, like, he was killing it … [we] were thinking if he can do that, we can make this' (2012). Humzah himself was working in his takeaway business at the time: 'So I wasn't involved. If I wasn't working, maybe I would have been tempted as well', he admitted. However, his long friendship with Liaquot and S Ahmed was a disincentive rather than an asset:

> Liaquot I know pretty well. I knew, something to do with business, something to do with money, I wouldn't be able to do it with him … S Ahmed was okay. I could have done it with S Ahmed. But S Ahmed I think started using it and all that, abusing it and stuff … He messed up like that I think … I didn't want to get involved with that group.

When S Ahmed and Liaquot were arrested and charged, Humzah told me, 'They turned on each other like rats. It was ridiculous'.

The complex, and often treacherous, intersection of friendship and business was particularly highlighted in M's relationship with his Stoneleigh friends as his drug business developed. As Humzah suggests above, M's highly visible material success was one of the motivating factors for S Ahmed, Liaquot and others to start their own, doomed, enterprise. M told me, 'I started doing this in 2001 and then in 2002/3 they start seeing me driving in big fucking cars and all that and so they wanted to get into it, do you understand?' (2012). He said that in the early days of dealing he would supply his Stoneleigh friends with cannabis and cocaine, but complained:

> Every single person owed me thousands of pounds. It was just to do recreational first … we used to be in Jadil's restaurant and … I used to blow a lot of money on everyone. And that's when I realized, hold on a minute, everyone's using me, Claire. I'm like, no one's pulling out no money, it's my money that's going on this for everyone's entertainment, fuck that.

While he knew his friends were starting to deal, he insisted he would never work with them: 'I locked them off', he told me. However, at one stage in 2002, M did employ Faruk's older brother Ashraf, who was part of Khalid and Shakiel's circle, and M's age group:

> Ashraf came to me begging, and he put that one, and guilt trip on me by saying he's getting married, his girlfriend's pregnant, they're going to have a baby, he doesn't have no money, blah, blah, blah. So I've gone, alright.

M gave Ashraf a large amount of cocaine to sell, but Ashraf later returned minus both drugs and cash, insisting that he had been kidnapped, robbed and beaten by a rival group. To make matters worse, he had driven the group to M's home, which they raided. M continued:

> M: I've helped him, next minute he's got some guys to come round. Apparently he got kidnapped by some black guys and they come in to my yard, you get me?
> Claire: You didn't believe that he got kidnapped?
> M: No, because if he'd got kidnapped, he could have told me something over the phone, so that I would have known and I would have been ready … And what pissed me off, I had my little baby in my yard and my missus, and they pulled a knife to us, you get me?

Robbed and humiliated, a furious M took swift retribution on his old friend: 'Afterwards I beat him up and I left him and I thought fuck that … But anyway, that's that. I locked him off.' I remember vividly at the time hearing about this incident from Shahin, and several days later I bumped into Ashraf on Abbey Street. He had a hoodie pulled up over his head, but I could see that one-half of his face was badly swollen and bruised purple. It was one of the most shocking sights I think I have ever seen. Ashraf himself, who was always shy with me anyway, hung his head and refused to meet my eye as he passed me, though when I spoke to him, he insisted he was fine.

Shocking though it was, and still feels, to me, the incident did highlight both the strength of the ties of friendship formed in earlier years and their fragility. Ashraf approached M on the basis of their earlier connections, M in turn responded on this basis, but this longstanding relationship was spectacularly fractured by the (perceived) betrayal on both sides. M's violent response in particular was motivated by his outrage at Ashraf's assumed treachery, but was also about maintaining his business reputation. Several of the young men I spoke to about this shrugged and apportioned blame equally: Shakiel, for example, who was close to Ashraf, simply commented, 'Ashraf did get attacked, he did get hurt, but M had to take the brunt of the financial loss, so M was upset about that' (2012). For M the biggest lesson was not to mix business and friendship: 'you see, that's why, when you try and help people, it always come back and bites you', he reflected (2012).

Over time, the relationships between the older lot loosened and dispersed further, and became entwined more with family connections and increasingly domestic lives and commitments. Many drew a line between the friends they would visit at home, with their families, and the broader networks that they met outside or on special occasions. For most, this was a relatively smooth transition, seen as an inevitable part of growing older. As Zohar told me, 'Everyone has got married, and they've become more and more family orientated, so everyone's moved to different places now' (2012). Nevertheless, these broader, older connections remained important, evidenced by their appearance – most usually without their wives and children – at weddings. This became a source of some amusement to me, and when I teased Humzah about this after Zohar's wedding, he told me that these occasions were a 'boys night out' – an increasingly rare chance for the friends to get together and relive their, occasionally chequered, pasts together. As he told me in 2012, 'Well, it's become like this – we'll either see each other at weddings, birthdays or maybe funerals, something like that …. I still see them as friends.' Shahin similarly told me, 'I think it's good to keep in touch … Even if you're doing something different, you know, there's nothing wrong with [pause] – I think it's a good thing if you can keep in touch' (2012).

The Ties That Bind

As Humzah and Shahin suggest, the friendships forged in their childhood and teenage years are both enduring and mutable but never inconsequential, and not lightly set aside. They highlight the changing nature of the relationships between these men across their adulthood, and their connection to their own individual and collective pasts. This is something that seems rarely to feature in accounts of racialized masculinity, which seem most often to suspend young men in some kind of atemporal aspic – as if 'the gang' (if it ever existed) was a reality that was unchanging and inescapable. These relationships are sustained over time through the mundanity of the everyday encounters, banter and exchanges – the 'stuff' that linked these no-longer-young men. At the same time they are rooted in the underpinning history of shared struggle, conflict, mutual understanding and reconciliation that is, in many ways, so profound that it did not even require overt articulation but which nevertheless conjured feelings of obligation and reciprocity, even across decades – what I think of as the ties that bind.

While the friendships had changed, in form, content and meaning, then, they remained a central part of the lives of 'the Asian gang', as they grew older. Their childhood and teenage years on the Stoneleigh Estate remained at the heart of this connection – work, marriage, the birth of children, the death of parents were and still are an important part of these relationships, even as they were reincarnated from the streets and corners of the Stoneleigh Estate to the virtual 'shed' of Facebook and WhatsApp.

The strength and depth of these ties were articulated to me during my often hilarious, often moving conversation with Jamal and Sayeed, whose closeness was apparent even as they finished each other's sentences and thoughts:

> Sayeed: I know obviously other people, colleagues and whatever not, but there is only one group of friends that's going to be involved in my life basically, yes.

Jamal: I think the lifestyle that we've lived, or the way that we are, we think, we wouldn't really, no matter how regular we see a person outside of our friendship [group], we would never class that person as a friend.

Sayeed: Yes, I think we've gone past that stage when we were nineteen.

(2012)

The Stoneleigh Estate itself remains a significant factor in sustaining these ties. As Ifti commented in 2012, even fifteen years after he had split from his friends, he still knew much of what was happening with them and, perhaps more importantly (and sadly, in his particular case), still cared:

Story flies. It's just someone has heard something or, you know, they pass it on. But eventually it comes to our ears … Everyone keeps a tab on people basically, or they will come up and find out what's the gossip … But it's just Stoneleigh.

Love and Marriage

A Suitable Boy

One Saturday afternoon in the summer of 1999 I dropped round to Humzah and Ifti's home, to see the sisters and maybe play *Tomb Raider* with Humzah. When I arrived, their mother asked me to drive her to visit a friend in Clapham Common. I had seen the friend, an older Pakistani woman, at the house a couple of times, though we had never spoken – she was one of the few women from outside the Stoneleigh Estate who visited, and was the only non-Bangladeshi woman I had ever seen there. With her husband frequently away from home on mosque business, Humzah's mother often asked me to drive her to see family or take her shopping, so I agreed without giving it a second thought. Tasnim and Tahiya accompanied us, stylishly dressed as usual, a glamorous contrast to my leggings and baggy T-shirt. When we arrived at a large house not far from the Common, the woman greeted us warmly and introduced us to her son, a handsome bearded man who hovered in the background. As Tahiya, Tasnim and I piled onto a comfortable sofa, his mother instructed him to go and make tea for us. My ethnographer's ears pricked up, and I glanced at the sisters, wondering if I was witnessing the preliminary introduction to a possible match for Tahiya. Tahiya herself looked uneasy, convincing me I was right.

Several minutes later, the son reappeared with a tray of tea and snacks. His mother then asked Tahiya and Tasnim to move to an adjacent sofa, instructed her son to sit next to me and serve me tea. The girls moved, smirking, while their mother laughed openly, and I sat aghast as the man obediently took a seat and poured me a cup of tea. After a few moments of acute embarrassment for us both, my empathy (and my research instincts) took over and I attempted to engage him in some conversation. He was, he told me, an engineer, in his early thirties, who had recently returned from working in Germany. 'How did you find that?' I asked him. 'It was okay', he responded, 'but I found the society too liberal'.

When we eventually left, the mother asked me to visit again and later asked Humzah's mother if I would be interested in a match. I could not help wondering what on earth he could have done that was *so bad* that matching with a (slightly older) thirty-something non-Muslim woman of uncertain background seemed like a good idea to his mother. Recounting the afternoon's events as an amusing story to Humzah later that day, he asked me, seriously, 'So what do you think?' Surprised, I told him I definitely was not interested. He continued, 'Well, I have an uncle in Bangladesh, you'd like him. He's very funny, he will make you laugh.' 'Does he speak English?' I asked. 'Oh, no' came the reply.

*****

During my time with 'the Asian Gang', I had occasionally wondered how the mechanics of an arranged marriage worked, though I had never expected to be on the receiving end of them myself. As a visibly South Asian woman growing up in Oxfordshire through the 1970s and 1980s, it had often been assumed by white people I met that I would have an arranged marriage, and was frequently asked about it (usually just after they had told me how good my English was). Assumptions around South Asian women's sexuality during that period were fixated on arranged marriages, underpinning racialized state immigration policies and practices such as 'virginity testing' (CCCS 1982), which continue to echo today in immigration legislation that has explicitly targeted South Asian marriages and curtailed rights of family reunification.

These stereotypes have perpetuated a culturalist and problem-oriented view of South Asian (and later Muslim) marriage practices through the dual lens of 'forced marriage' (Samad & Eade 2002,

Chantler, Gangoli & Hester 2009, Gill & Anitha 2009), and transnational marriage as 'importing poverty' and undermining 'community cohesion' (Alexander 2010, 2013). This has led to the imposition of increasingly draconian restrictions on marriage migration, including language competency for migrant spouses and an earning threshold on spousal sponsors, which has particularly impacted low-earning Pakistani and Bangladeshi communities. Most academic work has focused primarily on women, and particularly women of Muslim (Pakistani and Bangladeshi) ethnicity (see Dale & Ahmed 2011, Pichler 2011), with a similar focus on forced marriage (Chantler, Gangoli & Hester 2009, Gill & Hamed 2016) and marriage migration (Dale 2008, Charsley et al 2012, Alexander 2013). This research most often ignores men completely or positions them as the perpetrators of oppression (Macey 1999, Beckett & Macey 2001, Macey 2009) rather than its victims (but see Charsley & Liversage 2015, Samad 2010, Idriss 2022).

The past decade has seen the emergence of work challenging this problem-oriented approach, particularly by and on South Asian Muslim women, exploring issues of marriage and sexuality, and how diasporic marriage practices are undergoing contestation and change (Alexander 2013, Ali et al 2019, Maznavi & Mattu 2012, Kibria 2011, Shams 2020). This work has highlighted the complexity of contemporary gender and sexual identities and marriage practices, and notably the role of Islam in opening up new forms of connection for South Asian Muslims in Britain and elsewhere in the diaspora.

The proliferation of desi dating apps, marriage websites and Birmingham billboards aside,[1] marriage remains a crucial, and often contentious, point in the transition to adulthood for Bangladeshi Muslims, both men and women, in Britain. As Humzah's solemn reaction to what I thought of simply as an amusing anecdote demonstrates, the assumption was that everyone – even middle-aged academics – would inevitably marry, and that this would most likely be arranged. To *not* marry was almost unthinkable, particularly for (and by) women. Certainly, when I was working at the youth project my marital status and prospects were a subject for widespread interest and speculation amongst the Stoneleigh matriarchs. Later, Humzah's sisters, and Shahin's mother and sisters, would often quiz me about the (non-existent) men in my life, my plans for marriage and discuss what I, or they, might wear at my wedding. Shahin's mother told me, after my mother died, that when the time came her family would pay for my wedding and honeymoon.

Marriage was, then, very much a family affair. In research on 'Family Formation in Multicultural Britain', Richard Berthoud notes 'the very high rate of marriage' in South Asian communities, with around three-quarters of Bangladeshi and Pakistani women in partnerships by the age of twenty-five. Of these, he states, 'virtually all are in a formal marriage' (2000: 16). Berthoud notes, 'for South Asians the key questions are not whether they are married but how they are married and who they chose' (2000: 16). He argues further that arranged marriages are more prevalent amongst South Asian Muslim communities than other South Asian groups, although they decline amongst young people born or who have grown up in Britain (both men and women). Berthoud describes these patterns as, 'old-fashioned', both in reflecting older forms of British family values and 'in the sense that loyalty to their own communities' histories and traditions is one of the driving forces behind the preservation of these cultural patterns' (p21).

While the *how* and the *who* of marriage has undoubtedly diversified in the two decades since Berthoud's research, the *whether* seems less debatable. The 2001 and 2011 Censuses show that Bangladeshis have the highest rates of marriage of all groups – at over 54 per cent of households in 2001 and nearly 51 per cent in 2011.[2] Marriage matters, and is made to matter, even as its meanings and modes transform. And family remains at its heart. For the young men I knew, their romantic lives and their marriage choices (not always the same thing) were profoundly shaped by family and community: sometimes directly, through the interventions of family in the choice of partners, but also more implicitly through the pressures of parental expectations or the internalized obligations of family position (particularly for older sons/

brothers). Broader issues of caste/class and religion were also factors, but very much filtered through the lens of familial acceptability and community accountability. This amounted to an often complex set of checks and balances which factored in not only immediate family but extended family in the UK and in Bangladesh, as well as the ubiquitous gaze of the Stoneleigh community, and a broader imagined notion of the 'Bangladeshi community' nationally. These choices were almost always constrained, to differing degrees, and could come with painful personal costs. Their consequences could reshape broader relationships, around, for example, extended family arrangements, sibling hierarchies and care for ageing parents, as well as providing a home for the next generation.

While the first book explored familial connections through the lens of fictive kin and the public performance of 'respect' – the obligations and expectations of uncles and aunties, brothers and sisters – this chapter examines some of the ways in family was reconfigured through the transition to adulthood, and specifically through the lens of marriage and fatherhood. The focus here, then, turns inward to the intimate spaces of home, love and care, but places these seemingly personal domestic considerations in the broader web of family, community, ethnicity and religion.

Marriage: The View from 1996

Even during my first project, and at the age of fifteen to sixteen years old, the question of marriage was a live one for my participants, which shaped both their imagined futures and their present tentative forays into the world of love and sex. All expected to marry – twenty-six years was mentioned by several (Hanif, Mohammed, Jamal, Faruk) as their ideal age for marriage, while others saw it as a minimum (Shahin), with their preference stretching to thirty or, in Ismat's case, thirty-five. Fifteen-year-old Hanif reflected a common view amongst the little ones that twenty-six was an age: 'When you know you're going to settle down, you know, no more times fucking about and that, I think that's a good time' (1996). Jamal, who was in the same interview agreed,

> I want to live my life to the extreme, you know, do everything I want to do before I get married and settle down. I wouldn't want to be like them East End boys, you know, getting married as soon as you leave school and that kind of stuff.

Jamal's evocation of 'them East End boys' works to highlight the perceived difference between himself and his friends from the Stoneleigh, and the large Bangladeshi community in Tower Hamlets, which was seen as a haven of what they would describe as 'typical' – or Berthoud might define as 'old fashioned' – values and practices. To some extent too, this reflects tensions closer to home, with the expectations of their parents, and within their peer group, particularly those whose families were more 'traditional'. These fractures might broadly be characterized as emerging 'class' differences, although, as we shall see, in many cases the consequences were not at all what might have been expected, even within the group.

These distinctions were a subject for discussion, and teasing, and occasional tension, amongst the little ones themselves. Hanif reported one discussion within the group, which spiralled into a full-blown row:

> Everyone said Ifti's going to get married first … And they started saying to us, 'Who's going to get arranged marriage?' I goes 'no', Jamal goes 'no' as well. It's like we started asking them lot … and like they all started getting moody, like shouting out, 'So what we're going to have arranged marriage, if our parents want us to have arranged marriage, then we'll have one, we don't care'. It's like because they probably know they won't have one, a love marriage, it's like they're really taking it out on us. We're going like, 'There's no need to bite our heads off, it's only a question'.

> (1996)

The how and where of marriage was a significant division – arranged or not, 'back home' or not – and issues on which their younger selves had clear opinions. Amongst the older lot, most were in favour of love marriages: eighteen-year-old Shahin, for example, told me that he was 'not really happy' with the idea of an arranged marriage, while his younger brother Khalid commented, 'I wouldn't like to get an arranged marriage. I think it is totally stupid ... you don't even know each other or whatever, and you just getting married and sleep in the same bed' (1996). Khalid's best friend Shakiel agreed, 'I ain't looking for an arranged marriage, anyway ... You're marrying a complete stranger for one thing ... you might not have the same interests and that, [it's] completely different' (1996). Zohar, who was already seriously committed to his Pakistani girlfriend Humaira, and hoped to marry her, noted that love marriages were becoming increasingly common: 'It's all changing already innit? Enough people are having love marriages, where ten years back no one would have that' (1996). He acknowledged, though, that some never had a choice, 'some parents force them'. Others, such as Humzah, were less clear: a Bollywood-inspired romantic in some ways, but also quite conservative in his outlook, I think he would have liked a love marriage but also knew that his family would never allow it – an attitude reinforced by his place as the eldest son. He sighed, resignedly, 'It's all luck. I might get married here; I might get married in Bangladesh' (1996).

Amongst the little ones, the views were unequivocal. Jamal and Hanif told me:

> Jamal: I don't think anyone should have one. If they don't want to, don't pressure people into what they don't want to do. That's what I say.
> Hanif: That ain't following the prophet. The prophet chose his own wife and done everything his way ...
> Jamal: I think you should get to know them, then marriage, so that way you know where your future stands.
>
> (1996)

Mohammed similarly told me, 'It's always better to know a person before you get married. I wouldn't really think of an arranged marriage because it's like someone you don't know so you could be stuck for the rest of your life with like someone who might not be the right person' (1996).

They agreed, however, that some of their group would have arranged marriages – specifically, Ifti, Shafik, Enam and Sayeed. Ismat commented, 'They might turn different when they get older, you know, turn their own way. I'm not sure, but what they said probably they want to get arranged marriage' (1996). Mohammed similarly told me,

> Like we say to [Ifti], 'Here's your time to enjoy, you might as well take it, cos after that you're going to Bangladesh'. We joke around ... He don't say nothing. He goes, 'No I'm going to get a love marriage.' But we don't know, we just think.
>
> (1996)

Ifti and Sayeed largely agreed with their friends' assessment. Ifti shrugged and said, 'You're going to get married to a Bengali girl anyway. Your parents are going to sort it out' (1996). Sayeed reflected (probably optimistically) that 'there's a fifty-fifty chance' of his marriage being arranged, although he continued that he 'wouldn't mind ... if she's nice' (1996).

For all of the young men, as Mohammed suggests, 'arranged marriage' was synonymous with marriage 'back home' in Bangladesh, and this was a key source of the reluctance of those who favoured love marriages. As Shahin said, 'I can't really see myself going back home and getting a girl from there. Don't know. I would have communication problems, man, number one' (1996). His younger brothers both agreed. Khalid noted, 'I wouldn't have nothing in common with someone from Bangladesh, cos I would have to speak to her in Bengali and I can't speak that' (1996). Hanif explained, 'You don't know how your partner is, you know, you might have nothing in common plus you're from here, she's from back home, she will see things different from you and you can't really relate to her the way you'd relate to someone from here' (1996). His best friend Jamal insisted that a wife from Bangladesh would be 'into cooking and washing. I wouldn't want my life to be like that' (1996).

Nevertheless, their imagined future love match was not an entirely free and open choice. All insisted their wife would have to be Muslim, or convert to Islam, and that they would have to accept the conventional daughter-in-law role within the family. Shahin said he expected, as the older son, for his wife to live at home and 'I'd like her to support my mother' (1996). Although he had never dated a Bangladeshi girl – or indeed had many South Asian girlfriends – he speculated,

> I don't know, but I think I will marry an Asian person. I can't really see myself bringing a white person home, or something. She just wouldn't fit in … But who knows, man, you never know what can happen.

Mohammed, another eldest son, similarly told me, 'I've been out with white girls, but I wouldn't consider marrying them, firstly because it's going to be hard for them to adapt to our culture, and then it's like they're white, innit, it's like religion and thing' (1996). Shakiel similarly commented that as the only son it was his duty to stay at home and look after his parents, and that his wife would be expected to accept this: 'I've got five sisters and that's it ain't it? I mean, like if they're married away and the house is empty, I would probably want to stay with my parents anyway' (1996).

As the young men recognized, marriage is intricately bound up with broader familial relationships and responsibilities, including towards siblings. Many also acknowledged that their aspirations were very different from their parents. Jamal summarized, 'They expect me to [have an arranged marriage], my mum expects me to, but she knows I ain't going to have it' (1996). However, the young men saw this as a space for negotiation and manoeuvre, on both parts. Hanif told me that he had told his mother he did not want an arranged marriage: 'She goes, "Well let's see when the time comes" … She will say probably that she wants to see the girl or something' (1996).

All were adamant, however, that their own aspirations should not directly conflict with their parents, and particularly their mothers. Khalid commented, 'It's like you have to think of your mum as well' (1996).

Nevertheless, striking a balance between parental expectations and their own, more personal hopes was, even in these early years, recognized as challenging and was to prove tricky in the years that followed, particularly for those who were forging new, less conventional pathways. As Jamal summarized, reflecting on the difference between himself and his more conventional older brother, 'He'll do things to please my mum, and I would want to do things that would please my mum *and* please me' (1996).

******

When I spoke to them in 2012, now in their early to mid-thirties, all of my participants, with the exception of Ismat (whom I did not interview) and Khalid, were married. Most had married later than expected – in their late twenties or very early thirties (indeed, thirty seemed to be the 'cut-off' age for Bengali bachelors). The pattern of marriage – the who and the how – was, however, more complex, and in some cases unexpected, than their teenage selves could have (or, indeed, had) predicted. Amongst the older lot, a number had arranged marriages in Bangladesh – Humzah, S Ahmed, Liaquot, Salman, Jadil, Big Hanif, Mustafa, Ashraf – while their remaining cohort, Shahin, Zohar, Shakiel, Mehraj and M had love marriages with women from outside the Bangladeshi community. Amongst the little ones, the pattern was very different, and perhaps more surprising: while Sayeed and Enam married 'back home' as expected, Ifti and Shafiq had love marriages, Mohammed married a long-time British Bangladeshi girlfriend, and Hanif and Jamal had arranged marriages with British Bangladeshi women. When I asked some of the little ones about the almost complete inversion of their teenage aspirations, Sayeed replied:

> Obviously when we were growing up we all wanted love marriages …
> but you know, when I grew up, when I understand my reasoning a
> bit more, it's not about love marriage, it's about arranged marriage.
> Because arranged marriage is the way that we're supposed to do it …
> you build your relationship when you're married and then, you know,
> love happens.

(2012)

Love and Sex on the Stoneleigh Estate 1996–2012

While, for 31-year-old Sayeed, the choice of an arranged marriage was clear-cut, and integrally bound up with his faith – 'I take the Islamic view', he told me – an exchange with him and Jamal later in the interview painted a more complex picture. Jamal had married a couple of years earlier, having broken up with a long-term girlfriend shortly before the marriage was arranged. He reflected,

> When I was younger, I remember telling you, you know, I'd always love to get a love marriage, and had I'd had maybe a Bengali girlfriend I would have had a love marriage. Or maybe not Bengali, but a Muslim girl, I would probably have had a love marriage. But because I didn't have that my only choice was to have an arranged marriage. I wasn't looking to go back on the market and find myself another girlfriend and build something up and then get married because, you know, time was wasting away …
>
> (2012)

The conversation continued:

> Jamal: And also, you know, as I grew older, as we all grew older, we
> stayed away from girls a lot more towards the end of our lives.
> Sayeed: Because Islam influenced us; that's the thing.
> Jamal: You know, we wouldn't go to a nightclub or we wouldn't go to a
> bar, or socialize with girls in that sense.
> Sayeed: We actually never did actually go to a nightclub.
> Jamal: Yes, we never – we was never like that in the first place, but we
> never did do that, so there wasn't an opportunity …
> Sayeed: Do you know the other thing was, between us, the reason
> why I think we didn't find any female companions, you know, was
> a lot of us were shy.

This endearingly honest discussion captures the more complex and hidden hinterland to the marriage choices of the Stoneleigh young men – where arranged marriage was seen (by the young men and their parents) as at once the default option, a choice of last resort, and the only Islamically acceptable form. It is interesting to compare Sayeed's insistence that arranged marriage was 'the Islamic way' compared to Hanif's defiant assertion sixteen years earlier that 'the prophet chose his own wife and done everything his way' (1996). The balancing, or confusion, of culture and religion (Bengali or Muslim?), and the weight of parental expectations of marriage as 'time was wasting away' are also apparent. These elements are explored below: what is of interest here, however, are the later comments on dating and falling in love, and how these shape and are shaped by family and community expectations around marriage.

As Sayeed and Jamal suggest, dating on the Stoneleigh was fraught with difficulties. Certainly during my first project, for the little ones at least, dating options were limited: their school was 80 per cent male, and the opportunities for meeting girls outside were constrained by the seemingly constant vigilance of the Stoneleigh matriarchs. As noted in Chapter 5, the spaces where the friends could meet, let alone bring girls, were few and far between, and likely to be intruded upon by suspicious mothers at any time. With little money, and relatively circumscribed geographically, the pool of prospective girlfriends was comparatively small, and made smaller by the cultural norms which ruled out local Bangladeshi young women. Bangladeshi women who were related to friends, or friends of family, were automatically classified as 'sisters' and considered sexually unavailable. Ifti told me that he would never date a friend's sister: 'No way, that's liberties … that's stupidness … I'd be like an idiot' (1996). Hanif explained, 'Your friends' sisters are like your own sister … if they were nice I probably would [look at them] but I would never go out with them' (1996).

Those few that were not 'related' through blood or friendship were considered risky prospects, because they were assumed to want serious relationships leading to marriage. Ifti told me, 'If you go out with Bengali girls … they will expect you to get married' (1996), and later expounded, 'I don't really go for Muslim girls … they're too tight, let's keep it like that … they won't even give you a cuddle'. This led to a widespread dismissal of Bangladeshi young women as possible girlfriends, even amongst the older lot. Shahin, who was a prolific dater, told me, 'A lot of the Bengali girls that went to the school – I don't know, I can't talk to them, man, they're just not my type' (1996), while Khalid laughed and said, 'There was girls in school, and all these Bengali girls liked me as well, they wrote all these shitty love letters and that ... I just ripped them up, didn't even read them' (1996).

While the little ones undoubtedly did have relationships with girls, this was largely kept out of sight, including from myself and Yasmin, and remained casual and short term, largely focused on sex (though, I suspect, often without any actual sex). Hanif, with the vast experience of his fifteen years, told me, 'Girls, they're just good for one thing ... it's natural innit', although he later confessed, 'Thinking back, I'm glad I never did it' (1996). Mohammed similarly commented: 'It's like you go with girls for a few kisses and that's it really. I can't be bothered, too much pressure now' (1996).

For the older lot, who were more mobile and whose social life extended beyond the Stoneleigh to college and work, things were easier. Shahin told me in 1996, 'Last year was really good for girls ... I've been out with a Chinese girl, Moroccan, Turkish, Asian, Pakistani.' Zohar laughed, 'Shahin ain't serious, nobody bothers about that at the moment. S[hahin] goes out with anything' (1996). As with their younger brothers, relationships with Bengali young women were usually avoided – particularly those from the Stoneleigh Estate – while other relationships were fraught with dangers. Humzah commented, 'No one will come with girls in this area ... one person sees it, the whole person knows, you get me?' (1996). He explained,

> I don't really mind boyfriend-girlfriend but it's just, you know how it is, how Bengali culture is – we don't really want that because it's strict ... it's our religion as well. Both of it, it's like you're trapped.

Like Shahin, Humzah was, in fact, very successful with young women, though he was careful to screen this fact from family and the community. The division between home, friends and his sometimes complicated love life was, however, hard to maintain. His sisters, who adored him (and watched a lot of Bollywood films), would often regale me with stories of lovelorn young women pining for their older brother, who loftily spurned their attentions ('Bhaya's not interested in girls', they assured me). Their favourite story was of a young woman who planted herself outside their house for several weeks hoping to talk to him. The truth, he confessed later, was that she was a girlfriend whom he had finished with, leaving her heartbroken. For Humzah, there was no question of marriage, or even of acknowledging the relationship to his family. As he told me in 1996, 'If I was to have a girlfriend, I wouldn't just have any girl, I'd look for a girl that my parents would approve of.'

There were of course some illicit relationships between the Stoneleigh young men and local Bengali young women. Jadil, for example, dated S Ahmed's sister for two years, though, as he told me in 2011, when he discovered the relationship, 'he [S Ahmed] was really pissed off'. The equation of ethnic or religious suitability and the granting of family or community approval was, however, far from certain – in fact, quite the opposite. A 'love' relationship was by default considered an unsuitable match. Big Hanif dated a local girl for five years, but the relationship was discovered. He told me:

> We didn't get caught, I think it was one of my friends who betrayed me and for some reason he told her father. So she got into trouble and I think her father then kind of called me in ... She was kind of scared, I guess, she was crying. She said, 'Well whatever you do don't say we went out' ... she told me, 'My parents don't want to agree to get married to you ...'
>
> (2012)

Big Hanif decided to claim that while he had pursued the young woman, it had not been reciprocated. He reflected:

> It was one of those things. I just knew because I didn't have a job those days, I was working part-time and I just knew her dad's not going to agree and my dad's not going to agree .... I just sat there and thought, no, I'm not going to give this girl a bad name.

Given the constraints on sexual or romantic relationships, which had to be kept secret from family and the community, and where even friends were a source of betrayal, such relationships were often short-lived and transactional – though this might partly been a function of age, and the desire to have as much fun as possible prior to marriage. Khalid told me, 'For me the ultimate enjoyment was to see whether I could sleep with that girl, nothing else, not to go on a date, not to have a relationship' (2012), though he acknowledged, 'My friends, in that department, they are a bit different than me, and they didn't mind the relationships'. Handsome and charming, Khalid had a string of sexual encounters with slightly older women in his twenties, and our discussion shed light on how the young men handled their romantic and personal lives:

> Khalid: I was always fortunate … to see people who had their own place, so I never had to have stories of me having to pay for hotel rooms.
> Claire: I often wondered how you lot manage those things, actually. Because it must have been tricky.
> Khalid: Shagging in the car, honestly [*laughs*] … Because I never brought a girl round to my house and I would never unless it was a bride of mine.

As he discovered later, longer-term relationships were fraught with unforeseen pitfalls. When we spoke in 2012, Khalid was still struggling with the fallout of his relationship with an older Black woman, Pamela. The two had met at a rave in 1999, when Khalid was twenty years old. He told me,

> She was ten years older than I was … so you're quite excited by that … With Pamela it was a bit different … it was really nice in the sense that I just felt comfortable and that was important to me.

He continued,

> Pamela was the first person that I didn't sleep with up to this day on the first night of meeting her on a date … I really liked her company, she was much older than I was, she didn't ask me questions, she wasn't ringing me non-stop, and it was all those things I hated in a girl.

Khalid spent more and more time with Pamela and her daughter, Amina, and finally moved in with her. However, as he himself notes, this was never a clear decision on his part: rather he drifted into the move partly because of problems at home, and the difficulties of balancing a more serious relationship with family expectations. This led to an increasing separation between home and personal life that became increasingly untenable. Although he attempted to resolve this by moving out from home for two years, Khalid told me that he never discussed his family situation with Pamela: 'She never knew what I was facing at home ever … and then me and Pamela started arguing and stuff.' These tensions exacerbated when Pamela fell pregnant with their daughter, Jasmine, when Khalid felt the separation from his family even more strongly: 'It's something I so wanted to share and I just couldn't … it wasn't an option to just come out and say it', and his relationship with Pamela deteriorated further. Nevertheless, he did consider marriage:

> I remember my younger brother saying to me … 'well just marry her' … So then at one point, when she had the baby, I did ask her to marry me. And she said, 'Yes'. And then things can just happen on a sixpence and things can just change and we never got married.

The relationship, and the birth of his daughter, profoundly impacted Khalid long after he and Pamela had separated. When we spoke in 2012, eight years after an acrimonious split, he was still single, and still struggling with the ensuing separation from his daughter (only recently settled). He told me,

> Life is just so hard now … I don't know how to explain it. I've just kind of lost my trust with women … I've always hoped that in a fantasy world that I was able to call Pamela, Amina, me, Jasmine as a family. I would so love that. And then there's a part – it's a little part, but any little part like that could play a big part – is not going through what I did … I just couldn't go through that again.

For Jamal too, tensions between his love life and his home life were to cause conflict and pain. He told me, 'I've had girlfriends … well, I very much liked one of them but circumstances wouldn't allow us to get married and looking back on things in hindsight it was the best decision not to marry that person' (2012). Through his twenties, Jamal had been involved, on and off, with a local woman of Greek descent. They had first become involved when he was nineteen and she was twenty-five, dated for a year and a half, and reconciled five years later for a longer period, which ended shortly before he decided to have an arranged marriage. He told me,

> Jamal: Ultimately, I think we did really, really like each other a lot and it's just circumstances that we couldn't have been together
> Claire: Was it the fact that she wasn't Muslim?
> Jamal: Yes, I mean that was number one barrier. Number two was that she had children from other relationships, which would affect our family unit if we was to have one.

Nevertheless, Jamal told his family about the relationship, and that he wanted to marry her:

> And when I told my family they was very much against it … Everyone that I spoke to said, no, it's not a good choice, and my mum was really distraught about it and so, you know, I really thought about it. I wasn't happy but, you know, we decided to end things … it was a very difficult time.

Having decided to separate, and feeling that 'time was wasting away' as he approached the advanced age of thirty, Jamal agreed to an arranged marriage, insisting that the decision was a joint one between his family and himself. He told me, 'They did put me under pressure to marry, and I also wanted to get married as well to get her out of my system.'

While, for Jamal, marriage marked a break from his previous emotional life, and continuity with the expectations of his family, for others the transition was not so clear-cut. Most struggled to balance family and personal wishes, with greater or lesser success. This situation was complicated by the fact that 'family' did not always constitute a uniform point of view, while for the young men themselves, their personal wishes were inextricably bound with a complex set of familial roles, expectations and obligations. This was true whichever path to marriage was selected – arranged or not, 'back home' or not, willing or not – and had a range of outcomes, some of which could be predicted, but others less so. It is to these complexities I now turn.

A Suitable Girl

Marrying 'Back Home'

While their younger selves largely eschewed the idea of arranged marriage – and, even more so, marrying 'back home' – many recognized that this was something that their parents wanted and expected, and that lay in their future. For some, like Mustafa, having a marriage arranged in Bangladesh was welcome. He told me, 'It suited me because I thought, I'm a conservative man, I want a wife who is good at moving, you know. What I realized about the women in Bangladesh, they get up and go' (2012). When I asked what he looked for in a wife, he identified two key factors: social position and religiosity. For Mustafa family status was something he was clearly very aware and proud of, while religiosity was a more personal imperative. He explained he wanted his wife to be from

> A good class. Where the family is all good, honourable people with status … I said, I'm going to be religious … I don't want her to come and then I have to force her to pray. No, I want you to be praying five times before you know me … Attractive is no problem, but my primary is religion. That was my primary criteria.

Zohar commented that such a decision was inevitable for his friend, who had a difficult teenage and twenties and was shy around women: 'You never think how he's going to marry – he never had a girlfriend in his life' (2012). Mustafa's choices were likely limited too by his spell in prison, which would have restricted his ability to marry well in the UK. Nevertheless, when I met his wife, a very pretty young woman who was pregnant with their second child, both seemed happy and settled. Zohar agreed,

He seems very thing on his wife, very happy with his wife, which is a nice thing. [He's] devoted [to his son] and it's amazing, and he loves his wife, you can see that. We say, 'what are you doing?' He says, 'I went shopping with my wife.'

For Jadil, who also married back home, things were more complicated. He told me,

I got married in Bangladesh, so no one was at my wedding. It was one of those emergency weddings, or something.
Claire: What do you mean by emergency wedding?
Jadil: It was just like more my parents' idea. I was there at the time and I just done it there and then. No one knew.

(2011)

Unlike Mustafa, Jadil had a long-term girlfriend at the time his marriage was arranged. The woman was Greek Orthodox, and the couple had been together for seven years. When I asked if he had wanted to marry her, Jadil replied, 'If I had wanted to I could have done it, but my parents were like she will have to be Muslim and … she didn't want to convert'. He reflected,

Marriage for me is more like a religious thing, and a family thing. So if I'm going to hurt my family … then I don't think it's going to be a good idea. Because I want to maintain my relationship with my family. I don't want to let go and I'm the only brother, so I don't want to leave them. So I thought I'd make some sacrifices and that's what I done.

On a family visit to Bangladesh in 2001, his parents pressured him to marry, 'and then I just got married out of the blue'. For Jadil, this was more a pragmatic than emotional decision: 'I thought, I need to go back to London and I might as well get this over and done with, seriously. And I just done it and I just came back.' It was only on his return that he told his girlfriend what had happened: 'No, when I told her, obviously she didn't take it well', he told me, without any apparent irony. Now married for a decade, he said, 'She [my wife] is a Muslim and just a nice person with a good heart really … She was very beautiful'. Nevertheless, he admitted, 'I wasn't really ready to get married'.

As Jadil suggests, the expectations of his parents were stronger given his position as the only son in the family. To marry badly, in the eyes of his family and the community, would be to jeopardize his sisters' marriage prospects and reflect poorly on his parents. The same pressures were apparent with Humzah and Big Hanif, both of whom married in Bangladesh. In fact Big Hanif married 'back home' twice – once through pressure and the second time through choice. Big Hanif told me that his parents pressured him to marry in his early twenties, in part because of the unsuitable romance discussed above, but also because he had been in trouble with the police, and his parents thought marriage might settle him down. Returning to Bangladesh for his sister's wedding in 1995, when he was twenty-two years old, the family pressured him to stay and get married. He told me:

> I didn't want to get married. I wanted to come back and then my mum said, no don't go .… There was family pressure onto me, got married, came back and it only lasted a week … There was nothing wrong with her, it was just I wasn't ready to settle down. You see, the mistake my parents made at that time, they thought if they get me married, it will make me settle down, but I wasn't ready to settle down.
>
> (2012)

The couple separated after only a week, and then divorced:

> I did pay her quite a bit of money of my own. I worked and paid her off slowly. It was around about, in those days money, I paid nearly three and a half grand. Because I didn't want her to – [upset] her parents, you know. So I looked at it, her life was destroyed. I know it's going to be very hard for her to get married, so I did pay her … a significant amount of money to get divorced.

A decade later, Big Hanif married again – another arranged marriage in Bangladesh. He told me that in between these marriages he had been seriously involved with a Bengali girl from North London for five years. He told his parents about the relationship and wanted to marry her, but they separated when he realized her family were, he told me, 'very low caste'. If he had married her, he continued,

They [his parents] would have just told me to leave home … There's certain things my dad compromise and certain things my dad don't compromise. And that was one of those areas that my dad would just say, 'Pack your bags, go and never come back in my house. I don't want to know you'.

When I asked, slightly incredulously, if these things still mattered, he insisted, 'Certain things doesn't matter … but certain things does matter. And as you go older you realize'. Even as he facilitated the love marriage of his younger brother, being the eldest son meant that Big Hanif had to follow his parents' wishes: 'I had less choice and I knew that I had to compromise', he reflected. In 2004, Big Hanif returned to Bangladesh for nearly a year and met his current wife:

I went to a friend of mine. We were just normal hanging around, and I saw her. He said, 'Oh she's my cousin from next door' … And I said, 'Oh, really, she's quite nice', and he said, 'Oh yes, she's just finished college or something. If you want I can put in a good word for you'. And I says, 'Is it?', and that's it, a few months later we got married.

Like Jadil and Big Hanif, Humzah's marriage was arranged during a family trip back to Bangladesh. Approaching thirty years old, we all suspected that this was on the cards when he went 'back home', ostensibly to organize the sale of some family land. He told me,

I thought that might happen. I thought this time they might try and get me.
Claire: How did you feel about that?
Humzah: If it happens, it happens. I wasn't really fussed. When I got married I only stayed two weeks after I got married. I came home.

(2012)

While age was most likely the primary factor, his younger brother Ifti's recent love marriage, discussed below, was an additional pressure. As the eldest son, it was for Humzah to maintain the family's reputation, particularly as his sisters Tasnim and Tahiya were of marriageable age. He explained:

I'm their only chance … I was the only one that maybe can adapt … Even though with my one [Ifti] he's already fled, I still had to do it. It was like a tradition just to show that, look, I was on that path … [For my] sisters to get married, it's got to look good for them … It matters because people see all that and they see who you marry, where you marry.

His parents were happy, he noted: 'They knew their son married how they wanted to … so it sort of stabilizes everything.' Nevertheless, Humzah was unhappy with the process and the pressure. He confessed, 'When I got married, I thought, why did I get married? I didn't want to get married. I was like, oh my days, I felt like I was chained or locked … it felt terrible, bad.' Back in London, he dragged his heels over bringing his wife for over two years. Although now happily settled, he reflected:

> I think I'm made for a love marriage. I wanted to have a love
> marriage, really. It was just never finding them or it never happening
> Claire: You never found the right person?
> Humzah: Not even that. It just never happened.

Amongst the little ones I interviewed, only Sayeed married back home, albeit slightly reluctantly. The first in the group to get married (in his mid-twenties), apart from Ifti's love marriage, Sayeed married in 2005. He told me, 'I wasn't always thinking of getting married, but Islamically you have to do it … and I didn't have no girlfriend or nothing like that to get married. Even if I did … ' (2012). Feeling the family pressure after his father's death, he visited Bangladesh and was encouraged to see a prospective bride: 'So I went down there and my mum was telling me "have a look at her, your cards are open but you can choose anyone you want".' Having previously resisted the match, which was with a cousin, Sayeed was persuaded by his mother to reconsider, because his father had been in favour of the marriage. He told me,

> I wasn't planning to, thinking I'm going to get married straightaway,
> sort of thing, but I went down there and I spoke to her and I did like
> her … I don't know if my decision was affected by my dad's saying, to
> be honest with you … but it was my choice that I got married to her
> and I felt comfortable with it.

His friends painted a slightly different picture. Hanif told me,

> I know he didn't want to marry his cousin, and I said to him, look you
> know, your mum should at least be happy that you're willing to go and
> marry, but at least let you have that choice of who you're marrying … So
> then he married and I don't think he was initially pleased with it … If
> you saw his wedding tape, he was the most angry man [*laughs*] … But
> since he's really happy.
>
> (2012)

Sayeed certainly seemed content when we spoke in 2012. When I asked
him what he liked about his wife, Sayeed described her,

> She was a nice person … she was caring, she was loving and …
> I knew she would look after my mum, she would look after me,
> properly, she'd be a good mother sort of thing and Islamically she'd be
> great. So put them all together, and it's the perfect wife.
> Claire: Is she attractive? I've never seen her.
> Sayeed: She is attractive, but she's not *greatly* attractive, you know
> what I mean? … She's like me – I'm not beautiful … so we make a
> good couple sort of thing.[3]

Marrying Out

If marrying 'back home' seemed often like a capitulation to family
pressures, for those who married 'outside' of their community, or against
their parents' wishes, these pressures were even more apparent. While
the number of 'mixed' marriages are growing amongst the Bangladeshi
community, the percentages are still very small (an estimated 7 per
cent in the 2011 Census – the lowest percentage amongst South Asian
communities)[4]. 'Love marriages' were still frowned upon by the older
generation, a source of family embarrassment and community censure,
even when these were with Bangladeshi young women. Nevertheless
a surprising number of the young men I knew did marry for love,
particularly amongst the older lot where there were broadly equal
numbers of arranged and love matches. Amongst the older lot, Shahin,

Zohar, Shakiel, M and Mehraj all married non-Bangladeshis, while amongst the little ones, Ifti and Shafiq married 'out'. It is worth noting that only Shahin and Mehraj married White British women, with the others choosing other South Asian or minority ethnic partners – reflecting the very ethnically diverse communities in which they moved. Nevertheless, even marrying closer to home, ethnically or religiously, was often as frowned upon as choosing someone from across ethnic or religious divides.

When I completed the first study, only Zohar was involved seriously with a girlfriend, Humaira, whom he later went on to marry. In 1996, when they had been dating for about two and a half years, Zohar confided to me, 'I would love to marry Humaira if it carries on. I'd love to get married to her if everything stays sweet. If it does, I will fight for it … I'd leave home'. Although he had told his two older sisters about the relationship, he acknowledged that his parents and eldest brother and sister were likely to be against any marriage: '[They] would blow up most probably, innit … it's going to be hard, man', he prophesied.

As it turned out, Zohar's fears proved fully grounded, and this caused difficulties for the couple as the years passed:

> Any relationship you have your issues, ups and downs, and you have your arguments and your debates, and you break up and you get back together … And then the whole marriage thing came along. I think my parents never accepted it, and her parents were wary about me.
>
> (2012)

For Zohar, the obstacles were two-fold: first, because Humaira was not Bengali. When I asked Zohar if part of the reason was because of historic animosity between Bangladeshi and Pakistani communities in the wake of the Bangladesh Liberation War (see Alexander et al 2016), he demurred:

> They were anti, but I think the thing was because it was their pride in the whole Bengali thing and this was the first time marrying out of the culture… It could be white, Black, whoever. It's just out of the culture, not because she was Pakistani.

Second, his father and older brother were against the match because it signalled a loss of their patriarchal control. Zohar recalled:

> He [my brother] was against it. My dad was against it ... You know what? I don't think they were against it; they were more angry with me, not with Humaira. It was the way I carried on a bit, because I was out of their control. Because you start to grow up, become a man.

Humaira's family were equally reluctant, and there was some negotiation before the marriage was agreed. Zohar recalled, 'I took my dad to go and meet her dad. It was awkward, obviously. It's like two different cultures, two different languages ... but I had to do that to make sure that they met.' Even then, there was some uncertainty about who would come to the wedding, with Zohar's older brother being particularly obstructive: 'We fell out a little bit. He made that obvious at the wedding.' Even several years later, the tension was still there. Zohar commented,

> It's difficult isn't it? It's every family, they're always going to regret it and they're all going to say, 'If maybe I'd done it that way, maybe it would have been happier for him'. I'm not sure my brother has got any regrets, giving me so much tension, but he's never going to say that because he's old, proud.

Nevertheless, Zohar asserted that his marriage 'was the best thing of my life'.

While Humaira was at least Muslim, religious difference was an additional hurdle. Interestingly, for all of the young men, irrespective of their own religiosity and how or where they married, that their wife was a Muslim – and more importantly, that their children would be raised Muslim – remained non-negotiable. Religion, and religious conversion (or reversion), was one of the key ways in which an unsuitable match could be 'made' suitable, and was used to challenge parents' ethnic or cultural expectations as being 'un-Islamic'. This seemed to be true even when the individuals concerned were not particularly religious themselves. However, religion intersected with other factors such as family position, family status, sibling support and the financial independence of the young men. Zohar, for example, was able to marry

Humaira in part because he no longer lived at home and was financially independent. With Shakiel, the situation was somewhat different – his status as the only son, but financially important to the family, both constrained and facilitated his marriage choices.

Shakiel met his wife, Naima, while he was working as a minicab driver. Six years his senior and of a Sikh background, Naima worked as an account manager in central London, and Shakiel once collected her from work. He recalled,

> I just picked her up once and we had a chat, and we had a laugh, and then she called me up a couple of times after that to drop her home … it was a gradual build-up. I let her know I'm there and yes we started spending time.

(2012)

Twenty-three years old when they met, Shakiel commented, 'It was different, you know, an older woman and everything', and Naima had guided him through some difficult times at work and with his friends:

> She's just a nice person, and she was a good influence on me … She was a person who could deal with things, who was able to give me a bit of insight … We didn't always agree, but it was good to bounce off someone who … had gone through all those things. And you know we had a laugh, we had a lot of fun.

When I interviewed Shakiel in 2012, they had been together for twelve years and married for four years. I met Naima once, at a wedding, and liked her – a forthright, funny and warm woman, who seemed very settled with Shakiel and at home with the Stoneleigh young men. Nevertheless, the path to their marriage was often difficult. Shakiel told me,

> We were together for eight years before and I have to say up to the seventh year we still weren't sure whether we was going to get married. There was no question whether we could get married and get along and live happily ever after. It was a case of do we actually now want to go through with it because there's going to be a lot of baggage from both sides.

As the only son, Shakiel particularly felt the responsibility of going against his parents' wishes. His three older sisters had all had arranged marriages, and knew about the relationship and supported their younger brother, but there were two younger sisters still to marry. Being the only son, and a family breadwinner, however, gave him some room for manoeuvre:

> Because I'd taken on responsibilities in the house and everything from a young age … I was never disrespectful or anything at home but they, kind of, knew that I wasn't going to let them put me in a corner and say, 'You have to do this'.

While his parents, and Naima's, suspected there was someone – 'they knew there was someone but they didn't *know*', he explained – his mother and sisters continued to try to persuade him to marry back home:

> This went on for a number of years. I'd say, probably five. And I had little feelers poke me to see what happened. And then they finally decided, you know what, you're not going to walk away from her, then we need to make it legal … So in the end they kind of pressured us into it in a sense, because then it came to the point where my family weren't nagging me to break it off, they were nagging me to marry her and bring her home.

Nevertheless, Naima's Sikh background was a stumbling block – 'It's not ideal for them, it was not ideal', Shakiel confessed – and Naima converted, but 'secretly'. Shakiel told me,

> Her parents don't know …. Her mum and dad are very old and I wouldn't want this to be the thing that sends them to their grave …[5]
> It's not ideal for them either that I was a Muslim, but they met me and they like me.

Marrying out, then, necessitated a fine balance between parental expectations, family obligations and the judgemental gaze (and consequences thereof) of the wider community, seasoned with a large pinch of 'not knowing', trade-offs and occasional deceit.

There were two very different love marriages I saw close-up across the years, and which illustrate these complex positionings: Shahin's with Emma, and Ifti's with Ana.

As noted earlier, Shahin had a rich and varied love life in his teenage years and into his twenties. As someone who had perhaps moved furthest from his Stoneleigh roots, educationally, through work and financially, it was perhaps unsurprising that this distance (and distancing) was reflected in his romantic choices. When younger, his girlfriends represented a desire not to get 'caught' – the reason he would never date Bengali girls – and even as a teenager he was adamant that he would never have an arranged marriage. As he matured, there was an additional element of aspiration: a desire to find a woman who embodied his success and could understand and support his social ambitions. As he laughed in 2012, 'Well, I think I always knew I probably wouldn't end up with a Bengali lady.'

Shahin met Emma through work, while he was still a paralegal and struggling to get a training contract. Emma had already qualified as a solicitor and worked in the personal injury department of a large respected city firm (where Hanif and then Shahin himself would later work). A very middle-class English young woman from the Home Counties, Shahin told me, 'She was just different and we just got on very well … we had a completely different upbringing … we are complete opposites, a bit like chalk and cheese probably, but … we get on very well together'. They dated for several years before they married, and the relationship was kept secret, although, as Shahin commented, 'Mum always knew there was somebody. It's just the done thing, you don't ask'. As with Zohar, Shahin bought a flat and moved out from the family home, although he insisted that this was not because of his relationship with Emma. 'I just wanted, you know, it's just to have a bit more freedom, a bit more space and my own space … I just wanted something of my own … It was just more like a crash [pad]', he told me.

Shahin introduced me to Emma shortly before he took her home to meet his mother and older sister – perhaps as a kind of dress rehearsal. The couple came for lunch at the London School of Economics, where

I was then working, and I liked Emma at once. Petite, very pretty, intelligent and quietly spoken, she clearly adored Shahin, though seemed a little confused by our relationship and the shared history of the Stoneleigh Estate that (always) dominated our conversation. By this time, the couple had been dating for over five years. When he took her home, Shahin recalled,

> The first thing mum said was, you know, 'as long as she's a nice lady, it doesn't matter if she's white, but Islam is, you know – do you think she'll convert?'

Emma's whiteness and Englishness did not seem to be a barrier, though language was a practical issue, and her vegetarianism was, and continued to be, a cause of some perplexity for Shahin's mother and *boroapa*, who were both avid feeders of anyone who passed their doors. Shahin's family met Emma's parents and sisters, and, Shahin reflected, 'Family value wise, it was very similar'. Emma did convert to Islam before they married, though this seemed largely a symbolic gesture, and I never saw any sign that she practised her new religion.

While the family welcomed Emma, Shahin's position was not entirely straightforward: as the eldest son, his marriage choices were seen as a reflection on his mother and the wider family, although it is clear that none of his siblings or close friends had ever expected him to have an arranged marriage. This situation was made more complex by the fact that, apart from his eldest sister, none of the other siblings (including his two older sisters) had married, and that Rukhsana and Khalid had both had children out of wedlock. Hanif, who knew Emma from work, was supportive, but worried about the way the marriage would be viewed by his extended family, and the blame that might be directed towards their mother because of the unconventional choices her children had made. He commented, 'It's always a worry about what people are going to say, and it's like, you know, they're going to say more of the same' (2012). This was compounded by more practical concerns over the traditional role of the eldest son in caring for ageing parents, which was closely tied to marriage and the role of daughters-in-law, and some anxiety about Shahin having moved out from the family home. Many of these concerns were short-circuited by Hanif's own – arranged – marriage, which took place the previous year, and which made Shahin's marriage more possible. However, Shahin was clear that he would have married Emma regardless. Married two years and with a young son, he told me in 2012, 'It's going pretty well actually … I'm glad we got married and Emma's obviously the right lady'.

While a large proportion of Shahin's cohort chose to 'marry out', comparatively few of the little ones did so. Ironically, it was Ifti, who had always declared he wanted an arranged marriage, and who was expected to marry early and 'back home', who was the first of his peer group to marry (aged only twenty), but in a tumultuous love match. Something of a charmer, Ifti met Ana when they were both working at McDonald's, when they were in their late teens. Ifti, with his usual swagger, told me,

> She was eyeing me … but then she didn't know how to come to me. So I came to her direct, and said, 'You know, you're the only pretty girl in this restaurant' … So I just asked her out and said, 'I want an answer straight. I don't want it long, tomorrow or whenever. I know there's a queue behind you, but you tell me now, or you know, forget it'. And then she thought about it and she said yes. And we went with that. That was it.
>
> (2012)

Ifti told me he liked Ana because 'she was a straight girl, she was, you know, a simple girl as well … She wasn't too headachy … She had my respect, that's what it was'. Ana, who is Turkish-Cypriot, was herself under pressure from her family to have an arranged marriage, and was briefly engaged, but fell pregnant with Ifti's child. Panicked, Ana left home. Ifti recalled, 'And one day she just came with a bag'. It was at this point that I met Ana: Ifti called me and asked me to 'lend' him some money for rent on a flat where Ana could stay. I met the couple in Gaol Park, and liked Ana at once. Quiet and pretty, thoughtful and with a sweetness that endeared her to me at once, she looked terrified. She settled briefly in a small flat, found by Shafiq. Ifti told me,

Ana's parents just went to my home, knocked at my door, just went in demanding their daughter … My mum and my brother called me. They asked me, my brother said to me, 'Ifti, tell me the truth. If you are with her tell me, we'll fix it right now'. And I didn't know at that time, because we had respect, and you know, I was quite fearful of them. I didn't realize that they would have been very helpful actually, and I didn't know what to do. And so I said no, and she was sitting right beside me.

Ifti's parents decided to send him back to Bangladesh soon afterwards. He told me that the trip, supposedly for three weeks to see a sick grandmother, was not related to his relationship with Ana, but then temporized,

It was nothing to do with that. I don't know. Maybe it was, it kind of was, but they didn't put it like that … My brother said, 'Don't worry, just go and come back'. Then I told her [Ana]. She was crying.

The day before he left, Ifti asked me to speak to his older brother, Humzah, about the situation, and to ask for his help in pleading his case with his parents. Humzah met with Ana, and told me,

I saw her, I thought, ok she seems nice. We had a chat and everything, she likes him and stuff … Family wasn't really – because he was like very thingy, secretive, and he was doing it in a panic situation, pregnant and all that. Why not do it properly, and introduce her and that, instead of getting her pregnant?

(2012)

Meanwhile, Ifti went to Bangladesh with his father and with the situation unresolved. His grandmother died while they were there, and he and his father stayed for the necessary forty days of mourning. Afterwards, his father stopped him from returning, 'they were holding my passport and everything', he told me. Eventually, with his grandfather's support, Ifti returned to marry Ana:

It came to a point where I said, 'Look … there's no ifs or buts here. That baby's not coming into the world without me being married' … Then it looked to me like it was wasting time. So I went ahead, isn't it? I went ahead and done it.

Ifti and Ana were married in a local registry office, with his sisters and close friends (including Faruk and Shafiq) present, and afterwards I took them to Brick Lane for a celebratory meal. Their son Kenan was born shortly afterwards, in May 2000.

Marrying 'at Home'

While arranged and love marriages can be set up in opposition, the reality is more complex, and there are shared concerns around family responsibility, parental expectations and personal choice that underlay both routes. The issue of individual choice, and constraint, is present in both, while there is significant variation even within 'arranged' or 'love' marriages. Opposed ideas of 'traditional' or 'modern' forms of marriage – family versus individual, 'forced' or freely chosen, Bangladeshi or British – do not capture the complexities of these arrangements, nor the personal and familial stakes at play. Still less do they guarantee happiness or stability. Furthermore, it would be misleading to see marriage as simply an arena either of conformity or conflict: rather, it was a process of negotiation and of – sometimes slow – change. This change was not, however, a simple nor uni-directional one, moving towards the mainstream British way of life and rejecting traditional values. Rather, new forms of dating, of making matches and marriage emerged.

This was clearly apparent amongst the little ones: as noted above, of the young men I interviewed from this group only one, Sayeed, had an arranged marriage 'back home', while only Ifti had a 'love match'. While the numbers are too small, and perhaps too idiosyncratic, to draw any broader conclusions, the 2012 interviews suggest a degree of reflexivity and change around marriage across the cohorts that was quite striking. The three remaining little ones, Mohammed, Jamal and Hanif, are considered together here – although their routes into marriage were in some ways quite different – in part because their choices reflected a shift in focus and the emergence of a new 'third way' in the marriage stakes.

Mohammed was the third in the group to marry (after Ifti and Sayeed), aged twenty-six – the ideal age, according to their fifteen-year-old selves. He told me he met his wife 'met through some mutual friends' at university (2012) – although Jamal insisted they actually met through an online dating site – and the couple dated for four years before marrying. Having finished university, Mohammed decided it was time to settle down: 'I'd finished all my education and was working – my mum and dad were starting to get on my case.' Although he had previously been involved with a Pakistani young woman, when choosing a wife he deliberately looked for a Bangladeshi partner, who would be acceptable to his parents. He reflected, several years later,

> The strange thing is probably no one in my generation group would have [married out] but now it's such a common thing, like people marrying in and out, that if my brother married out I don't think my mum would have been overly upset. But I think when I was ready to get married it was still quite a taboo.

As the eldest son, Mohammed was particularly attuned to his responsibilities towards his parents, aware of the pressure to marry, but also signalled the change that has taken place in the five or six years since he married. While careful not to criticize his friends, like Sayeed, who married back home, he viewed this as a 'the worst case' scenario, commenting,

> Everyone knew that was the last option ... everyone knew in the back of their heads ... that, you know, things are not so bad for us. In the worst case you could be thirty, still go back home and still get married.

At the same time, although his was technically a love match, Mohammed viewed his choice as very different from those in the older lot who 'married out'. Indeed, he explicitly defined his choices against the older group:

> They were like second generation and we're like third generation, kind of thing, so they probably tested the boundaries and we've said, hold on a minute, it doesn't actually work, let's stick to what we know.

When I asked him if he had been surprised by Jamal and Hanif choosing arranged marriages, he told me,

> I wasn't really surprised because no one had serious girlfriends … I think our age group has been quite orthodox … our age group was a lot more focused than our elders … Like in the great spectrum of things … we're going back to our roots, kind of thing.

I, on the other hand, had been very surprised when Hanif and Jamal both decided to have their marriages arranged, in the UK, at around the same time, since they had both been so set against this option when they were younger. Of course, they had kept their love lives very private across the years – even Hanif, whom I was close to, had never given any indication of any interest in, or involvement with, the opposite sex, and I had never asked. Indeed, the two friends even married on successive weekends, although their routes into wedlock were strikingly different.

As discussed above, Jamal settled on an arranged marriage partly on the rebound from a long-term romantic relationship, which his parents had refused to accept. Reaching his thirtieth birthday, and under pressure from his family to marry, he decided on an arranged marriage to a young British Bangladeshi woman from a neighbouring borough in South London. Initial searches proved tricky because of his lack of formal qualifications and his employment in a betting shop. He told me, 'In Asian culture, it's word of mouth first … my mum was like finding that she was going to a dead end everywhere, so, you know, I had to change my job role very quick' (2012). The initial introduction was arranged through a third person: 'You know, they said, "Oh so and so's looking to get their daughter married", so they just passed it along to my mum'. He liked the family of his future wife because

> The family that I married into were very humble and very, you know, straightforward, and it was based upon me as a person rather than what I was earning or what job I was in.

After the initial introduction, things proceeded quickly: 'I met her the first day and then I told my mum that I said, yes, I will marry her and after that we married after a month', he told me. Ironically, the speed of the wedding led others to believe the marriage was a love match – 'when we got married all her side thought we was dating', he laughed. When I asked him about the speed of the marriage, he explained:

> You see like for me I don't believe in the concept of free mixing before you marry, like all this getting to know each other on the telephone and all that stuff ... I don't need to know her in that depth, that's not a worry for me because once I'm married I'll have time to find out about you anyway.

Leaving aside the unconscious contradiction of this statement given his recent relationship, Jamal's comment also implies criticism of his best friend Hanif's choices. Hanif had also elected to have an arranged marriage, with Khadija, a young British Bangladeshi woman from North London, and they married the week before Jamal. The couple first met on Hajj, where Hanif had accompanied his mother, who was recovering from breast cancer. He told me, 'When I went to the Hajj seminar she was there as well, actually, and I did see her and I did think, "Wow, you know, she's ... " and I can still remember what she was wearing' (2012). The families met up on Hajj, in the tents set aside for British pilgrims:

> So she went with her father and her older brother, who were in the same tent as I was, and Khadija was in the same tent as my mum and my mum got to know her quite well ... And the funny thing was whenever I was pushing my mum in the wheelchair around she'd say to me 'oh, have you seen that girl?' ... I was saying to her, 'mum, this is wrong'. It's one of the things that's prohibited actually, you know, to discuss marriage and stuff whilst on Hajj.

On their return, the families remained in contact, and Hanif spoke to Khadija regularly over the phone (although they never met up in person). He explained, 'We kept in contact ... not thinking at the outset, oh I'm going to marry her ... but I suppose the further you went on, the more you obviously started thinking about that. And then I thought, you know I should get married.' Hanif felt that their meeting on Hajj was fated:

> To think, you know, of all the places where millions of people have got together, and … I've sort of come to know *her* there – I don't know it just seemed right really … I've always been someone who sort of tries to follow signs and think things happen for a reason, and so I sort of follow things in that way.

Fate aside, the speed of the decision did take us all off guard. Shahin commented, 'I was a bit surprised, because I said, "Oh, are you sure?" … It was all done really quickly' (2012). The decision seems partly to have been made on religious grounds: Shahin told me that Khadija's father, in particular, was keen for the couple to marry quickly:

> He was just well, if her and Hanif are going to talk to each other – because they were becoming more religious – and he thought it just would be better if they got married. And I think Hanif felt the same, and rather than being boyfriend and girlfriend, they wanted to get married.

While the religious expectation/constraint was undoubtedly a key element, age was also an issue: 'I thought, I'm not getting any younger, actually I should really marry, settle down' (Hanif 2012). Hanif was also keen to start a family and to have someone to support their mother at home – especially after Shahin had moved out. Indeed his deepening faith was inseparable from his sense of family responsibility. He explained,

> I was always the youngest. My sisters had sort of done what they had done, and so as I started, you know, growing up more, and Shahin was doing what he was doing and Khalid was doing what he was doing. And then … the more I started to focus on my religion, the more I started appreciating more home responsibilities in terms of my mum, for example.

While he did not criticize the relationship choices of his older siblings, he continued:

I think being the youngest you can sort of … see maybe mistakes that others have made and so you can learn from it. So maybe it's easier for you because other people may be making the mistakes that you may have made, but you've had the chance to sort of look and think, ok well that's not the right thing to do.

Nevertheless, he acknowledged that an arranged marriage was not something he had really considered for himself until quite recently:

Claire: Did you think that would be something you'd do?
Hanif: I didn't. I would have seen something like that as being
    not glamorous, or not the way to be, but that's probably more
    reflective of where I was at that stage of my life, really. And I'm
    really happy it did go the way it did go and it wasn't any other way.

I did not meet Khadija before their wedding day, but have come to know her quite well since she moved into the family home. A stunningly beautiful, intelligent and articulate young woman, of strong faith, and with a quietly wicked sense of humour, she seems ideally suited to Hanif. A psychology graduate, now a primary school teacher, she once told me she had studied *The Asian Gang* at university and wanted to know which of the pseudonymized participants was her husband. So I guess that cat is now well and truly out of the bag.

Happily Ever After?

As Hanif indicated above, a key factor in his decision to marry was to fulfil his wider familial responsibilities, particularly around care for his mother as she aged. This was a common concern articulated by most of the young men, no matter which route to marriage they took. This was particularly the case for eldest sons, on whose shoulders, traditionally, the expectation of parental responsibility fell. Big Hanif told me that when his mother fell ill with cancer it was his role to take her to hospital and doctors' appointments and look after her until she died, 'as a traditional Bengali would say, as the oldest son it's fallen to me to look after [her]' (2012). This was a key pressure in his decision to have his second arranged marriage: 'I had less choice …. Basically I had to keep my family happy.' This freed his younger brother to have a love marriage and move out from the family home. Big Hanif told me, 'He says to me, "No, I'm going to get married and move out. You're the oldest, you should stay home and look after parents" … He just blatantly told me that. I just said, "Ok then".' This is not to suggest that the young men felt this as a burden, and most embraced it as a positive duty. Shakiel, for example, who married for love, had brought his wife, Naima, to live at his family home with his mother and younger siblings. While this was expected as the only son, it was also something he wanted to do (and had remained constant since I first interviewed him in 1996). He stated,

> One of the things I'd made clear to Naima before we got married was that, you know, my mum was always going to stay with me. We're not going to move out … That's never going to change … Even if I had older brothers … I reckon I still would have ultimately, you know, taken her home.
>
> (2012)

The expectation that their wives would take on a traditional role of daughter-in-law was not restricted to eldest sons. M, who was a younger son and who married a mixed-race (white/Thai) woman, also brought her to live at the family home. He told me, proudly,

> She used to make tea and iron my dad's shirts, and my dad loved her … You know when you get old, you get lost in the sense of time. He used to get up sometimes, three o'clock in the morning, knocking on my door wanting tea and that. So my wife used to go and make it for him …
>
> (2012)

He reflected, 'She's like how a Muslim girl should be – very quiet, modest.' Hanif, Jamal and Sayeed, who were all youngest sons, were also keen to take on the primary caring role in the family. As suggested above, for Hanif, this was strongly connected to his faith: 'I see it as a blessing for me to be able to look after my mum' (2012), he reflected, while Sayeed told me:

I'm the one that's living at home at the moment … I think in Asian families it is sort of expected but me, personally, I would never leave my mum … even if I was the oldest I wouldn't leave my mum because I feel that I'm too attached to my mum.

(2012)

Jamal's older brother left the family home after Jamal married and brought his wife home – something that was particularly interesting given that Jamal had always described his older brother as more traditional than him. Echoing Sayeed, he said,

My brother obviously is more financially equipped than I am so he moved out. But anyway it would have been him that moves out anyway because, like I'm more closer to my mum and dad – well, my mum anyway, so my mum would rather have me at home than my older brother, I guess.

Taking on this role was a central expectation of his arranged marriage,

I've told my wife, you know, there's not going to be that feeling that I'll move out, so don't ever get stupid ideas … A lot of girls nowadays would encourage their husband to move out from their mother's home because mums are very demanding on them, the daughter-in-laws … But it's not like that in our family.

This transition was not always straightforward or successful, particularly where the wife was not Bengali. Ana, for example, moved into Ifti's family home for about eighteen months, and while both she and Ifti's mother tried to adapt, Ana found the expectations of her mother-in-law and sisters-in-law hard to manage, especially with Ifti being so often out of the house working. Ifti sighed, 'I guess she just found it hard to adjust and it was hard for everybody' (2012). The couple moved to a flat several miles away, and later separated. They reconciled for a couple of years after Ifti was released from his first spell in prison – 'We got back together but we didn't tell the families, because it was broken off for a long time', he told me – and had two more children. They separated again, permanently, shortly after our interview in 2012, and the relationship between Ana and Ifti's family deteriorated over the next few years.

Of course, and as Jamal suggests, these tensions are not necessarily rooted in cultural or religious differences, but in the act of displacement that patrilocal marriage entails for women, and the difficulties around adapting to a new family (Alexander 2013, Alexander et al 2016). Indeed, Humzah's arranged marriage 'back home' also faltered in London, leading him and his wife to move out to a flat in East London. Ifti commented,

> He [Humzah] gave everyone the shock of their lifetime moving out with his wife. She found it difficult … I think she was young and naïve and now where they are – because she had it cushy, comfy and now they're struggling … They've come like where, like they've run away or something, or they're a love marriage, but they've made it difficult. And so they're feeling it.

Humzah himself shrugged:

> I just thought basically she'd be able to at least help my mum out. She was good with all that stuff. She'd be someone to lend a hand … That didn't work out.

(2012)

'Moving out' was often seen as bringing shame on the family, and was rarely acknowledged publicly, even though these practices were becoming increasingly common. This is in part because of changing employment and financial positions, or because of the incapacity of the social and rental housing sector (where Bangladeshis are concentrated) to provide houses of sufficient size to accommodate multi-generational households (Shankley & Finney 2020). A number of the young men I knew moved out of the parental home, both before and after marriage. In fact, the numbers of those living outside the parental home outnumbered those still at home broadly by two to one, although it is impossible to characterize either group by their marriage pathways, family circumstances, employment or financial position or other axes of differentiation. Irrespective of their residence, all were insistent that this did not impact their role and responsibilities towards their families. Often, living situations changed over time, and for a range of different reasons. Mohammed, for example, lived at home after marriage, but moved out to a nearby flat after his first child was born. He told me,

I ran out of space ... it's not like back home where I can build an extension ... Once you're married, you just need a bit of space to yourself as well ... I thought this is probably the best compromise because I'm close to my parents – they're literally two minutes up the road. But I just needed a bit of space.

(2012)

As the eldest son, he continued,

Mum and dad were really upset ... it was quite difficult for them to let go ... It was just upsetting for them to see me move on, but I think they love it now because it's just another place that they can go and visit ... We pretty much live there anyway – we eat and everything else round there ... there wasn't really any tension or guilt.

There were other tensions too as the young men settled into married life. Especially for those who had married back home, adjusting to life with a wife from a very different background could prove difficult. As Humzah noted, 'I went back home to get married – it's very hard, it's like they're from another planet ... They won't understand nothing, none of your jokes, none of your stuff. It's very tricky' (2012). Some adjusted by keeping their married life and their outside lives completely separate. Shahin told me that he had not met many of the Bangladesh-married wives of his friends:

Some of their wives, I've been to their houses but I've never seen their wives, which is quite odd I think ... they would just stay in the kitchen or something ... It's a bit like being in the Dark Ages ...

(2012)

However, he temporized, 'if it's for religious reasons and the lady doesn't want to come in front of a man, that's fine. So that's probably why I've never sort of questioned it or said anything'. His younger brother Hanif told me that neither he nor Jamal knew Sayeed's wife: 'No one's really met her' (2012). Even Sayeed himself explained, 'My wife comes from a different part ... She's like alien compared to the other wives, that's why' (2012). While this was not a source of tension amongst the close friends, this did mean they spent less time together after marriage, and especially as they entered into fatherhood. Sayeed attributed this in part to his wife's shyness, to her commitments with their three young children and to her lack of English: 'She don't actually like you know to go out and mingle and things like that … it's not worth putting someone in an uncomfortable position', he insisted. It is worth noting too, however, that Hanif and Jamal's British Bangladeshi wives also did not know each other well. Jamal explained,

> Both our wives are completely different. You see his [Hanif's] wife is much younger than my wife, for example. Also his wife is more inclined to the way Hanif is as well, like she's very religious … So those kind of views, they don't [*Pauses*]. I don't mean to say they have bad attitude to each other but they just don't get along.

Sayeed concluded, revealingly:

> We three have always said when we get married, you know, our wives will go to each other's houses, but it didn't turn out like that. You know, our wives have different views as well … There's not an attachment like the way we are attached, you know.

There were exceptions, of course, across all the marriage types. Shakiel told me that he and Mehraj's wives and children were close and went on holidays together, while Mohammed said that his wife and Jamal's wife were friends, 'I think my wife and her meet for coffees and whatever the young mums do these days' (2012). Zohar and Shahin and their wives often met up for dinner. Big Hanif and Mustafa were both adamant that their wives accompany them to their friends' houses, and if they felt this was not possible, the friendships would be axed. Mustafa, who was a devoted husband and father, stated,

> There's nobody out there I'm not taking my missus there. When I go to their house, my missus is coming to see their missus. My kids are coming to see their kids, and I'm coming to see them. It's on that basis, end of story.

(2012)

He insisted, 'Your conduct, your behaviour should be clear as water. My behaviour, my conduct is clear as water with my life, end of story.'

For many of Mustafa's peer group, however, things were more opaque, particularly those who had chosen arranged marriages. As noted with Jadil, above, those who had married 'back home' often had ongoing romantic relationships that were disrupted – or in some cases, not – by their marriage. Several of the men I knew whose marriages were arranged in Bangladesh maintained their London relationships after marriage or found new girlfriends. This was a widely recognized (if not accepted) practice, and one that was often justified by them because of the nature of their marriage choices. Humzah told me of his friends, 'Everyone's married, but everyone's still got their girlfriends' (2012). One participant,[6] for example, confessed to having a number of affairs since he married, but was careful to keep these worlds separate:

> It's like I lead two lives. I lead one life at home, and then I do lead the other life outside of home … Whatever I do outside, I do outside … it's a bit risky. I mean, but it's not like I'm having serious relationships … I don't let that happen because I know I've got three kids and I've got my wife at home, so I want to maintain that.

While, as above, these were often relatively casual, in some cases these were long-term, committed relationships. Humzah described one close friend who had married due to parental pressure but spent most of his time with his girlfriend: 'He's got a serious relationship with one person and he's married to one person …' (2012). Humzah explained, 'I think you get certain things from a certain person. With your girlfriend you get another way of relaxing, or whatever, feeling, understanding … Morally, I can't really say.' Shahin similarly speculated,

> Maybe they want the best of both worlds and they want someone that's going to be at home, to cook and they'll stay at home, you know, look after the mother, all the homely stuff, but then … they want somebody at the same time that they can converse with and who's interested in the music they're listening to … And they want that as well.

(2012)

However, he and others – especially those who had fought for their love matches – were critical of these choices. Shahin continued:

> I would have thought they would have been strong enough to have said to their parents, 'I don't want to go to Bangladesh and get married'. So I think there's always that excuse. I see that as an excuse … It might be a bit harsh but you know … you can say no to your parents. … There is pressure, there must be pressure, but I think, you know, I think it's probably a personal choice, with a bit of pressure.

When I asked Mustafa about this practice amongst some of his friends, he was outraged, and demanded who know which of them I was speaking about. Backpedalling furiously, I tried to make it sound like a more generic query, though I suspect he was not convinced. An interesting example of the 'not-knowing' and 'not-telling' that seemed to function to maintain relationships between friends, and within families – as well as a testament to the respect (and fear) in which Mustafa was held (particularly since his religious reversion) – Mustafa told me, 'To tell you the truth I don't know about any of these issues. And if that is, I'm totally against it and disgusted to tell you the truth' (2012).

Fathers and Sons

While care for ageing parents – and especially mothers – was a key factor in the decision of when, where and whom to marry, an additional consideration was the production and raising of the next generation. Most were clear that, for them, marriage was an essential precondition for having children – as reflected in Ifti's insistence on marrying Ana before the birth of their son Kenan. M told me that a former girlfriend had become pregnant and had an abortion:

> And that used to dwell on me. So I didn't want to go through the same kind of scenario ever again. So I thought, If I'm going to get married, I'm going to get married properly the Islamic way and then have a child and that, have a family. I've always loved kids.

(2012)

Most of the men I interviewed in 2012 were fathers, some very recently so – or were hoping to be in the near future – and were fully involved in their children's lives. Shakiel, whose son was two and a half, told me, 'I've always wanted kids, you know. He couldn't come soon enough really. As soon as I got married, I was ready to have a family straightaway' (2012). Khalid spoke of the birth of his daughter, Jasmine, 'I can't tell you how happy I was when she was born … I just can't tell you how happy a feeling that was … how happy I used to wake up and just hold her and feel so content' (2012). Even the usually cynical Jamal, whose baby daughter was only four months old when I spoke to him, rhapsodized:

> It's the best thing in the world, you know. She's away at the moment … but I miss her so much everyday. It's amazing how a baby's smile can lighten your heart so like … I didn't think that I was going to have that, so when it hit me, it was a bit of a shock.
>
> (2012)

Zohar told me his daughter Maryam was 'a daddy's girl. People say I spoil her'. Maryam had been born prematurely, weighing only three pounds, and Zohar reflected,

> I was overprotective. I took about four weeks off work and sat with her and done everything possible … you don't know what fatherhood is until you have the baby and Maryam, it was just wow, your stress levels are 100 per cent increased.
>
> (2012)

Later, he said, 'I think you just grow into it. I don't think you plan it … at the end of the day with your child there's this immense love that you can give, that she can give back to you and then you just forget about everything else'.

Becoming fathers had led many to reflect on their role, stressing their 'fully hands on' (Sher Khan, 2012) approach to fatherhood. When I asked him what kind of father he was, Shakiel replied, 'I think I'm a good father, you know … I've got a lot of time for my son … I made an actually, real concerted effort to make sure I can do everything that my wife can do, apart from breastfeeding .... My dad was shocked that I was so hands on, because he wasn't' (2012). Sayeed similarly told me, 'I would say I'm a good father ... they're always with me. The only time that my wife takes them is when they have to go to sleep, because if I go there they won't go to sleep, they just want to be with me' (2012). He added, 'I can be a better father and I think with time I will be.' Zohar was very devoted to his daughter, and described their relationship, 'We do our own thing. We just go out for a drive, or we go out to see my friends. That's the thing. That's how close [we are]' (2012). Mustafa told me 'I'm very practical. I overlook everything, and I take key responsibilities, because my son's got eczema, I bath him all the time to make sure I get it under control' (2012). I was personally witness to this care when I interviewed Mustafa at his home: I had rashly taken his son an Easter egg, which he ate and then promptly vomited back up, and it was Mustafa who leapt to look after him and clean him up. His care and gentleness with his son was genuinely touching, and very at odds with his fierce reputation.

Many reflected on their aspirations for their children's futures, stressing their desire for an experience very different from their own, particularly in terms of money and education. Mustafa told me that he wanted three children only because 'I can't afford too big'. M, who already had three children, told me:

> You know how the mentality of our parents were, save money for their education, their future ... Like I never used to get that, and my dad used to go, he used to save for me for the future, for my education and that. I thought when I get married, when I have kids, I'm going to do the opposite. I'm going to waste money on buying them everything I can.
>
> (2012)

Big Hanif also reflected on his desire for a more affluent future for his little boy, then aged two: 'I'm not interested in a big family, I'm not interested in having children for the sake of having children. You know, if I'm going to have one or two, I want to give them a good education' (2012). Jadil, who has three children, admitted, 'I don't get to spend a lot of time with them, with my commitments and my business' (2011), although when I interviewed him he had spent the morning building a chicken coop for them in the garden. Nevertheless, he said he was hopeful his eldest son would take over from him: 'With my son, I would like him to take over my business ... I want my son to like come into my footsteps.'

Fatherhood was also tied up with the desire to be a good role model and protector. Jamal told me,

> I want to be a good father, obviously. I want to give her everything that I physically can in terms of financial support, in terms of emotional support and also just the spiritual guidance as well.
>
> (2012)

Shahin similarly reflected,

> I'd like to help, you know, like make sure he's on the right track ... I've probably done it with my brothers as well; just if there's something that I failed in, at least I can keep that knowledge and say look, I was there, it didn't work, and you know, be able to guide him.
>
> (2012)

As the father of a mixed-race son, Shahin was particularly keen to connect him with his Bengali heritage:

> I'd like him to grow up ... knowing that he's of mixed race origin, and that he has a connection to his Asian side as well ... So I said to mum when she sees him she should speak to him in Bengali so he can pick it up and at least he will have some connection to his Asian side. I think it's important.

For Shahin this represented an interesting shift: he spoke little Bengali himself and had said when younger that he was not particularly interested in the connection with Bangladesh, although he had been born there, and the family still held land in Sylhet. Now he spoke of wanting to visit Bangladesh with his son, to explore his roots.

For others, faith was an important part of their role: as discussed above, the desire to raise their children as practicing Muslims was a key factor in their marriage choices. The father of three daughters in 2012,

Sayeed told me that 'obviously I would like a boy, but I'm happy the fact that our Prophet used to have three girls' (2012). He continued, 'I want my daughter to handle situations, that's the thing, Islamically … I want her to live by Islamic rules.' Similarly, Mustafa described his fatherly responsibility as 'the Islamic way' of providing 'Guidance, A role model' (2012).

Becoming fathers had also led them to reflect, often very movingly, on their relationships with their own fathers, and how this pointed to a generational change. Their fathers were often considerably older than their mothers, and older when their children were born than my participants. In many cases, the fathers were absent for extended periods, leaving their young families in Bangladesh, or worked long, antisocial hours. This led to distant, and often difficult, relationships with their sons. Humzah told me, 'That generation was just terrible. We weren't connected with our parents. It was just beating the crap out of you to make you understand something' (2012). Zohar similarly commented,

> Dads or fathers I know from Bangladesh, they're very distant, and that naturally happens because of the era and culture. There was a big distance … My dad, because he was working all the time, and that time he was being responsible for your children and making sure you had enough income coming in, to support here, to support back home, to do everything you want to do.
>
> (2012)

Cultural hierarchies of respect entrenched the gap between father and son – something my participants were determined would be different with their children. Big Hanif told me,

> I used to love my dad, but I was scared of him, so I couldn't go up to him and tell him [sic] for advice. I don't want my son to do that … I want him to respect me but also love me, but I don't want him to be scared of me so much.
>
> (2012)

M similarly reflected,

My boy is going to learn from it, you know why? Because my old man was more harsh and never explained things … But with my boy, I'm going to not try and be so fatherly, but like a friend as well … instead of being so strict, I'm going to be more like a friend with him and explain things.

(2012)

As Big Hanif and M suggest, these relationships could be particularly conflictual. Jamal, for example, told me,

If I look at my own relationship with my father it's very distant, you know. We don't speak so much and also that's partly because when I was growing up my dad used to beat me a lot because I was naughty. So that kind of relationship was never there in that sense and that's something I do want to have with my children. I want to have a relationship, I want them to be able to speak to me and tell me things are not right.

(2012)

Reflecting on his own childhood and his own very different views of fatherhood, Zohar commented, 'I think that's a generational change, so that's part of taking that culturalism out of that' (2012).

Of course, not all of my participants' fathers were from the same cultural mould. Shahin spoke of his father as quite different from most Bangladeshi men of his generation:

He was quite calm, quite laid back but very focused, and knew what he wanted … there wasn't that detached relationship which some of my friends have had … So when he was around at the weekend … he would take us to the park or a shop … we'd go out and actually spend time together … He was quite hands on as well. So I mean he would help out with household tasks, to help my mum out, whereas not many Bengali men of that generation would do that.

(2012)

Sayeed also noted that his father was his primary carer, although he noted that, as the youngest child, his relationship was very different from his older brothers':

> My dad was really good with me, what he used to do I teach my kids
> same thing ... [My older brothers] they had a more distant relationship
> with my father ... they never used to talk to him, but caring-wise my
> father used to take more care of us than [my mother].
>
> (2012)

I was particularly touched by Mustafa's reflections on his father, and
his determination to make a change with his own children. Mustafa's
father was acknowledged by many of my participants as being
exceptionally harsh with his sons, even by Bangladeshi standards.
Mustafa described the relationship vividly, though without any rancour:

> My dad used to beat me, you know, very aggressive, very strict. Beat
> me for anything, boom, boom, boom, bam, bam, bam. And the
> majority of my friends, I see it was like that as well. I don't want that
> kind of relationship. That is not the Islamic way ... I would rather have
> a father-son relationship.
>
> (2012)

His relationship with his own young son seemed very different, though
I did wonder if these dynamics would change as the child grew up.
Recently, when his name came up in a conversation, I asked Zohar
about this. Zohar told me that Mustafa was an affectionate and devoted
father to his (now) four children, especially his youngest daughter – a
testament to Mustafa's transformative faith and love.

****

These are, of course, necessarily incomplete stories. The accounts
offered above are based in most cases only on the accounts of the
young men themselves since, by their nature, marriage and fatherhood
are private and personal domains, outside of the gaze of the curious
ethnographer – however nosey she may be. The stories presented here
do not include the voices of the women that loved and/or married
'the Asian Gang', nor the views of the wider web of family members –
parents, siblings, extended family – who were integral to the choices
made, and what happened next. It recognizes, but does not explore,

the experiences of the Bengali young women from the Stoneleigh estate, although my limited knowledge of some of the participants' sisters suggests similar (if significantly more constrained) processes of struggle and change. As far as I am aware, none of the young men I knew were gay, but I recognize the very different and difficult struggles that this might lead to.

As these stories – however partial and still-changing – reflect, family remains an unfinished and ongoing project. Marriage and fatherhood provide revealing insights into the changing identities of these men, highlighting both transformation and continuity from the hopes and expectations of their teenage selves. In many cases, these paths were very different from what they had imagined for themselves and each other back in the mid-1990s. Nevertheless, the importance of family remains a central part of their adulthood, even as (and perhaps because) it is a locus of struggle, negotiation and reconciliation. And hopefully, as Sayeed commented 'love happens'.

Religion

The Missing Muslims

On the wall of the tiny back office of the SAYO project in the mid-1990s there was a small black-and-white cartoon printed on A4 paper. Titled 'Common assumptions and stereotypes about the Asian community', the line drawing depicted two South Asian men, one with goatee beard and *kufi* addressing the other: 'I suppose with you being Gujerati and me being Bangladeshi and being born and brought up 4500 miles apart, you can forgive them thinking we're the same.' At the time, and when writing the first *Asian Gang* book, the poster captured for me the sense of fracturing within the category 'Asian', and the emergence through the 1990s, of the figure of 'the Muslim' – usually figured as young and male – into the forefront of political and public concern. My comment then was that 'the reification of Islam as one of the key markers of difference in contemporary British racial discourse has proved pervasive and politically potent, providing the impetus for renewed public debates around immigration, integration and the requirements of citizenship' (2000: 6). Twenty-five years later, and over two decades into the War on Terror, the phrase 'overtaken by events' leaps to mind.

Looking back, the poster captures a web of implicit tensions that were to surface in the following years, reconfiguring the landscape of racial and ethnic relations and profoundly reshaping the lives of 'the Asian gang' participants as they grew to adulthood. Pausing only briefly to note the need for the qualifier 'South' to the term 'Asian' in recent years,[1] the poster title and caption encapsulates the ongoing balance between external misrecognition and stereotyping, and internal identities and community fault lines. On the one hand, there is the homogenization of racialized discourse in the notion of 'the Asian community', wherein all Asians are imagined as 'the same'; on the other, there is the assertion of difference, configured here in the layering of ethnic ('Asian'), national/regional (Bangladeshi/Indian-Gujerati) and religious (Muslim/Hindu).[2] From the mid-1980s and through the 1990s this apparently benign assertion was to solidify into a more antagonistic reification of difference, encoded along racial (Black/Asian), national (Indian/Pakistani/Bangladeshi), religious (Muslim/non-Muslim) and, increasingly, socio-economic lines – what Sivanandan has powerfully characterized as the retreat to 'ethnic enclaves and feuding nationalisms' (2000).

The contemporary construction of 'the Muslim community' as a coherent entity – and as a problem (Alexander, Redclift & Hussain 2013) – is most usually traced to the demonstrations around the publication of Salman Rushdie's novel, *The Satanic Verses*, in 1988, and the Gulf War protests of 1991 (Kundnani 2014), although there are longer historical and cultural roots (Sayyid 2015, Ansari 2018). Arun Kundnani has described South Asian Muslims as constituting 'an ideal enemy' (in the 'clash of civilisations' ideologue Huntington's (1996) words), being 'ideologically hostile, racially and culturally different' (2014: 27) – visible, alien and angry. Certainly by the mid-1990s, when the moral panic about 'Asian Gangs' reached its peak, the nexus of racial, cultural, social and political 'crisis' (to borrow Hall et al's evocative 1978 term) was encoded as Muslim. As discussed in Chapter 1, by the time we entered the new millennium, this implicit code became increasingly explicit, and hostile. Such shifts were already apparent during my first study – Runnymede's landmark report which first popularized the now ubiquitous term 'Islamophobia' was published in 1997, tracing the emergence of anti-Muslim racism into the political mainstream. The report defined Islamophobia as 'unfounded hostility towards Islam … [and] the practical consequences of such hostility in unfair discrimination against Muslim individuals and communities' (1997: 4). The following twenty-five years have seen the entrenchment, intensification and banalization of Islamophobic sentiments, with Sayeeda Warsi arguing in 2011 (when I started my second round of interviews) that anti-Muslim prejudice had become acceptable across the mainstream – passing the 'dinner-table test' of respectable racism (Batty 2011). In 2017, two decades on from the original report, Runnymede published an influential collection of short essays, arguing that Islamophobia was 'Still a Challenge for Us All' and calling for action to tackle anti-Muslim racism, and disadvantage, across all spheres of public life (Elahi & Khan 2017). The introduction notes that in the intervening twenty years, 'anti-Muslim prejudice has grown further and wider' and has developed in 'new and toxic ways' while 'the Muslim community' itself has grown in size, visibility and organization (Elahi & Khan 2017: 5). This has been matched by increasing data on or about British Muslims in all aspects of their lives.[3]

Nevertheless, as discussed in Chapter 1 and further below, the hypervisibility of Muslims has also led to their invisibility, constructing them primarily through the dual public discourses of 'threat' and 'victim'. Most academic research on Muslim identities, which has proliferated from the 1990s onwards, has reinforced this dualism, with a focus on either extremist or fundamentalist ideologies, or on the practice and impact of Islamophobia, at a state or individual level. The private life of Islam – what it means to individual Muslims, how and why it is practised, how its meaning changes over time, and in the encounter with the discourses of the past three hate-filled decades – has been less explored. By this, I do not mean an exoticist anthropological narrative of ritual and gift giving (Werbner 1990), nor analyses of theological tenets and debates (Ansari 2005, Eade & Garbin 2005, Bhatt 2013, Sayyid 2015), but an exploration of how faith is lived in the mundane spaces of everyday life. While its impact has been noted in previous chapters, or left implicit, in this chapter, I try to draw out its role more explicitly, focusing on the individual roots, routes and transformations of faith. My emphasis here, then, is less on the political or institutional dimensions of Islam, and more on its biographical aspects, while recognizing the inseparability of the former from the latter. In particular, I will explore the way that faith has shaped and impacted on 'the Asian gang' as it grows older and across all aspects of life, including work, friendship and family.

It is unsurprising, of course, that religion should feature more prominently in this later book, given its ubiquitous and inescapable significance in contemporary discourse, and its (connected) increased importance in the lives of 'the Asian gang' participants. Perhaps more surprising was its absence in the earlier study. Reflecting now, and having re-read the earlier transcripts, this absence has two reasons. First, and as discussed below, religion was not as strong an element in the identity of my participants at the time – at least not in the public spaces in which my ethnography was mainly set. Second, and relatedly, religion was more situated in the private spaces of home, family and community, which, as a woman and a non-Muslim, were less accessible to me. While the question of faith was discussed – and is revisited below – it never made it to the final text in any substantial way. In discussions since, several of the participants have argued that this was an oversight on my part, and that being Muslim was always a key – or *the* key – part of their identity. While I remain only partially convinced by this – or rather, think that *the way* in which being Muslim mattered changed in the years after the first study, as it did in the world outside – I nevertheless acknowledge the criticism, and my own myopia. As Mohammed commented during our 2012 interview:

> You probably missed a trick there, to be honest with you. I know for a fact subconsciously it's always in someone's head, but I think through the course of our discussions you've just probably never prompted the right question to bring it up.

Being Muslim 1996: The Roots of Religion

Looking back, Mohammed was right: my interviews in 1996, reflecting by the dominant discourse of the time, were focused primarily on issues of ethnicity and race, rather than religion, as a key framing of identity.

While I asked how the young men described themselves – Asian, British, Bangladeshi, Black – I only occasionally asked them where 'Muslim' featured in this hierarchy of identifications. The top self-ascribed labels were balanced between 'Asian' and 'British', with 'Asian' probably the top choice. 'Asian' was often conflated with Bangladeshi or Bengali. Zohar told me he generally used 'Asian' as his primary identity, but reflected, 'It's a hard question innit? Born here and being born in a Bengali family' (1996), while Khalid, in contrast, insisted, 'I describe myself as Bengali – there's nothing wrong with that, that's how I grew up … I won't lose my roots or nothing' (1996). Black rarely, if ever, featured as an identity, reflecting the fragmentation of political blackness and solidarity from earlier decades (Alexander 2002, 2018), or perhaps Modood's assertion that Asians had never considered themselves 'black' in the first place (Modood 1988). Or perhaps it simply reflected the very tense relationships with local Black young men in the area at the time (Alexander 2000). When I did – inconsistently – suggest Muslim as a label, most claimed it, but rarely offered it as an identity marker themselves. Again, this may be because Bangladeshi (and even Asian) was often seen as synonymous with Muslim.[4] When I asked Khalid about the label Muslim, he replied, 'That's one of them, yeah' (1996), suggesting a multiplicity of equally valid identity choices, while Ifti, by contrast, insisted on a hierarchy 'I'm a Muslim, then Bangladeshi' (1996). Mohammed did not initially describe himself as Muslim but, when I raised it as a possibility, he responded, 'Yes, of course, that's a priority. I'd have to say that first' (1996).

Labels aside, the interviews clearly show that religion was an important part of their everyday lives. As Zohar insisted, 'Everyone knows something about it' (1996), although knowledge and practice varied widely within the group. According to Zohar, Shahin and Humzah were the most religious amongst the older lot, with Mustafa and Salman the least knowledgeable: 'He don't know nothing … he don't know how to pray', Zohar commented on Salman, though without judgement. Amongst the little ones, it was acknowledged that Hanif was the most religious, with Sayeed (Salman's brother) the least informed.

Religion was most closely associated with their family and home life. As Mohammed stated, 'It's very important to know your religion because that's how you've been brought up' (1996). Most spoke of their parents, in particular, as important religious role models. Zohar's parents had been on Hajj twice, and Ifti, Mohammed and Hanif all noted that their mothers were key to their religious practice (if with sometimes limited effect). Ifti told me, 'My mum will always tell us to pray anyway, she will remind us' (1996). I would often witness this when I visited their house – though she often met with shrugs and evasion from her children. Mohammed similarly told me, 'My mum wakes me up in the morning, like some mornings I have to pray and that. Sometimes I lock my door and just go back to sleep' (1996). Religious education in their childhood took place at home and was bound up with childhood memories and family bonds, and with the cycles of family life – Ramadan, Eid celebrations, Friday mosque. Mohammed linked his early religious education with memories of his grandfather, who lived with the family: 'I used to go to the mosque with my granddad but then he moved out and he couldn't make it to mosque, so I stopped.' Jamal was very clear that religion begins at home, and was a key parental responsibility, and was critical of those parents – like Sayeed's – who had not fulfilled this duty:

> Some people, like their parents don't even teach them the right prayers … like Sayeed, they come out and say how do you do *wudu*, you know, the washing, … That's a basic thing, your parents should teach you that kind of stuff.
>
> (1996)

Religion was, then, modelled at home and first taught in the home. Shahin recalled, 'I used to see my mum pray, my dad pray and I used to get a teacher come in every Saturday and Sunday, and they used to teach us about religion and everything' (1996). Extended family was also significant. Both Shahin and Khalid spoke of the influence of an older cousin, who had become much more religious, and whom they wanted to emulate. Shahin told me,

What influenced me was my cousin – like he was fucked up, you know, and like we hadn't seen him for quite a while and I see him after about three or four years and he just changed. Like before he was getting into so much trouble and then he just changed suddenly. *And I thought, if he could do it, that means I could do it as well.*

(my emphasis)

Khalid similarly spoke of the importance of his cousin, but also how his influence on Shahin compounded Khalid's own interest in learning more about the religion: 'We just looked at him as a role model sort of … And I thought, why not? Why shouldn't I do it if my older brother's doing it as well?' (1996).

Nevertheless, these accounts also suggest if not ambivalence then at least a variable engagement with the religion – or at least its performance and practice – in the mundanities of everyday life, and the trials and pleasures of teenage years. As Shahin's comment above suggests, religious belief often carried with it a residual sense of guilt, of not doing enough, and of being insufficiently Muslim. As Mohammed noted, 'I would say, I'm a Muslim, but then you can't be a Muslim if you are not practicing the religion, so it's quite weird' (1996), while Hanif echoed, 'It doesn't mean if you're born a Muslim you are a Muslim. You should practice it' (1996). However, religion also offered the prospect of transformation at some unspecified future date. Religion represented at once a sense of past comforts, present failures and the possibility of future redemption. It did never *not* matter.

In the present of 1996, for many of the young men religion represented a spectral presence animated by a feeling of lack and guilt at their current lifestyles, linked closely to their public lives and friendships. Several spoke of being more religious when younger – for the older lot, this was around three or four years earlier (the early 1990s, when they were aged around fifteen). Shahin said,

About three years ago I was really into the religion … I was attending a lot of conferences, you know. And I've got a few cousins. They're religious as well. I used to go to their house and started reading about religion a lot, and then started praying four or five times a day. I haven't opened the Quran for four or five months now but like at that time, I was constantly going through it ... Now I try to pray about once a day.

(1996)

Zohar similarly told me, 'It's really important to me. I studied it. I was quite religious back when I was sixteen, fifteen. I used to go to Mosque and all that' (1996). Then, life just got in the way: 'I feel guilty, but I don't pray ... I just stopped cos I started hanging about more, just messing about ... It clashes with everything as well – college, doing your work and everything.' He continued, 'It's hard innit, like you've been brought up not to do them things, but then you go out and do it.' Khalid similarly confessed, 'I used to be a strong believer before – I still am really, but I'm not practising or nothing. It's like before I used to pray five times a day ... now I don't really pray at all ... I feel bad, man. I still like it and I still believe strongly, but I don't really practice it' (1996). When I asked why, he replied, 'That's the only thing I can blame, really, because of friends and that', although he later added 'it's just that I'm probably lazy'. His friend Shakiel echoed Khalid: 'It is important to me, but I ain't making enough effort today. I ain't really taking it too seriously ... I couldn't fit it in' (1996).

Their sentiments were echoed by the little ones. Hanif told me,

I used to be kind of religious before ... I used to do my five prayers a day ... [Then] I started coming out more, I started missing prayer times. Like, before, if I missed it, I made up for it at night-time, but now I've started thinking, 'So what? Forget it'. Lazy, whatever.

(1996)

Sayeed, who told me, as Jamal indicated above, he knew only 'a little bit' about Islam, stated,

I'm trying to learn it, but like every time I get a chance to learn it, yeah, there always something going wrong .... Like the teacher that's supposed to come to learn us, like, I'm never on time, something like that, cos like there's fun outside and my friends, and I keep forgetting when it is.

(1996)

However, it would be misleading to assume that religion became less important: rather, it was the gap between what they aspired to, or felt they *should* be doing, and what they actually did, that became a palpable source of tension. Sayeed told me,

> From the age of seven I should have learned everything … [but] my mum didn't get a chance to take me to the Mosque. They moved around London too much having problems and all that … I always wanted to learn my religion, culture and everything, but I never get the chance to.

He sighed: 'I'd like it if my whole family were more religious, my brothers and sister knew more about Islam, than anything else, but it ain't like that.'

While critical of Sayeed's lack of religious knowledge, Jamal told me that his own variable religious commitment caused him moments of acute anxiety: 'Sometimes I wake up, I have nightmares, I wake up in the middle of the night thinking, you know, how's my life going, when I'm dead, I'm dead, I ain't going to come back, let's change things' (1996). However, these anxieties rarely survived the light of day. Mohammed, who described himself as 'medium' in terms of his religiosity, explained, 'That's how everyone thinks out of us lot – I should try harder … It's like think and try is two different things. It's hard' (1996).

Humzah summarized, 'I'm religious. I believe in my religion a lot. The trouble is, when it comes to it I don't practice it. I don't do it, I believe it' (1996).

As Humzah suggests, religious practice in their everyday teenage lives was patchy. Several told me they prayed, or tried to, most days. Shahin told me,

> It does make you feel a lot better – you're more relaxed and everything, but I'm just not paying enough attention to it now. I still say to myself, you know, oh, I didn't pray today, and I say, 'Allah please forgive me'. But I try to get it in once.
>
> (1996)

Mohammed stated, 'I normally do two, three prayers a day. I try to, anyway' (1996), while Sayeed insisted, 'If I knew how to pray, I would pray' (1996). Most attended Friday prayers at the local Abbey Street Mosque, although Mohammed confessed that the popularity of this amongst the little ones was largely because they got a lunchpass to leave school early. For the older lot, Friday prayers were a chance to meet up with friends ahead of the weekend's socializing. As Shahin commented, 'On Friday, we meet up there, come out the Mosque and you might just grab a spliff or something.' He acknowledged, ruefully, 'There's a difference between knowing it and practicing it' (1996).

Most fasted during Ramadan, but only Zohar told me he kept all thirty fasts. The others averaged over twenty fasts, though as Khalid confessed, 'I do break some of them. I can't hack it sometimes' (1996). His younger brother Hanif commented that it was hard to maintain fasting during the school day: 'I felt bad because I started off keeping it – my intention was to keep it, and I used to break it at lunchtime, breaktime, cos everyone else used to do it' (1996). By contrast, Sayeed told me that he did try to fast 'occasionally' because of his friends: 'I don't want to be left out. I want to still be with the religion and all that' (1996). Eid celebrations were, of course, highly anticipated and enjoyed by everyone, irrespective of their religiosity – and after prayers were over were determinedly secular occasions, focused on cars and friends and food and girls (and sometimes, drugs; see Chapter 5).

While they acknowledged their present failings, all of the young men looked to a future where they would more fully embrace their religious duties. All, for example, said they wanted to do Hajj, but tied this to a time when they would, and could, fulfil its incumbent expectations. This meant a time when they could put aside what Shahin described as 'sins', or what Zohar referred to as 'those stupid things'. Shahin explained, 'I would like to go but it's like when you come back you're going to be, you know, making more sins or whatever, so I think it's not actually a good idea for me to go now' (1996). His younger brother Hanif similarly said, 'If I go back now, down there, it's like when you come back you would be a changed person. You wouldn't be doing the things you do. And I think that would be like hard to do that at the moment' (1996). When I asked, 'What things?' he said, laughing, 'Chasing girls'. Ifti, who told me that after Hajj 'I'd be a better person, I'd be good', had a longer list of 'things', 'Drugs, alcohol, lying, thieving' (1996). For most, this magical transformation was slated for around their mid-twenties (or what Zohar referred to as 'when I'm well old') – not coincidentally the age at which they expected to settle down and get married. Jamal, who thought he would go on Hajj around the age of twenty-four or twenty-five, explained,

> Cos once you go Hajj you want to change, you don't want to go there and like lie about everything, you want to go there and really make an effort and change. And around them times I reckon I will be able to change.
>
> (1996)

The previous year, 1995, Humzah had undertaken *Umrah* with his mother. On his return, head shaved, he spent several months at home, and stopped contact with most of his friends. Later, though, he drifted back into his normal patterns. When we spoke about it in 2012, he reflected,

> That was pressure. I didn't even know. They forced me. She [his mother] said 'you've become too bad' … When the day come, I wasn't ready. I was still into all the other stuff. Then suddenly, what the heck? Then I tried, alright, I'll try I'll see if I can do it. So I think that was ok for the first six months … It drew me to the right path for a little while.
>
> (2012)

While his friends were sympathetic to his struggles, they felt it was a clear example of why doing Hajj at too young an age was a mistake. Zohar commented at the time, 'He went, but he can't hold that religion' (1996), while Shahin echoed, 'I'm not sure his back's in it … When he come back he was like staying away from everything … but now he's just normal like. I don't think he really wanted to go. I don't think it was his decision' (1996).

At the same time, however, they resisted the idea that religion was important only for those of advancing years. Shahin told me,

> This is the way Bengali people see it – a lot of my mates see it this way as well – when we are old, got kids, we will go to Hajj, grow our beard,

then we 'll come home, go to the Mosque. But you might not live for
that age.

His younger brother Hanif similarly said of some older Bangladeshi
men in the community,

> They're hypocrites, cos this is how most Bengali men think – like
> they'll fuck about and that when they're like in their twenties, young
> and that, then when they're like forty, they think yeah we're going to
> die ... so they start praying; that's how most of them are.

> (1996)

As Hanif and Shahin suggest, there were some generational
differences emerging in terms of how the young men, their parents and
the broader Stoneleigh Muslim community thought about Islam. In
particular, there was an articulation of the difference between Bengali
'culture' and Islamic religious tenets and practices that was to become of
increasing significance in the following decades (see Riaz 2013, Kibria
2011, Hoque 2015). Hanif, for example, told me that 'our culture's a bit
like Indian culture; it's a bit like Hindus, quite a lot of things like mixed
in' and commented of his friend: 'Mohammed knows quite a lot, but
what he knows is what his parents teached him, and ... he still thinks
the typicalish things. It's like religion mixed in with culture, that's his
point of view' (1996). The young men were sometimes critical of the
local mosque elders who they felt privileged Bangladeshi culture and
politics over the religion, and who were resistant to outsiders, and to
change (a view that was to become more vocal in later years). Shahin
commented,

> I don't really like the imams at the Mosque, you know. You can see
> them on the street and you do salaam to them and they won't do it
> back ... They see themselves on a higher level. It's stupid really, cos
> sometimes they don't know what they're talking about as well.

> (1996)

As Shahin intimates, the reputation of the local young men as
troublemakers was widely embraced by the Mosque elders, even when
they attended for Friday or Ramadan prayers. Some admitted this

viewpoint was not unjustified: Khalid, for example, stated that 'they [the elders] think that we are just totally moving away from Islam and all this. That's what I would think if I was in their position' (1996), while Hanif temporized,

> If we go there, they think we've come there for a different purpose … They think we come there to muck around. I can't really blame them cos like during Ramadan prayers like we used to go there … but most of them fuck about … It's like, if you're doing your prayers, they'll come behind you and like push you and make you laugh, come in front of you, try and make you laugh. I think that's really bad.
>
> (1996)

Ifti agreed, 'When you're praying, they still piss around, and when you're praying, you have to concentrate on your praying. You can't have your mind on something else, or it's not worth praying' (1996). Shakiel insisted, 'We do take it seriously' but then laughed, 'It's the little ones that mess around in the back' (1996).

Some of these generational tensions within Muslim communities nationally have been traced to the increased significance of Islamist groups in the UK throughout the 1990s and that have been particularly influential on British born-and-raised Muslim young men (Husain 2015, Kibria 2011, Riaz 2013, Kundnani 2014, Hoque 2015). Groups such as the Jamaat-e-Islami, which had political roots in Bangladesh (Kibria 2011), or Tabligh Jamaat, which shaped the Young Muslim Organisation (YMO) in East London (Riaz 2013), were active in East London through this period. They even made their way onto the Stoneleigh Estate, just before the start of my first study in 1994. Indeed, the senior youth worker at the SAYO project when I began my research, Hassan, was a member of the YMO. The project then was strongly focused on religious education, and a number of the older lot had been away on weekend retreats and camps and to conferences to teach them about Islam. While some were initially positive – Shahin, for example, told me, 'I used to respect him at that time because I thought he was alright. He's got a lot of knowledge about the religion, knows what he is talking about' (1996) – the glamour soon wore thin. Shakiel mused,

They were alright when we first met them. They come to the Mosque and that and they talked quite good ... Then after like Hassan and that come, *they used to like think they know too much, bit more than like your mum*, and they used to come out quite rude. And you think, no.

(1996, my emphasis)

Shakiel's statement captures the layering of community and parental loyalties, seasoned with a healthy suspicion of 'outsiders' and what I think of as sheer Stoneleigh cussedness, that saw the YMO disappear from the Estate in short order. In their interviews a couple of years later, this scepticism was very apparent: Zohar referred to YMO as 'just troublemakers', while Humzah dismissed them as 'all crap ... they're just doing it for the name'. His brother Ifti scowled: 'We hate them ... they were bringing out new stuff.' Shahin, who was more positive than most, agreed that Hassan had been inappropriate in bringing his religious agenda into the youth club: 'I think that wasn't a good thing, he tried to force people, force his religion' (1996). Jamal concurred, 'I think everyone should find their religion within their own time, you shouldn't force them' (1996). Hassan himself was ejected from the project, and the Estate, after a violent encounter with Mustafa, shortly after my arrival (see Alexander 2000, Chapter 3). Ifti reflected, with some satisfaction: 'We was giving the respect we can, but he wanted more and more ... He went over the top, and he asked for it, and he got it' (1996).

Nevertheless, it would be misleading to see this conflict as an absolute rejection of change. Rather, it suggests that religious identity was in a state of flux, discussion and negotiation (Riaz 2013). Shahin commented that 'a lot of the young boys, even the ones that aren't religious, they still respect the ones that are religious' (1996). In a telling, and amusing, encounter, Khalid told me that the day before our interview he had been approached on the Stoneleigh Estate by some YMO members from East London,

We got stopped yesterday by some people come from other areas to preach, and they just go out to bring all the youngsters to the Mosque ... They stopped me, and I was on my own and I didn't really feel like going to the Mosque that day. And they was just talking about religion ... and after they go, 'Come with us, we're going to the Mosque after, let's just try knock on some doors, bring us some other people'. And I goes, 'I have to go somewhere.' They go, 'You can go there after.' And then after I see Ashraf, and I goes, 'Yeah, this boy knows everything.' And then they caught Ashraf, and I see Ashraf's face like 'you bastard'.

(1996)

When I asked Khalid why he had not just told them 'no', he replied, 'I wouldn't say that, probably out of respect'.

These generational shifts and uncertainties do suggest a changing climate for young Muslims through the 1990s, which was to become hugely significant in the first decades of the new millennium. When I interviewed them the first time around, most spoke of their awareness of the increasing resentment towards Muslims, especially in the media. Humzah noted, they think Islam is hate ... Muslims are just known as terrorists' (1996), while Hanif stated, 'The media and that try and put Islam down a lot' (1996). Zohar insisted that, in the face of growing media hostility,

I would stick to my religion. I wouldn't diss my religion no way ... but I wouldn't diss no one else's religion. I would respect it cos that's your religion and you follow it, and I respect you following your religion.

(1996)

However, for most, this remained peripheral to their everyday lives. When I teased Sayeed, 'So you can't imagine getting really militant and growing your beard and donning your outfit?' he replied, earnestly, 'No, not in this age anyway' (1996).

Making Muslims: Institutional Continuity and Community Change in the New millennium

When I saw Sayeed fifteen years later at Shahin's wedding, he was sporting a dark suit, shades and an impressively bushy beard. I asked him where his wife was – she had been similarly absent from Hanif's wedding the previous year because of childcare issues. He told me she was unable to come because she was pregnant with their third child. When I commented that it was a shame because I had never met her, he shook his head in mock regret, and pronounced solemnly, 'Yes, I think I will have to get a second wife so I have one to bring to weddings'.

Sayeed's transformation reflects the increased – or increasingly explicit – role of religion and faith in the lives of my participants in the years between the first study and my interviews in 2012. This, in turn, reflects the growing significance of religion in political, policy and public discourse in the UK, entrenching and broadening the nascent Islamophobia of the 1980s and 1990s, and cementing anti-Muslim racism as an inescapable, 'normalised' feature in the everyday lives of British Muslims (Meer 2015, Cohen & Tufail 2017). As discussed in Chapter 1, the growing public and political hostility across the first decade of the millennium has seen unprecedented state-sponsored targeting of Muslim communities through this period (Kundnani 2014, Meer 2015, O'Toole et al 2016, Cohen & Tufail 2017, Miah 2017). This has been met in turn by the growth of a visible and vocal counter-narrative from an increasingly confident and well-educated British Muslim civic society and an emergent British Islamic identity (Hoque 2015, Meer 2015, Rashid 2016, Allen 2017). The Muslim population also grew across this period, from just under 3 per cent of the population of England and Wales in the 2001 Census to nearly 5 per cent in 2011 (Muslim Council of Britain 2015).

This national picture was writ small on the Stoneleigh Estate. The number of Muslims in the Borough rose from 6.85 per cent in the 2001 Census to 8.5 per cent in 2011 – broadly in line with the city's average. The increased influence, and increased diversity, of the Muslim community locally was reflected in the proliferation of mosques across the Borough, with an estimated eight to ten mosques in 2010, catering to an estimated 20,000 Muslims from over twenty different ethnic and national groups.[5] The dramatic expansion of the Abbey Street Mosque in those years is an indication of the institutional presence and influence of the Stoneleigh Bangladeshi Muslims during this period.

The first mosque in the area, founded in the 1980s when many of the Bangladeshi families moved to the Estate, was located in the basement of a local grocers – what Humzah referred to in a recent 2022 phone conversation as 'the Red Shop'. By the 1990s, when I did my first research, there was a temporary purpose building on a small square off Abbey Street, opposite the Stoneleigh Estate Play Association, which catered to 400 local, almost exclusively Bangladeshi, men. The Mosque expanded from 2006 and by 2014 occupied the whole of the Square, with a capacity of over 2500 people, with facilities for both men and women.

The significance of this public sphere, and the historical and political events that shaped it, should not be underestimated in understanding the emergence of British Muslim identities at this time. Most research has focused on these external factors as shaping a British-Islamic identity forged through political resistance to the global and national context – notably the wars in Iraq and Afghanistan and the intractable issue of Palestine abroad, and anger at ongoing racism and marginalization at home (Riaz 2013, Hoque 2015, Meer 2015). Indeed, my participants reflected on this context in terms of shaping their individual sense of what it means to 'be Muslim' in the twenty-first century. Speaking of the attacks of 11 September 2001, Shahin, for example, told me:

> I think it's encouraged people to become more religious. Even those Muslims that were not practicing have said, 'Oh, let's read about it. Let's learn about the religion so if we're speaking to our non-Muslim friends we can actually explain and tell them Islam is not all about war and this sort of killing innocent people, and it's the complete opposite'. I think 9/11 has pushed people more to the religion, those that may not have thought about religion in the past.

> (2012)

Jamal similarly commented that after 9/11, 'A lot of people that wasn't practising, they found an attachment to Islam, especially with the negativity that was being thrown at it' (2012). Always religiously inclined, Hanif became more interested in Islam in his first year at university, which coincided with the events of 2001, and he and his friends went to a number of rallies and talks in Hyde Park. Of 9/11, he recalled,

> Even on the day, I still remember it, I was doing playwork … and Shafik called me … I went into work and one of the more elderly members of the staff team, she was saying, 'Oh it's those Muslims' and I can remember I was really, really angry. And I said to her, 'How can you know it's Muslims?' At the time they hadn't known.

Shakiel, who was minicabbing at that time, and was at the sharp end of the Islamophobic backlash, said the hostility he received led him to learn more about his religion: 'It put you on the defensive because after that happened, I was still cabbing and obviously … you know, you had to be ready for it' (2012). Mohammed similarly told me that the events, and the backlash, led to a stronger political engagement amongst his friends:

> I mean, racism always existed, you know, whether passive or active. It was always there but I think you saw it a lot more. Like I felt it a lot more, probably after that, and you slowly started to realize the differences … The obvious thing was the colour of our skin but I think that our social values came to light as well … We went through a phase when we were going to a lot of talks … We went to a shitload of marches and Palestine marches … political is probably more upfront.
>
> (2012)

He noted that this increased religiosity amongst the group:

> So I think that's probably when a lot of things started to change, and you kind of started to think of what your true values are … The stance was we're not going to give up what we've always believed in, we might not have practised it as much but we certainly won't give it up.

It is significant that much of this debate and engagement took place outside of the formal institutional spaces of the Mosque. Ajmal Hussain has written recently about the ways in which young Muslims in Birmingham have engaged with civic and informal spaces – arts centres, radio stations and social media (2014, 2016) – to shape contemporary discourses around Islam and challenge institutional religious authority.

He has also examined the growth of 'street salafism' in which religious debate takes place on 'the street', and in everyday spaces, such as restaurants and shisha bars, importantly as a way to 'evade easy capture of authorial gazes', both external and internal to the Muslim community (Hussain 2022). While this form of street preaching did not seem to have influenced the Stoneleigh young men – perhaps because of the history discussed above – it is certainly true that they shared some criticisms of the local religious institutions. While Big Hanif noted the continuing role of the Mosque for the local Bangladeshi community – 'everyone comes to local Mosque, so you get to see them on that day. Yes, so I will go to, outside, just hang around outside the Mosque and get to meet pretty much everybody' (2012) – others commented that the expanded Abbey Street Mosque had done little to reflect the changing context of the Estate or the Borough, and offered little for younger British-born Muslims. One of the most trenchant critics, Silver, told me,

> My feeling is things haven't changed too much around that Mosque. It's just now looking like a Mosque rather than a shack. I think the people that run those mosques, and that Mosque particularly ... they're just not embracing change.

Speaking in 2012, he was critical about the lack of facilities for women (which has since changed), but more so about the closed ethno-cultural mindset of the predominantly Bangladeshi Mosque elders, who did not reflect the changing demographics of the Muslims who used it (now, according to Silver, 40 per cent Somali). He explained,

> Nothing changes in that Mosque for me from when it was a bit of grassland ... Because I think the building's there, the religion's there, it's God's house, but I think the mindset of how we must educate and how we must embrace multicultural London in 2012 hasn't changed ... The power base in the Mosque is still Bengali ... Islam isn't based on race.

Hanif, who rarely attended the Abbey Street Mosque but was actively involved in a more inclusive, multicultural Mosque in a neighbouring borough, dismissed the development:

We've got a fantastic new building, massive structure, but it's soulless, there's no soul within the Mosque. You know, there's no activities, nothing goes on. They just lock the doors as if this is *our* Mosque.

(2012)

At the same time, the young men were strongly critical of what they saw as more informal, 'extremist' elements in the wider Muslim community, especially those who espoused separationist ideologies. They particularly resisted those who sought to circumscribe what a 'Muslim' was, or should be. Zohar told me, 'I've always prayed, went to Friday prayers and religion was a big part of me, but I've never exposed it to anyone that it's got to be like this or like that, or this is wrong or this is right' (2012). Shakiel commented,

As a Muslim, I think, it is your duty to perform all your religious activities, and you do have an obligation to invite others to your religion, but you don't invite someone to the religion by grabbing them by the throat and marching them in through the door.

(2012)

Shakiel, who had always struck me as a phlegmatic and laconic person, was unusually strident on this topic. He insisted,

Religion is important to me. I mean, I know I could be a better Muslim in practising it, but I'm not and that's something I need to work on. But I know what I have become better at is identifying good and bad Muslims … And I don't think all Muslims are good and I think the good Muslims are too quiet.

When I asked what he meant by a 'good Muslim' (aware of all of the pitfalls of such Manichean dichotomies; Mamdani 2004), he clarified, 'Like, moderates. People who are quite happy to perform their religious activities and live by the rules and just get on with life'.

While Shakiel was surprisingly vocal on this matter, his views were echoed by many of the others, including the more actively religious men. Shahin commented, 'So you've got the aggressive side which is no different from the English Defence League, for example. It is an extreme and they're actually bad for Islam' (2012). Zohar similarly felt that this promoted division within the Muslim community: 'It brings out debates that are unnecessary. We don't need them debates, you know what I'm saying? … It's all one, isn't it? Religion, Islam, same, different sects' (2012). He continued,

> I say to them, you do not have to be here. If you feel this is not the way Islamic life is, you are allowed to go to Saudi Arabia. You are allowed to go to Egypt, to get a visa. You are allowed to go to Yemen, go there. But don't do it here. You're making it hard for everybody else that's just trying to live a peaceful life.

He insisted, 'You are part of the problem, so you're not part of resolving it. The way you can be is obvious, being a good person.' Even Mustafa, who was widely recognized as the most religious of the older lot, opined, 'I think they're saying the wrong things, they don't have any right to say that living in the UK' (2012).

From my interviews and discussions across the years with several of the participants, it seems that there was little, if any, influence of more hard-line Islamist ideologies amongst the group. While there were rumours that S Ahmed had been approached to be an informant for the security services, and on one occasion Jadil's pub was raided in the wake of a nearby terrorist incident, any encounters with extremism seemed to be mainly at one or two removes, or had the status of hearsay. The closest to home these issues came was through Liaquot, who upon leaving prison had adopted a strong religious identity influenced, according to Shahin, by Salafist teaching he had picked up from a friend of Humaira. His friends were largely critical of his stance: Zohar, for example, described Liaquot's beliefs as 'not collective opinion, it's what he believes, it's a biased, kind of, one person. "I said this, and I believe this, and I interpret this"' (2012). Shahin commented,

> I remember having a discussion with him and some of it was just, 'You can't wear a suit and tie'. But why can't you wear a suit and tie and be religious? … So he's obviously not read into the religion properly, and just, you know, going to a few talks.
>
> (2012)

Amongst his peers, this was largely a matter for collective teasing rather than concern, and several members of the older lot laughed that they had nicknamed him 'Mullah Omar' because of his radical beliefs. Shahin recalled,

> Even at Zohar's wedding, do you remember you came to my flat and Mustafa was there and Liaquot was there as well and Liaquot wasn't taking pictures and we were joking saying, 'Oh, he's Mullah Omar; he's worried about the FBI, you know, like he's wanted … '. He's not saying no to the pictures because it's unIslamic.

For Shahin this was a matter not of too much religious belief, but of the need to learn more: 'I've always said to him, "Oh just, you know, read yourself, so you understand"', while Mustafa mused, 'He's going to burn himself out because he's taking things in and he doesn't know that – he should be more calm. He gets too excited. He sometimes says things that he shouldn't say' (2012).

At the same time, however, all agreed that Liaquot's increased religiosity was a positive thing, especially in the light of his chequered past. Shakiel commented,

> I don't think it could ever be a bad thing … He's still working … he's still providing for his family … he seems a lot more pleasant now and he talks to me, you know, he's very polite.
>
> (2012)

Hanif similarly noted, 'It's made him better for it, because at least he's not doing the things he was doing' (2012), and Sayeed and Jamal agreed, 'Islam can only benefit you' (2012). Sayeed continued, 'He's doing his own thing now, and just working, he's in the masjid, he's with his family … from what he used to do before it's like a whole turnaround.' However, Shakiel temporized, 'It is a bit odd'.

Becoming Muslim: The Routes of Religion

While it is clear that the global and national events of the new millennium indelibly marked the religious consciousness of my participants, it would be misleading to reduce this transformation solely to the political and social context of the period. Certainly, external events foregrounded elements that had, perhaps, been taken for granted previously but, as the discussion above suggests, this was also very much an individual journey, linked to personality and personal biography. While religion became a more overt and significant part of their lives, the men found their own ways through this hotly contested terrain. For some, this was seen as an inevitable part of their growing up, and a deepening of their family background. Zohar told me, 'This has always been part of everyone's growing up. It's been part of it and as you get older, you start discovering religion a lot more yourself' (2012). Silver reflected,

> Even if you drank and you smoked weed, and you had sex outside of marriage – which most of them did – they would still go on Friday and pray, and they would be fasting where they could, and they would still do their Islamic duties.
>
> (2012)

As he grew older, he was able to recognize the influence of his faith across all aspects of his life:

> I think it was always there. I probably wasn't able to articulate where my value base comes from but as an older man I probably recognize now more: how did I come to think and buy into the things I think and buy into?

Big Hanif attributed his deepening religiosity to his age, rather than any external cause:

> I do pray, I would, if I have days off on Friday, I would go and pray. I study, I read a lot of religious books. I wouldn't say I'm a Fundamentalist, but … I used to drink, drink, drink before but I stopped doing that … if I buy meat now, or eat somewhere, I will make sure it's halal. I don't know, is it because of my age?
>
> (2012)

Having undertaken Hajj in his early thirties, Big Hanif married and settled down and his increased religiosity was part of this shift. He told me, 'I came back and afterwards I gave up drinking, smoking cigarettes and everything. Kind of cut down … on going out clubbing and all that.' He noted that these changes were part of a general shift amongst his peers: 'I guess as we got older, people wanted to make money and get settled, I guess. Everyone wanted to move on, make something of themselves, that's what it was.'

Shahin commented of his friends: 'Look at them when they were sixteen. They probably weren't going to the Mosque. But they're going now' (2012).

For others, there were more personal triggers. Sayeed and Hanif, for example, spoke of how the deaths of their fathers had been central to their search for faith. Hanif, whose father died when he was only nine, told me that this loss had been fundamental in shaping his religious belief from a young age:

> Quite early on in secondary school where I was sort of praying five times a day and I can remember on the weekends I'd go out and wear my *topi* and wear the *kameez* ... I think it was more sort of – my dad passed away and yes it was more after that, and then we started doing the Koran classes at home and stuff.
>
> (2012)

Although as he grew older, Hanif became well versed in Islamic politics, culture and history, undertaking Hajj and visiting Palestine as part of a charity relief programme, it was this more personal biography that animated his faith. He told me, 'It was more a case of having lost our dad. I don't know. You felt the only way to help him was to do good things ... From an early age I can remember, that was drilled into me.'

For Sayeed too, his father's death led to a long-desired, but often postponed, exploration of his religion. Along with Mustafa, discussed below, Sayeed's was perhaps one of the more dramatic religious reversions, marked most visually by his impressive – 'huge' to quote Shahin – beard. When his father died in 2003, Sayeed told me,

> I wasn't really interested in religion at that time ... and after my dad passed away, it wasn't a sort of overnight thing. Well, I switched basically. It took the time, it took about another three or four years for me to grow a beard and, you know, get serious in my religion.
>
> (2012)

He continued, 'I think the turning point was my dad. It changed my whole mentality of thinking, of, you know, you're wasting time, do something.' 'Doing something' meant settling down in work, getting married and learning more about Islam:

> I started learning more about my prayers, started learning about the Quran, the hadiths, the stories of the prophets. What as a Muslim you have to do … I still don't know much of it. I'm still like willing to learn, really learn.

He told me that for him, faith was a personal, not a political, exploration: 'What is your purpose? You've got to find out for yourself, that's the thing … it's a personal journey', and one that was ongoing: 'As a Muslim you have to search, you have to search. If you don't search, you ain't going to find the truth, simple as that.'

For others, the disruption of prison life served as a catalyst and a chance for reflection – if, in some cases, only temporary. Ifti told me that during his short spells in prison, he practised his faith more;

> I believe in God and you know I believe in my religion, but I know I don't practise it. But when I was inside, I was doing it. Everyday I was doing it, because that's what I like to do, that time will go. And you come out of your cell more, and it wasn't even that. It was I was repenting, I guess, inside … it made me feel good.
>
> (2012)

As was typical with Ifti, his faith was a combination of a sincere wish to be and do better, combined with a more pragmatic agenda – a way of getting out of his cell more often, and of finding support from fellow Muslims to negotiate life inside. As Shahin commented, peer group influence was particularly important to Muslims in prison, and the relatively large numbers of Muslim prisoners could be a powerful protective force.[6]

> I think they need a Muslim community in prison. It's quite powerful as a group identity and they like that to feel – because when they're on the street, they're always with friends, and when you're in prison nobody knows anyone. But then you've got the religion that sort of brings everybody together.
>
> (2012)

M, too, who was just embarking on a long term sentence in a high security prison, told me that he was trying to learn more about Islam: 'I'm learning it again now, mashallah ... but I always knew I had to pray.' He insisted, 'I've always had a good intention in that department, you get me?' (2012). He was attending Arabic classes (as well as the gym) and told me he hoped that this new-found faith would continue when he was finally released: 'I want to start meeting people that are on like Islamic terms where they pray five times a day, so when I come out, that's good. They're the kind of people I want to hang about with.' More than this, and with M's characteristic mix of bravado and enthusiasm, he assured me, 'When I come out I don't want to stay in this country Claire, no more. I want to move to a Muslim country'. To date, this has remained a pipedream. For Ifti too, unfortunately, the effects dissipated on his release: 'When I came out, for some reason I just got busy with life again' (2012).

For others, the impact was life-changing. Liaquot, as noted above, became more religious when in prison and built on this after his release. The most dramatic impact, however, was undoubtedly on Mustafa. In prison for three years of his six-year sentence (see Chapter 5), Mustafa determined to use his time to effect a profound transformation. He told me,

> I immediately said to myself, three years. What am I going to do with that three years? I made up my mind at that time ... I wanted to change and I did want to make my way, away from all this scene and evil and neglecting my family. I wanted to head straight towards, and I want to practise Islam and learn about Islam. So I started praying five times a day ... I got a copy of the Quran, loads of Islamic literature, read the translation of the Quran. I was loving every single bit of that ... then I'd read it about eight times over, different scholars' opinions, translations ... All I was doing for three years was just reading the Quran, reading Islamic texts as much as I could.
>
> (2012)

He continued, 'All three years. ... I learned a lot. It was a blessing. And I don't regret it. To tell you the truth, on my heart, sincerely, I don't regret one single second of prison.' His friends were uniformly positive about the changes. Humzah commented, 'When he became religious, I was happy for him', while Shahin told me,

> Mustafa changed ... found Islam when he was in prison and I think it's helped him, actually ... he's a different person. So when you speak to him, he's calm, not as worried as what he used to be ... So Islam is part of his life, so it's probably a way of life for him.

> (2012)

Of all of my participants, Mustafa led his life according to his interpretation of Islamic principles. He told me, simply,

> It's the most important aspect of my life, period. There is nothing else more important than that ... You fall under that and everything else falls into line, and you don't need to worry about nothing, nothing whatsoever ... Because Islam is a very practical religion. Do's and don'ts are quite clear. The principles are clear and easy to follow. And, basically, that's how I live now.

> (2012)

Of course, not all of my participants gravitated towards religion. Humzah, for example, confessed that he had become less religious as he got older: 'We've always had religion in the family. I was more religious before. I've become less religious for some reason, I don't know why. I am trying' (2012). Although his religious practice had been patchy in the years I knew him, he traced a steeper decline to the period after he got married and he and his wife moved out of the family home. 'I've not been able to pray and all that, all the stuff. Not having time. But I still have the belief and I'm still trying my best to do better', he told me. Jadil similarly noted, 'I do describe myself as a Muslim and I believe in Islam, but I don't practice ... I used to, but now I don't do anything' (2011), and traced this to his work. Sher Khan too was clear: 'I've never been religious ... I don't know why, it's just me. I give back, and I still go to the mosque when I can, or when I feel like, Eid and things like that, but I'm not very religious and I think everyone knows that' (2012). Nevertheless, he told me he gave money to his local mosque and was insistent that his children should know about their religion:

If I give them the basics, my kids, and then if they want to pursue that, all good and if they don't at least they can turn round to me and say, 'Look, dad, at least you taught us the basics'. At the end of the day the worst thing is for my kids to turn around and say, 'Look dad, you didn't even teach us anything about religion'.

As is discussed further below, even in its absence, religion and faith shaped the men's everyday lives, and were seen as positive influence. Zohar summarized,

Some came back, some went to it ... and then some went into it in more depth than others. Some have it as a part of a sanctuary for them, to feel more happier, which I think is the best way because it does work.

(2012)

A Note on Beards

Of course, the boundaries between religion as an institutionally framed, external facing/ascribed identity and faith as a more personal spiritual state of being are porous and uncertain. While many of my 'Asian gang' participants had been led to re-examine their personal faith through the clamorous political context of the 2000s, this faith was shaped too by family and community relationships. As is explored below, faith in turn reshaped the mundane interactions of everyday life – work, family, friendship. Moreover, the profession of faith, especially through the external markers of religion – beard, *topis*, dress, were recognized as often inadequate guides to belief or behaviour. Hanif noted,

You've got people wearing, outwardly looking very Islamic. They wear the long, you know, the *salwars* ... They've got a really big beard, they've got, you know, a hat, and the minute they open their mouth it's completely against the teachings of Islam.

(2012)

The wearing, or not, of beards was a telling lens into the religion/ faith dynamic, and a topic for discussion amongst my participants. Many of the men had grown beards in the period between the two sets of interviews, with greater or lesser success. Hanif often commented to me – only half-jokingly – that his own attempts had been less successful than he wished, particularly in comparison to his friend Sayeed's marvellously bushy whiskers. Mustafa and Liaquot had both grown impressive beards. Others, like Zohar, Mohammed, Silver, Khalid or Shakiel wore carefully trimmed goatees, which constituted a nod towards their faith (or, indeed, a keen sense of urban hirsute fashion, or both), but expressed a degree of caution around how this might be read. This caution indicates the racialization of beards (akin to the racialization of the hijab for Muslim women) (Tarlo 2009, Rashid 2016) as a sign of religious extremism, which sits in telling contrast to the parallel fashion for hipster beards amongst white middle-class men through the same period. Mohammed, for example, felt that having a full beard like Sayeed's would be impossible for him because of where he worked in the City: 'Like if I did have a big beard like him, I'd find it quite hard to work where I'm working with the stuff that I'm doing … why should I burden myself with something?' (2012). The idea of a beard as a 'burden' suggests the highly freighted meaning that facial hair carries for particularly brown/South Asian Muslim men in the context of the War on Terror.

At the same time, beards were widely recognized as a sign of religious adherence: Shahin, for example, described Liaquot, 'He's like really religious now and is growing a beard' (2012), while Sher Khan captioned the growth of religion as marked by 'the beards and all that and the little hat' (2012). However, and as Hanif commented above, a 'good beard' was not always an indicator of good practice.[7] Shahin noted, 'You know, just growing a big beard doesn't necessarily equate with having a lot of religious knowledge' (2012), while Zohar insisted lack of a beard was not a sign of lack of religious commitment:

> People have said, 'You don't look Muslim'. I said, 'Why does it actually matter? How do you know that … because I haven't got a beard, I don't pray whenever I can, so I'm not Muslim?' … There's no one but God can say that to me, if I'm a Muslim.
>
> (2012)

Mohammed was similarly critical of his friend Sayeed's beard:

> Different people approach religion in different ways ... There's nothing wrong with having a beard but he [Sayeed] feels, for example, to me it's like a way of expressing the way he is, but I could do equally the same thing without having a beard.

However, in a long discussion about his beard, Sayeed and Jamal explained the importance of beards as less an external symbol than a personal reminder:

> Jamal: It's to constantly remind you that you are a Muslim man and you should behave as a Muslim man.
> Sayeed: It's to help you become stronger in your faith and to avoid doing bad things ... You're giving a bad name to Islam. So you shouldn't take it light heartedly growing a beard. It's not easy.
>
> (2012)

Jamal, like Zohar, denied that having a beard reflected his faith:

> I don't think physically I need to have one for people to say to me, oh you're a practising person ... For me it's all about personality of how you are as a person ... Someone who's nice without a beard is more of a brother to me than someone with a beard but has an aggressive attitude.

Nevertheless, he also took the symbolism of the beard seriously enough to feel he could not commit to what it represented:

> I don't think I'm an ideal person; I have my faults, you know; I swear a lot. So for me to keep a beard and then be out there swearing, for example, I'm actually doing more negative to the religion than positive.

Where for Jamal a beard was a sign of an end-state – something to be lived up to, or failed – for Sayeed, in contrast, his beard was a living reminder of his ongoing struggle. He followed Jamal's statement:

> The way Jamal thinks about religion is quite different than me because he thinks, like, you know, if I do this am I going to live up to this person? But I think I have to do it, if I don't I'm not going to change.

For Sayeed, who in 2012 had worn a beard for six years, it was a guide to action. He told me,

> You know when I first kept it, I found that a lot of things that was appealing to me when I didn't have it – like falling in love with girls [stopped] … When they look at me, they would know I'm a Muslim and they would look away. So it would sort of help me in a way from doing bad things. And I quite liked that.

It is worth reiterating, however, that these differences were rarely a source of conflict amongst the men. Indeed in most cases, even for those who were not particularly religious, the matter was one at once of personal choice, and of collective endeavour – all felt that religion was a good thing and the pursuit of faith something to be supported, no matter how convoluted, or occasionally misguided, its path. Sher Khan, who as noted above described himself as 'not very religious', captured this position well. Having long sported a straggling goatee that made him look like a particularly mischievous djinn from the Arabian Nights, he told me, 'It's second nature, it's not religious in any aspect at all … it's basically a trademark now. If you don't know me, you know my beard!' (2012). Nevertheless, when I asked him about the increased religiosity within the Muslim community – 'the beards and all that' – he shrugged, 'I don't know what's behind it. Again, it's good, if that's for them and they want to be religious, then so be it. I'm not going to judge anyone … good luck to them.'

The Sacred and the Profane

While the symbols and practice of religious belief became more explicit as my participants grew older, it is also true that religion and faith shaped their everyday lives in less overt ways – in ways of thinking, acting and interacting with others, in the public places of work and in the intimate spaces of friendship, love, marriage and family. While these were rarely discussed, or experienced, as constraint, it is clear that religion shaped these choices in indelible ways. These were often linked to upbringing or family and community expectations, but also to the changing political and social context, in which being Muslim came to matter, blurring the boundaries between the personal and the social, the mundane and the political, the sacred and the profane.

These constraints are perhaps most obvious in the arena of work, where the encounter between the individual and the world beyond the Stoneleigh was thrown most sharply into relief. Negotiating external perceptions of what it means to 'be Muslim' in British society was a ubiquitous, implicit and often unremarked part of work (see Chapter 4). It is there in Mohammed's decision to avoid the 'burden' of a full beard, or to not go for drinks after work, or Shahin's decision to incorporate his wife's English surname into the name of his new law firm. It is there more explicitly in Shakiel's preparation for expected violence when mini-cabbing, or the routinized racism facing Mustafa or Big Hanif or Sayeed when they drove London's buses. It is there too, more positively, in Silver and Zohar's choices around careers dedicated to helping others, or to Jadil's donations from his restaurant and pub business to the Shapla Foundation, founded by Silver and his friends. And it was there, as a spectre, in the background of the men who, like M and Ifti, who chose a more illicit path. M told me, 'I felt like the devil was on me … I asked Allah, make me a good person, I don't want to sell drugs' (2012).

While most of this was an unspoken, perhaps taken for granted, part of being Muslim in Britain, at points this was more consciously articulated. Sayeed, for example, told me that he left one of his early jobs working for a catering firm because, 'I told the manager, "Look, I can't deliver alcohol. First of all, it's against my religion, second of all, I just hate the smell of it" … I just walked away' (2012). Mustafa similarly refused to work in the family restaurant because it sold alcohol, and admitted that this had caused problems with his parents and brother: 'As usual, people, if you say something to them that affects their income … hostility is always a factor' (2012). Jadil claimed that his business had impacted his religious practice:

I think it's this pub. This pub changed me a little bit … Just with the late nights and everything, it's hard to catch prayers and everything … I suppose if I had more time, I'd go back to religion and try and practice a little bit. But when I'm busy with this pub and everything, I haven't practiced for the last eight, nine years.

(2011)

Although I suspect Jadil was not particularly religious to begin with, his work had brought conflict with other Muslims – the members of the Mosque who objected to him selling alcohol in his restaurants or off-licence or owning a pub – and, as discussed below, with some of his friends. When I asked Sayeed if it were true that he had stopped his brother Salman from opening a pub like his friend, Sayeed insisted,

I told him it was haram at the end of the day, what Jadil was doing. You may be making millions, but you're sinning millions, you know, it's not worth it at the end of the day. And he [Jadil] knows it as well as everyone. Every Muslim knows it, but yes, they do it for the money.

(2012)

His best friend Jamal too had struggled with working for a bookmaker (see Chapter 4) and had eventually given up this work to enable him to make a good marriage. Even his current work, at a bank, caused some problems. In an exchange with Sayeed, he explained,

Jamal: I try my best not to do much loans, but I do what I need not to raise eyebrows … I don't really like selling interest to anybody.
Sayeed: Obviously, Islamically, if we're going by Islam basis, we should avoid it …
Jamal: But I think the whole world's eaten up by the whole interest system, you know it's a capitalist ideology … Even Islamic banks … I don't believe in my heart that there is an Islamic mortgage, because there isn't.
Sayeed: not unless you pay for the mortgage what the actual price of the house is without interest – until that's done, it's not halal.

Sayeed continued, 'I mean, I'm uneasy, but I know he's trying to do his best and I can't give an opinion on him ….I think it's better than what he used to be doing, definitely …. Even working in that environment was bad.'

As the above discussion suggests, religion was a factor to be negotiated between friends and impacted on these long-standing relationships in a variety of ways. While all of my participants recognized the importance of religion and were supportive of their friends' struggles with their faith, there were points of tension. Jadil reported that since his reversion, Liaquot would not come into his pub – something that must have stung particularly, I suspect, since Liaquot and S Ahmed had once used the pub as a base for his drug dealing activities. He told me, 'Oh my God, he won't even come into my pub or anything … he's gone like really religious.' When I asked 'has that caused problems in your friendship?' he replied, 'I think it has a little bit, yes. Where I would have called him before, now I wouldn't' (2011). He was critical of what he perceived as his friend's judgemental stance,

> My opinion is you can become a Muslim, a good Muslim. You don't have to preach and all the other things. You don't have to start lecturing people … Like if I became a Muslim myself again, I would just do my prayers and I wouldn't advertise it. I'd just keep it to myself and just go about life the same way. I wouldn't want to make an image of myself.

He noted that his feelings were common amongst the friendship group who, as discussed above, did not necessarily share Liaquot's particular version of Islam:

> You can just be a Muslim and pray and do things, but sometimes when you go into religion too much, they say you are following Mullah Omar and he is following Bin Laden … and then, you know, they just clash.

Revealingly, though, Jadil was more generous towards Mustafa, suggesting his irritation came from issues with Liaquot personally. He told me, 'Mustafa has calmed down a lot from what he was before. He is a very calm person. Liaquot is like still hotheaded, he's ready to go to war.' Indeed, several of the older lot told me that Liaquot and Mustafa had nearly come to blows over a theological dispute in the car on the way back from Shahin's wedding.

Big Hanif similarly noted that there were points of disagreement with his friends on religious issues. While not identifying particular individuals, he commented,

> A few of them lives round here, and I do talk to them and we do disagree on a lot of things. Even though they have become religious, they still have that narrow view. Firstly they look from that narrow view of the street, now they look at narrow view from religious, and I always find that hard for some reason.

> (2012)

Later he was more specific: 'I will be honest with you, I don't really go into conversation with Liaquot on a religious view because we disagree on a lot of things.' However, the bonds of friendship were still significant in mediating these tensions: 'I don't really want to upset him … he's my friend, after all these years … I just try not to go there because we know we're not going to agree.' He continued, laughing, 'We know that even when we were young, we didn't agree with Liaquot.'

Like Jadil, Big Hanif suggests some of these theological disputes and stances actually reflect longer disagreements based on personality and personal history. Nevertheless, he also highlights the balancing of these longstanding ties (and animosities) with the choices of the present moment. As discussed in Chapter 5, this balance was achieved through a mixture of strategic silence and avoidance – not-speaking, not-seeing and not-knowing – but also with an acceptance of their friends as they were, with all their faults and failings. This was particularly clear in my discussions with Mustafa. He told me that one of the key elements in his religious reversion was 'for me to come out of the cycle of friends, gangs and that sort of social negative' (2012). He maintained these boundaries in part by moving away from the Stoneleigh, which gave him more choice about when, where and with whom to engage. He rarely went to his friends' houses (with some notable exceptions, such as Big Hanif, Zohar and Shahin), and never socialized outside, unless it was family occasions such as weddings, funerals or birth of a child. He insisted,

> I would never go where they would be smoking, I would never go where they were just talking about, you know, vain talk … I wouldn't participate. I would go to their weddings. If he's got children now, obviously I hope to see the child, inshallah … I'll go in that situation. But other than that, no, not to talk rubbish. Not just to hang about.

In their turn, his friends would not invite him to occasions where he might feel compromised and kept some of their more dubious activities (such as girlfriends or drugs) out of his sight. Mustafa recognized this clearly, acknowledging, 'They hide it from me; they don't reveal to me their habits … And if it did ever come to that, I would have to depart from them'. When I asked him about his friends' former drug dealing, he told me, resignedly,

> Somewhere I knew but nothing, you know, blatantly. And then I can't really do nothing … I can only admonish them, and then you do get tired. It's falling on deaf ears.

He continued, 'And they did realize after the mistakes that they'd done. They all ended up in prison.'

The little ones were more open, and perhaps more forgiving, around their discussions – perhaps reflecting the reconstitution of the smaller, tighter peer group in the years following school and college. Mohammed told me:

> I think we still had some core values and … most of us understood religion. It was always in our minds, whether it be in the back of the mind or the front of the mind, it was something we took values from, and I apply those values in everyday [life].

(2012)

As discussed above and in Chapter 5, religion had increasingly shaped the group's social interactions and activities. This was not to suggest that there were not debates and disagreements amongst the group and very different levels of religiosity. Mohammed continued,

Like even with religion, for example, there are some things that I significantly disagree with other people and vice versa, but it doesn't necessarily mean that we still can't eat from the same plate.

According to Mohammed, the friendship papered over the cracks caused by disagreements but also prevented any explicit exploration of these differences, and any clear resolution. He explained,

We can probably see that there is a grey area … I think we've just learned to get on with it. We've had some fierce debates … but I think no one wants to be that third person deciding … It's never been to a point where it's disrupted the relationship.

It was clear that he, and his friends, ultimately felt that maintaining their friendship was worth the cost of compromise, and occasional tactical silence. Jamal and Sayeed agreed:

Jamal: We have discussions about Islam, and we sit on two sides of the fence on loads of different topics but we don't fall out over it, because that's how it is

Sayeed: At the end of the day, no matter what we think, what differences we have, we have the same core belief, you know, we're doing it for Islam.

(2012)

It is perhaps within the intimate spaces of home and family that religion had its most profound impact. As discussed in Chapter 6, religion was a key consideration in the choice of a wife, and was a particular consideration in relation to children, even for those, like Sher Khan, for whom religion was not a significant part of their identity. However, it was also important in reshaping relationships with parents, with siblings and wider family. Silver, for example, noted that while there was some suspicion of traditional authority, this had opened space for discussion between parents and children, leading to generational change:

Children are telling their parents what to think. It's coming from people that look like they want to tell you. People that are knowledgeable and wiser and who are saying mixed marriages are not haram actually, you can talk about sexuality, you can talk about women's rights, you can talk about abortion ... Whereas growing up, it was all the prejudgements – squash it, don't talk about it and make it bad ... Education's the thing, Claire.

(2012)

A more global perspective also emerged amongst the younger generation – notably around Palestine. Shahin commented, 'It's quite a big thing amongst the new generation of Muslims. So my dad would never have thought about campaigning on Palestine' (2012). Similarly, Hanif told me that his generation of British Muslims were changing the ways that Islam was being taught, and learned:

Everyone's got smartphones and such – which is dangerous also because little knowledge is dangerous knowledge. But even if you just walk into a mosque, most mosques now, the imams, you know, they can speak English, they're more clued up, they're more knowledgeable.

(2012)

Shahin echoed, 'You've got a new generation of imams coming up that have, sort of, been brought up in the UK and I think it's a very good thing' (2012). Nevertheless, it would be misleading to see this as a generational split, and often differing practices and perspectives sat alongside each other. For example, Hanif commented that, amongst his close friends, Jamal still maintained many of the beliefs and practices of his parents:

[Jamal's] a bit like in/out, in/out ... He's the one that has more cultural traditional values than the rest of us ... He sometimes has difficulties with cutting away that cultural baggage and it's more a case of, you know, 'my father's done this, my father's done that'.

(2012)

Within families, levels of religiosity varied considerably, between parents and children, but also between siblings, though this was rarely a source of conflict. Shahin noted, 'Hanif's a lot more religious than I am' (2012), while Sayeed's faith was shaped by his older sister Sultana and her Algerian husband. The couple had a love marriage and later became much more overtly religious. Sayeed told me,

My sister wears the niqab … I'm shocked at that … It's out of her own choice she done it … And I say to her, 'Why do you wear it for?' She says, 'No, this is the way. My duty's following my husband and I'm married so no one has the right to see what's underneath, not unless I want to show it to them.'

Nevertheless, he shrugged, 'It's her choice at the end of the day' (2012).

In contrast, both of Sayeed's older brothers were much less religious. Interestingly, as the youngest child, Sayeed's relationship with his older siblings was partly reshaped by his faith. This was most clearly apparent when his older brother Salman was struggling with an ongoing addiction to crack cocaine and heroin. When I asked Sayeed, tentatively, about this struggle, he told me,

He's had a troubled history, so I mean for him to get back to that normal way of thing is going to take a long time … Every day I try, you know, to help him go down the straight path, but …

Sayeed's response was clearly shaped by his sense of religious and moral duty, and this clearly had some impact on Salman (as discussed above, in relation to the vetoing of his pub plan). Nevertheless, this seemed only to partially offset traditional sibling hierarchies of respect and authority (see Alexander 2000, chapter 6), and the lure of his addiction. Sayeed told me, 'So he would come and talk to me and I would give him advice and everything … Sometimes he will listen, but most of the times he won't.' Sayeed clearly struggled to balance his sense of right and wrong with his love for his brother and his desire to support him:

At the end of the day, I know my brother's doing a mistake … so he's trying his best to get off it. So I can't abandon him for that … I can't lose respect for that, he's my older brother. So I'm going to be there until one of us passes away, and you know, I'll help him until the end of time comes.

It is clear that within these family relationships religiosity changed over time and was in a process of negotiation with other cultural and interpersonal dynamics. This was apparent too within spousal relationships. While all my participants had insisted that their wives should be Muslim, or convert to Islam, the dynamics after marriage were often a complex balancing act. Sayeed and Mohammed both noted that their wives were less religious than they were, and had tried to address this after marriage. Sayeed told me his wife was 'not as religious as me … But I've tried to make her religious, so she can teach the kids and she can, you know, be content with herself' (2012). Mohammed similarly stated,

> [My wife] was a lot less religious … there was some conflict, and I was like 'you're not going to do this, or you are going to do that' … She didn't wear a headscarf when we married, for example … and I said, 'Ok fair enough, I understand that this is what you've done before but the … goalposts have changed, so this is something that I expect you to do'.
>
> (2012)

In contrast, Humzah felt his wife was more religious than he was and welcomed this as a way of keeping him more focused: 'You need someone a bit religious to keep us … to not go astray' (2012). Nevertheless, as noted above, she had only limited success in this endeavour. For others, marriage was part of a shared journey of religious exploration. Zohar, who had recently returned from Umrah when I spoke to him in 2012, told me that the pilgrimage had strengthened the couple's faith:

> We've always been strong … and we thought, what more can we do? … Humaira is covering her hair, I started praying a lot more. I started getting into religion a lot more. I started learning a lot more.
>
> (2012)

As with beards, discussed above, the wearing of hijab was a point of debate, particularly with their wives. Indeed, the wearing of hijab – even more so than beards – has become a hotly contested and highly policed gendered symbol of religious belief and practice within the community, nationally and internationally (Tarlo 2009, Rashid 2016, Bibi 2022). However, within the domestic spheres of my participants, there was considerable variation in practice and attitude. Mohammed's demand that his wife wear the hijab was uncharacteristic for the wider group, who insisted that this was a matter of personal choice for the women themselves. Humzah told me that his wife did cover her hair, but 'I don't want her to. I don't mind. She can wear however she feels comfortable. I've told her that so many times' (2012). Hanif similarly reflected:

> I would never have imposed that someone wear it because then it's not right because they're wearing it for the wrong reasons really ... I would have married someone who didn't observe the hijab ... so long as they were maybe religiously inclined and then you'd hope they'd make that decision themselves.
>
> (2012)

In 2012, it seemed more of the wives and female family members of my participants wore hijab than did not. However, practice varied within the families I knew well: only one of Humzah's four sisters wore hijab when I knew them, while amongst Shahin's nieces, 'the dots', it was the youngest two, Rabia and Sadia, who wore hijab, starting in primary school. Indeed, they were the first in the family to wear hijab, with their mother and aunties coming to the practice much later (and, I think, strongly influenced by Hanif's wife, Khadija). The older two sisters, Shamaila and Nasrin, did not wear hijab during their teens and twenties, and while Nasrin started to cover her hair after marriage, Shamaila still does not. This seems simply never to have been an issue for comment or tension amongst the sisters, nor the wider family. Shahin pointed to this as indicative of a further shift between his and the younger generation:

> Rabia or Sadia started covering their head before my sister did ... You've got a new generation of individuals that are actually reading about Islam, and I think they want to identify themselves as being Muslims despite the negative media image.
>
> (2012)

The intra- and inter-generational influence was very clear in Shahin's family. Hanif told me that he thought his increased religious belief had particularly influenced his sisters, and their children, although this was not something he had consciously tried to do. He reflected, 'I've never really sort of forced it on anyone. I think it's more that they maybe had seen a change in me and how I was maybe better for it' (2012). His wife Khadija, he told me, had also been a major influence on his sisters and nieces, and had taught them more about Islam – although he commented that his and Khadija's interpretations of the religion were not always the same and were often debated. Hanif held fortnightly 'circles' with his nephews and nieces to teach them more about the religion:

> Even now we do like a fortnightly circle … [with] all the girls and [his nephews] … We've just been going through the stories of the prophets … And it's quite nice because then everyone sort of gets together as well. And they enjoy it … If they have anything to discuss, you know, we'd discuss it.

His oldest nephew, Samir, had recently 'asked me to teach him how to pray'.

****

As Hanif shows, what it means to be Muslim in Britain is an ongoing dialogue, which crosses generations, families and communities. Certainly the global and national events of the past twenty years have placed Britain's Muslim communities at the forefront of surveillance, control and hostility – Islamophobic attacks are on the increase, and the spread of 'respectable' anti-Muslim racism permeates far beyond the polite confines of middle-class dining rooms. Such events have sharpened and shaped the consciousness and identities of a generation of British Muslims, and their engagement with their faith in a context of hatred and often wilful misrepresentation and ignorance.

Nevertheless, this is only one side of the story. The other is one of coming to terms with one's faith in the move to adulthood – of growing up Muslim, of facing life challenges and of rethinking what faith means in terms of intimate relationships, friendships, work and for the next generation. It takes place in the unremarked and unremarkable activities of daily prayer, of fasting, of paying zakat, of Eid celebrations or the 'bigger' experiences of pilgrimage. Being Muslim did never not matter, even as what this meant for individuals was a complex and shifting space. This is an unfinished conversation. As Sayeed insisted, 'You've got to find out for yourself, that's the thing ... it's a personal journey.'

Endnotes and Updates

Every book is a failure.

(George Orwell, 'Why I Write', 1984: 10)

New and Old Beginnings

This book ends, as it began, with a wedding. Taking place in the late summer of 2019, this marriage was between Khalid and Hanna. Hanna, a British Bangladeshi divorcee with, like Khalid, a teenage daughter, had grown up on the Stoneleigh Estate, and the couple, both in their late thirties, had known each other for many years, although they had only been dating, in secret, a few months. The wedding celebration was small – less than fifty people – with only immediate family and close friends present. My own invitation had arrived quite late, via a phone call from an apologetic Khalid, only a few weeks earlier. It seemed the marriage had been decided recently, and the wedding planned at quite short notice, but there was no way I would have missed it. I travelled with the rest of the family to the event, which took place in one of Silver's restaurants in Kent. Silver himself was there to supervise proceedings; the first time I had seen him since our 2012 interview.

Khalid was the last of the young men I knew well to be married, and it had often felt for all of us, especially Khalid himself, that it would never happen. After his tumultuous relationship with Pamela, and the birth of their daughter, Jasmine, Khalid seemed to have given up on love, and as the years passed, he had devoted himself to Jasmine and training to be a nurse. His relationship with Hanna came as something of a surprise, to me at least. As a young man, Khalid had expressed no interest in Bangladeshi young women, least of all those from the Stoneleigh Estate, and as he grew older he had kept any romantic relationships very quiet – if indeed there were any. On his wedding day, though, Khalid seemed more relaxed and content than I had seen him in many years, and the couple seemed well-suited, comfortable and happy together.

For me, the wedding had a sense of familiarity and of completion – of a circling back to earlier times, places and people, and to the Stoneleigh Estate in the mid-1990s, where my relationship with 'the Asian gang' began. In part, it was a sense of continuity – being with Shahin's family, chatting with Silver, reliving former times, catching up with the gossip and rehearsing old (and new) jokes. This feeling of circularity, or deja-vu, deepened when I discovered that Hanna's older sister was Shopna, who was one of the first youth workers in the SAYO project, and whom I had interviewed as part of the first study. 'Did I ever finish my project?', she asked me at one point, surprised to see me there (still/again?) after so many years, and even more surprised to learn about *The Asian Gang* book. The question was an echo of the conversation a decade earlier at Zohar's wedding that sparked the new research and a timely spur to stop prevaricating and start writing.

The answer to Shopna's question was both yes and no. Yes, I had finished the first project and written the book. Yes, I had started a second project, but no, this was not yet finished, and no, the book from this second project had, at this time, not even begun, though it always lurked ominously in the back of my mind, and took various shapes in my guilty imagination over the years – usually in the early hours of the morning. Clearly, in many ways, the first project had simply never finished, nor showed any signs of ever doing so, even until today. Like 'the Asian Gang', my history, memories and affections are entangled with the Stoneleigh Estate and its denizens, and I find myself circling back there imaginatively, emotionally and, lately, through my involvement with Zohar's youth charity, physically.

If I think of my involvement with 'the Asian gang' as a circling (back) rather than a linear narrative of arrival, learning and departure, this does not imply stasis. If proverbially one can never go home again, the same is as true of fieldwork. The field and its inhabitants have moved on, even as I have: the relationships have changed, or developed, or broken, and in every case need to be made anew, even as I shift from friend/family/once-familiar-face to researcher to writer and back again, knowing that the process of writing itself transforms, recreates and, possibly, threatens those relationships. There is no ending, no point at which the relationship stops, is transcribed and analysed, scripted and typeset, and set aside. If there is no going back, there is also no leaving.

It is this tension, of continuity and change, connection and disconnection, there and here, then and now, that has formed the core of this book. In revisiting 'the Asian gang' first fifteen years after the initial study, and then a decade later through this belated text, I have sought to explore how these now-no-longer young men have grown (up) together and apart – the ties-that-bind and the differences-that-separate-but-never-quite-divide them. It is this unresolved seesawing that underpins their forays into college and university and work, that sustains and fractures their friendships, that balances or upsets the complex web of obligations, expectations and desires around love and marriage, that recreates and sustains families (of blood and of choice), and that nourishes and challenges their faith. Or perhaps it is best imagined as a gyroscope, which both spirals outwards, from the Stoneleigh Estate in the 1990s, and back to the web of connections that lies at its heart, even as those connections change and fracture and the balance becomes precarious.

Tales of the Unexpected?

In many ways these stories are unremarkable, and deliberately so. In fact, it is in their very ordinariness that their power to challenge lies (or, indeed, to challenge *lies*). These are stories of the everyday – often funny, uplifting, moving, sometimes heartbreaking – exploring the mundane process of growing up and growing older in twenty-first-century urban Britain. These are stories of work, of family, of friends, of faith that are rarely told – in part *because* they are so mundane and unexceptional, but more because they do not fit within the dominant narratives of Muslim men that position them as Victim or, more usually, as Threat.[1] At the same time, they do not, and cannot, stand outside these dominant discourses: their lives are shaped through the encounter between what others think of them and the men they are, or strive to be. This may be the relentless onslaught of media, political and policy debates around who and what Muslim men are, and what they should be, set against a backdrop of a toxic post-Millennial political context of Islamophobia at home and abroad. The 'Others' may be their lecturers, employers or colleagues, or customers in their restaurants, on buses or in their taxis, who embody and enact these discourses at work or on the street, where racist stereotyping, suspicion and microaggressions are so much part of the everyday as to pass largely unremarked. Or, closer to home, they may be the 'internal others' of community, mosque elders, neighbours, family or friends, who are threading their own way through a changing society and its impact on the most intimate spaces of personal life.

The accounts presented are at once inconsequential and important: they tell of domestic dramas, and moments and choices that are not so much hidden as overlooked, or ignored. Yet individually and collectively they paint a portrait of a period of transition and transformation for the individuals, families and communities – and for British society at large. They illuminate the ongoing dialogue within and across generations at a moment when division and polarization are presented as the norm, and where nuance is drowned in the furore of ideological and political position-taking.

These stories are, then, both unremarkable and unexpected – they challenge the racist 'commonsense' (CCCS 1982) and offer a counterpoint, however partial and unfinished. They do not provide the other half of a Manichean fantasy, however – replacing the 'bad' with the 'good' Muslim, to use Mamdani's evocative phrase. Rather the picture that emerges is one of complexity, contradiction, change – of struggle, resilience, compromise, moments of triumph and occasional failure. Of what it means to be human. And Muslim.

Ethnography in 4-D

Ethnography has long laid claim to privileged insights into social and cultural realities – to offer first-hand accounts authenticated through 'being there' as participant, observer and narrator. While the older, objectivist accounts of ethnographic research, formed in the colonial fields of the imperial civilizing mission, have been under erasure since the post-structuralist turn of the 1980s (Clifford & Marcus 1986, Clifford 1988, Geertz 2000), there are still important and powerful claims to be made for ethnography as a 'necessary form of witnessing' (Behar 1996). Acknowledging the partial and mediated nature of the truths it offers, ethnography does nevertheless allow 'some kind of voice' (Willis & Trondman 2000:1) to those whose lives and experiences remain invisible, unheard or ventriloquized by (both internal and external) 'others'. My own attempt at ventriloquism is equally partial, equally mediated, equally flawed – an inevitable 'failure', in Orwell's terms – but a necessary testament to the lives of 'the Asian gang' in all their glorious humanity, at a moment when the lives of Muslims in Britain and globally are most often rendered two-dimensional and under erasure (imaginatively and, often, physically). Accordingly, I have tried to centre the voices of the men themselves, to allow their personalities, their histories, their emotions and their humour to emerge and, if not to actually speak for themselves (which the process of selection and writing makes impossible), at least to animate the text, to provide depth and resonance. For this reason too, I deliberately chose not to burden the writing with the weight of too much theory and analysis but to allow the stories to breathe, and the reader to draw their own (admittedly guided) conclusions about what they mean.

My aim, then, has been to paint a portrait of 'the Asian gang' in 3-D, but with an additional focus on change over time – what my friend Wendy Bottero once referred to as 'ethnography in 4-D'. This allows for a focus on complexity and diversity both at a given moment – the mid-1990s, the early 2010s, 2022–3 – and across time, as the pathways between 'then' and 'now' diverge and reconverge. While it is impossible to capture this fluidity on the written page, and while much of this movement happens off-stage and unwitnessed by even the most diligent (or nosiest) ethnographer, my hope has been to illuminate some of the key 'moments' on the journey.

As with the first book there are inevitably lacunae and silences. While there is more acknowledgement of the central role of family, for example, in most cases this has remained more at the level of (their) report than of (my) experience. For the individuals and families I know well, there have been difficult choices to make around what to leave unexplored, perhaps because the issues were too personal, too painful or have changed significance over time. A chapter on changing sibling relationships fell by the wayside because, on later reflection, the stories were simply too private; or because what I was told in 2012 no longer held true but could still hurt family members; or because the things we discussed openly then looked and felt very different written down in black and white, and were felt, in one angry early morning text message, as a betrayal. I struggled too throughout with what to say about people who were crucial, but unwitting, walk-ons in other people's narratives – friends, girlfriends, sisters, wives, parents and children. While I have tried to balance my ethnographer's instincts for a good story (or a good joke) both with what is 'necessary ... witnessing' and my desire not to cause harm, pain or distress to people I respect and care about, I doubt I have always got it right. The proof will be in the reading.

Failing the Riz Test: The Muslim Folk Devil

If the strength of ethnography lies to a large extent in the 'thickness' of its description (in Clifford Geertz's phrase) (Geertz 2000), there are two important caveats. First, that looking at what I think of as 'down and in' at the intimate spaces of people's lives, it is important to remember that these lives are necessarily and inescapably imbricated in the wider web of social, political and economic structures and relationships. Second, there is a need to place questions of culture and identity historically – to consider the ways that histories from below shaped, and are shaped by, the wider flow of 'big' historical events and narratives (Alexander et al 2016). There is a need then to look 'up and out' (and back) at the context in which individuals and groups live and breathe, particularly when the subjects of the research are – as they so often are – marginalized, excluded and discriminated against.

Of course these external structures are themselves complex and multi-layered: my participants were working within multiple frames of meaning, including local, national and diasporic (notably Bangladesh, but also the Bangladeshi community worldwide, and the global *umma*). Concerns around Palestine, or the Rohingya in Myanmar and Bangladesh, or Muslims in Modi's India, Syrian refugees or the cultural genocide of the Uyghur in China are part of the lives and minds of the Stoneleigh participants. In fact, the last time I saw Shahin and Hanif was in September 2022, when I invited them to hear Arundhati Roy speak at the Stuart Hall Foundation lecture in London on 'Things that can and cannot be said'.[2] Perhaps inescapably, one of her main themes was the complex formation of political and cultural identity structured through religion – most notably, in its current formation, the ambiguous, and often precarious, place of Islam in the world's increasingly hostile geopolitics. Her perspective on the policies of the Hindu Right in Modi's India, and the attacks on its Muslim citizens, held particular resonance to the UK audience in the light of the violent clashes in Leicester between young men of Hindu and Muslim descent the previous weekend (Puri 2022). Although investigations are ongoing, the clashes have been linked to diaspora politics, recent migration from the subcontinent and to established communitarian antipathies, with the blame being cast from both sides across the religious divide.

If the events in Leicester bring global politics close to home, they also reflect a wider British set of ongoing suspicions around race, religion and migration. Leicester itself has recently been announced as the first White minority city in the UK, according to data from the 2021 Census (Johal & Thompson 2022), with South Asians outnumbering the white population by 2.5 per cent. Amidst the expected outrage about the ethnic state of England's cities from right-wing commentators like Nigel Farage, ex-chancellor Sajid Javid asked, simply, 'So what?' (Nicholson 2022).

While I rarely find myself agreeing with Mr Javid on anything, the question is a provocative and timely one – about where, why and how race and ethnicity matter, and what this might mean for a sense of national identity or crisis. Given that the census also revealed that Britain (or at least England and Wales) was no longer a predominantly Christian country either (Duncan et al 2022), with the number of self-identified Christians falling to just over 42 per cent, the entanglement of ethnicity, national identity and religion adds complexity to these debates. The number of Muslims, according to the Census, has risen to nearly four million (6.5 per cent of the population of England and Wales), up from 2.7 million (4.9 per cent) in 2011.[3]

The question is if, why and how this matters, or is *made* to matter? The answer goes beyond a simple focus on numbers, or percentages, or proportions. It goes beyond the increasing diversity within the British Muslim population too, though questions of wealth and class, migration history, place and legal status are important faultlines within this imagined community, and likely to become more so over time. At its heart is the role that Muslims play in the wider national imagination, perpetuating a sense of crisis and – more than any other minority group – heralding a call to the cultural and civilizational barricades. Certainly in the decade since I completed my last interviews with my participants, issues of religion and discrimination have remained at the centre of political, policy and popular posturing, with devastating consequences for the everyday lives of British Muslims. Inequality in employment, housing, criminal justice, health and education remain entrenched and largely invisible and unremarked. Anti-Muslim racism is integral to the asylophobic pushback against refugees at Calais or crossing the Channel, or abandoned in camps, or under attack in hotels and hostels, or awaiting deportation to Rwanda. It is scorched in the overrepresentation of Muslims in the stripping of British citizenship by the state – perhaps most shamefully in the abandonment of Shamima

Begum, the Bangladeshi schoolgirl 'jihadi bride', whose appeal against
the revocation of her citizenship (by the aforementioned Sajid Javid)
was recently rejected by the Special Immigration Appeals Commission,
even while it acknowledged that there was 'credible suspicion' that she
had been trafficked for sexual exploitation. Sayeeda Warsi was quoted
as stating that citizenship-stripping powers 'have been used almost
exclusively against Muslims ... creating a two-tier citizenship system
completely at odds with British values of fairness and equality before
the law' (quoted in Siddique 2023). Meanwhile – and probably not
coincidentally – the recent Shawcross Review of Prevent has sought
to keep the focus of counter-terror legislation and action firmly on
Muslims rather than the growing threat of far-right extremism, arguing
that 'the most lethal threat in the last 20 years has come from Islamism,
and this threat continues' (cited in Katwala 2023). Clearly government
policy spectacularly fails the Riz Test.[4] Such failure is not accidental,
though – Britain's Muslims are being deliberately (and cynically)
pushed to the frontline of its war on terror (and associated culture
wars), which is almost indistinguishable from a war on Muslims. What
might be termed a 'Weapon of Mass Distraction'.[5]

So What? Some Tentative Takeaways

If ethnography prioritizes theory from below, allowing its findings to
seep from the data, rather than imposing its framing from above, or a
priori, nevertheless there are five key messages that I would highlight
here (recognizing that each reader may find their own alternative
readings). First is to challenge easy reifications of identity that seek
to label and circumscribe social categories – racial, ethnic, religious,
gendered, sexual, classed – and mobilize these at the barricades of
identity politics, and on either side of the culture wars. While labels
have resonance and utility, and can be used for good and for ill, they
do not, and cannot, begin to account for richness and humanity of the
people they claim to represent, or entrap.[6]

Second, and as a counterpoint, I would argue that while the deconstructive turn in social analysis has been important in, to use Stuart Hall's evocative Althusserian phrase, 'bending the twig' away from such homogenizing categories, the rush to celebrate difference, the subjective and the unconscious has betrayed its original critical and political intent and diluted its potential to disrupt and challenge (Hall & Back 2009). As I have argued elsewhere (2002, 2018) the appeal to a politics of difference is a necessary but not sufficient step to a politics of social justice and social change. While the personal can be political, it is not always so – particularly if that is where it stops.

Third, while identities are most usually conceived *either* as 'being' *or* 'becoming', there is a need to recognize *both* continuity, solidarity and the role of individual, collective and social histories *and* change, difference and diversity (Hall 1990). Hall has described this as the 'play' of history, culture and power, acknowledging that the encounter may be fraught, unresolved and incomplete – what I always think of as 'toe-stubbing' moments on the rocky path from a contested and fractured past to an as-yet undetermined future. Hall writes of identity as 'Not an essence but a positioning' (Hall 1990): perhaps best imagined as a kaleidoscope in which individual and shared histories, experiences, memories and emotions are configured and reconfigured, are paused and then shift again.

Fourth, where most studies suggest that change is a source of conflict – particularly in relation to intergenerational change, and more particularly still in relation to racialized communities (Alexander 2006, Alexander & Kim 2014) – this study suggests that this process is best seen as a dialogue or negotiation. Moreover, rather than a simple one-off transition, a break from a past most usually imagined as anachronistic and dysfunctional, this is an ongoing conversation which seeks to engage and blend tradition and change, the old and the new, into emergent, uncertain and shifting attitudes and practices. As my participants engaged in these transitions – unevenly and in different ways – with their parents, older siblings and community, so are these conversations ongoing with the next generation, and the next.

Obviously – though it bears repeating, particularly for racialized young men – youth is itself a transitional category, something that is passed through and passed on to others.

Fifth, identity necessitates a reckoning with emotion – with the hate that erects the borders within and between individuals, groups, communities and nations, but also with the love that underpins social life and connections (Ahmed 2004). More than anything, this has been a book about love – about friendship, acceptance and forgiveness, weddings and funerals, and the birth of children, playing football and going to the gym, about WhatsApp groups and Friday prayers. About being there for each other, still.

Updates: February 2023

Inevitably, things have changed, and continue to change, for 'the Asian gang' in the decade since the last set of interviews, and even as I write. The kaleidoscope shifts and the 'Asian gang' dissolve and settle again, for a moment.

This moment is late February 2023,[7] as I put the finishing touches to what I hope will be the final draft of the manuscript. As might be expected, the past decade has seen changes in the lives of my participants, as they mature into middle-age, though there are less than through the period traced by this book. Shahin's solicitor's firm has proved highly successful and has developed an established reputation in the field of employment and discrimination law. He and Emma divorced last year, but he shares custody of their son and is a devoted father (and dedicated football coach for the local under-12s team). He lectures part-time for a London law school. Zohar is now joint-CEO of a highly successful national youth charity, which is recognized for its work around youth violence and education. He still works on and around the Stoneleigh Estate. He is still happily married to Humaira and they have two, much-adored, daughters. Humzah is still living in East London with his wife and three children. He has drifted in and out of various jobs but most recently was working with Jadil at a restaurant in South London. Zohar is encouraging him to renew his sports coaching certificates and to come and work with his youth organization. Jadil closed his pub just before the first Covid-19 lockdown and bought a number of flats to rent. As mentioned earlier, he also opened a small restaurant in South London, with Humzah and Salman as employees. His mother died during the pandemic, and his father passed away last month, and Jadil is reportedly taking time away from his businesses to spend more time with his four children. Big Hanif still lives on the Stoneleigh Estate with his wife and son. He spends time at the local mosque and has recently returned to bus driving after a cataract operation. Zohar recently described his life as 'Mosque, work and his family'. Mustafa is also still working as a bus driver. He works night shifts so he has more time to spend with his four children. He is teaching the boys to box, and, according to Zohar, treats his little girl 'like a princess'. He has become something of a fitness fanatic and has a regular Friday session at the gym with Humzah, Shahin and Salman. M was released from prison in June 2021, having served half of his twenty-year sentence. He was rearrested less than a year later and is currently on remand, awaiting a court date.

Khalid completed his training as a nurse and is working in a South London hospital. His work during the pandemic was reported in the local press and celebrated by his local mosque. After their marriage, he and Hanna bought a flat, where they live with Hanna's daughter. In a recent conversation, Khalid told me that his life now is shaped by his faith. Shakiel gave up cabbing and currently works as a supermarket store manager for a major retailer. He has just returned from taking his wife and son to visit his father, who has retired to Bangladesh, and is suffering with dementia.

Among the little ones: Hanif moved to work with his older brother Shahin in 2016. He and Khadija have a beautiful daughter, Amara, and they live with his mother at the family home. Jamal works as a business accounts manager at the local bank where he was working in

2012. He has two children, a girl and a boy. Sayeed still works as a bus driver and is married with five children. His beard is still magnificent. When I spoke to Hanif, he was unable to tell me what had happened with Mohammed since the 'big split', and I have, as yet, been unable to contact him. Shortly after our interview in 2012, Ifti separated from Ana and had a drug-related relapse that led to a period of homelessness and a severe breakdown in his mental health. He was institutionalized for a number of months, and then returned to his parents' home for care, before moving to a hostel. His recovery is slow and precarious, but he is working and has a new partner and young daughter.

Elsewhere, Silver was divorced from his first wife shortly after our interview in 2012. Blaming his workaholic lifestyle, he has since cut back and is working part-time with Zohar as a training manager. He got married again several years ago, to a Moroccan activist he met through his international youth work. They have a young son and are expecting another baby soon. Sher Khan had a massive heart attack several years ago and has recently returned to his mentoring role in a school in Kent. He is still married and his children are grown, with his oldest son recently married.

In our recent conversation, Zohar told me that the past decades have been 'a real big journey'. While this book has, I hope, captured some of the essence of this journey, the 'Asian gang' has already moved on. As Zohar sighed, 'It is what it is'.

Notes

Chapter 2

1 https://www.gov.uk/government/collections/english-indices-of-deprivation.
2 'Multi Ward Profiles 2019', www.southwark.gov.uk.
3 As above.
4 Census data tables; Ward Profiles (2017), www.southwark.gov.uk.
5 It was not possible to find percentages of Bangladeshis living in the Ward, but constituted around 1.4 per cent of the borough profile based on the 2011 Census 9 (Public Sector Equality Duty, www.southwark.gov.uk).
6 All figures taken from Census data tables https://www.nomisweb.co.uk/query/select/getdatasetbytheme.asp?opt=3&theme=&subgrp=.
7 https://data.london.gov.uk/dataset/ward-profiles-and-atlas.
8 http://moderngov.southwark.gov.uk/documents/s85621/Report%20-%20Great%20Estates%20Improvement%20Pilots.pdf.

Chapter 3

1 In 1997, in the borough, 27 per cent of young people obtained 5 or more GCSE grades at A*-C, while Thomas More School had 22 per cent achieving 5 or more GCSE grades A*-C.
2 In 1995, the year after Shahin left school, only 22 per cent of the borough achieved 5 or more GCSEs, A*-C grades – half of the national average, and the worst performing borough in London. The school was reported in the TES as the worst performing school in the borough in 1994, his GCSE year, and was labelled a 'failing school'.

Chapter 4

1 https://www.ethnicity-facts-figures.service.gov.uk/work-pay-and-benefits/employment/employment-by-occupation/latest/downloads/employment-by-occupation.csv (accessed 20 August 2021).

2   A 2017 report on Diversity in the Legal Profession (Aulakh et al) notes that BAME solicitors have increased significantly in number over the past thirty years, but 'continue to experience fewer opportunities than white male peers, resulting in unequal pay and progression outcomes' (p5). BAME solicitors are overrepresented in High Street firms and regional firms and in sole practitioner firms. The report notes that 'the profession remains heavily stratified by class, gender and ethnicity' (p5). The report does not disaggregate the 'Asian' category by religion or nationality.

3   In 2010, at the time of Zohar's wedding, Liaquot was also working as a chauffeur for Addison Lee – and was becoming (in)famous amongst his friends for his 'Guess who I had in the back of my limousine' stories.

Chapter 6

1   Mohammed Malik, a bachelor from Birmingham, took out a billboard advertisement to find a wife in early 2022. Alongside a picture of a smiling bearded Malik, the tongue-in-cheek text read 'Save Me from an Arranged Marriage' with a web address 'findMALIKawife.com' (see metro.co.uk, 4 January 2022). The story was picked up by the national press and mainstream news channels (including the BBC), as well as by CNN and India.com.

2   This is calculated using the Household Reference Person (the person that is 'head of household', according to the census). These are compared to 36.5 per cent of white British and all categories in 2001 and 33 per cent of white British and all categories in 2011. The data were downloaded from Nomis (https://www.nomisweb.co.uk/) (accessed 9 June 2022). I am grateful to my colleague Dr Dharmi Kapadia, who generously did this analysis for me.

3   This statement was a source of some hilarity with Jamal at the time, and a week later, Hanif asked me, laughing, 'Is it true that Sayeed said that he married his wife because they were both equally ugly?'.

4   2011 Census analysis – Office for National Statistics (ons.gov.uk), accessed 3 July 2022.

5   The myth around 'forced conversion' of Sikh women by Muslim men in the UK is a long-standing Islamophobic trope (see Katy Sian 2013).

6   I have decided not to name him in case any members of his family read the book.

Chapter 7

1   Reflecting both the increased demographic and economic/political presence of East Asians in the UK and the importation of transatlantic terminologies.

2   This is figured in the drawing, although, of course, it is important – especially now – to note that Indian/Gujarati does not necessarily equate to Hindu.

3   A question on religious affiliation appeared for the first time since 1851 in the 2001 Census.

4   Ninety per cent of British Bangladeshis identified as Muslim in the 2011 Census.

5   This is according to a documentary 'Mosque: the Story of Islam' in the Borough made in 2010.

6   The Muslim Council of Britain notes that 13 per cent of the UK male prison population is Muslim, nearly three times their proportion in the UK population and around three times that of the white British male prison population (2015).

7   With a nod to the wonderful 'We are Ladyparts' classic, 'Bashir with the Good Beard'.

Chapter 8

1   Riz Ahmed has referred to 'stereotypical, toxic, two-dimensional portrayals' of Muslims onscreen (Pulver 2021). This has led to the launch of the Riz Test (www.riztest.com).

2   Arundhati Roy, 'Things that can and cannot be said: the dismantling of the world as we knew it', 30 September 2022 (www.stuarthallfoundation.org.uk).

3   This has risen to 6.5 per cent in the 2021 Census. The increase in Muslim population accounts for 1/3 of the population growth of England and Wales in the period 2011–21 (https://mcb.org.uk/2021-census-as-uk-population-grows-so-do-british-muslim-communities/).

4   The Riz Test measures how Muslims are portrayed on screen according to five criteria – all of which government policy in the past three decades has failed (www.riztest.com).

5   I came across this phrase from Chuck D of Public Enemy in a recent BBC2 documentary series 'Fight the Power: How Hip Hop Changed the World'. The urban dictionary defines this as (amongst other things) 'Something that distracts large numbers of people from thinking about important issues'.

6   I am thinking here of a recent piece by my favourite author, Terry Pratchett, who wrote, in a different context, 'We live in a venal world run largely by men who count numbers and because they can count people, they think people are numbers' (2014: 269).

7   What follows is based on a number of informal catch-ups with Zohar, Shahin, Khalid and Hanif at the time of writing.

Bibliography

Abbas, M. S. (2019), 'Producing "internal suspect bodies": Divisive effects of UK counter-terrorism measures on Muslim communities in Leeds and Bradford', *British Journal of Sociology*, 70 (1): 261–82.

Abbas, M. S. (2021), *Terror and the Dynamism of Islamophobia in 21ˢᵗ Century Britain: The Concentrationary Gothic*, Basingstoke: Palgrave Macmillan.

Abbas, T. (2002), 'The home and the school in the educational achievements of South Asians', *Race, Ethnicity and Education*, 5 (3): 291–316.

Active Communities Network. (2010), *Breaking Barriers: Community Cohesion, Sport and Organisational Development*, London: Active Communities Network. Available online: Breaking+Barriers+FULL+Report+-+Jason+Roberts.pdf (squarespace. com) (accessed 2 February 2023).

Agamben, G. (2005), *State of Exception*, Chicago: University of Chicago.

Ahmed, S. (2004), *The Cultural Politics of Emotion*, New York: Routledge.

Alexander, C. (1996), *The Art of Being Black: The Creation of Black British Youth Identities*, Oxford: Oxford University Press.

Alexander, C. (1998), 'Re-imagining the Muslim community', *Innovation*, 11 (4): 439–50.

Alexander, C. (2000), *The Asian Gang: Ethnicity, Identity, Masculinity*, Oxford: Berg.

Alexander, C. (2002), 'Beyond Black: Rethinking the colour/culture divide', *Ethnic and Racial Studies*, 25 (4): 552–71.

Alexander, C. (2004a), 'Re-imagining the Asian gang: Ethnicity, masculinity and youth after "The riots"', *Critical Social Policy*, 24 (4): 526–49.

Alexander, C. (2004b), 'Writing race: Truth, fiction and ethnography in "The Asian Gang"', in M. Bulmer and J. Solomos (eds), *Researching Race and Racism*, 134–49, London: Routledge.

Alexander, C. (2005), 'Embodying violence: "Riots", dis/order and the private lives of "The Asian gang"', in C. Alexander and C. Knowles (eds), *Making Race Matter: Bodies, Space and Identity*, 199–217, Basingstoke: Palgrave.

Alexander, C. (2006), 'Imagining the politics of BrAsian youth', in N. Ali, V. Kalra and S. Sayyid (eds), *A Postcolonial People: South Asians in Britain*, 258–71, London: Christopher Hurst.

Alexander, C. (2008), *(Re)Thinking 'Gangs'*, London: Runnymede Trust.

Alexander, C. (2010), 'Culturing poverty? Ethnicity, religion, gender and social disadvantage amongst South Asian communities in the UK', in S. Chant (ed.), *International Handbook of Gender and Poverty*, 272–7, Cheltenham: Edward Elgar Publishing Limited.

Alexander, C. (2013), 'Marriage, migration, multiculturalism: Gendering "The Bengal diaspora"', *Journal of Ethnic and Migration Studies*, 39 (3): 333–52.

Alexander, C. (2014), 'The empire strikes back: 30 years on', *Ethnic and Racial Studies*, 37 (10): 1784–92.

Alexander, C. (2016), 'The culture question: A view from the UK', *Ethnic and Racial Studies*, 39 (8): 1426–35.

Alexander, C. (2017), 'Raceing Islamophobia', in F. Elahi and O. Khan (eds), *Islamophobia: A Challenge for Us All: 20 Years On*, 13–16, London: Runnymede Trust.

Alexander, C. (2018), 'Breaking Black: The death of ethnic and racial studies in Britain', *Ethnic and Racial Studies*, 41 (6): 1034–54.

Alexander, C. and J. Arday, eds (2015), *Aiming Higher: Race, Inequality and Diversity in the Academy*, London: Runnymede Trust.

Alexander, C., J. Chatterji and A. Jalais (2016), *The Bengal Diaspora: Rethinking Muslim Migration*, London: Routledge.

Alexander, C. and H. Kim (2014), 'South Asian youth cultures', in J. Chatterji and D. Washbrook (eds), *Handbook of the South Asian Diaspora*, 350, London: Routledge.

Alexander, C., V. Redclift and A. Hussain, eds (2013), *The New Muslims*, London: Runnymede Trust.

Alexander, C., S. Carey, S. Lidher, S. Hall, J. King and S. Lidher (2020), *Beyond Banglatown: Continuity, Change and New Urban Economies in Brick Lane*, London: Runnymede Trust.

Alexander, C. and W. Shankley (2020), 'Ethnic inequalities in the state education system in England', in B. Byrne, C. Alexander, O. Khan, J. Nazroo and W. Shankley (eds), *Ethnicity, Race and Inequality in the UK: The State of the Nation*, 93–125, Bristol: Policy Press.

Ali, N., R. Phillips, C. Chambers, K. Narkowicz, P. Hopkins and R. Pande, (2019), 'Halal dating: Changing attitudes and experiences among young British Muslims', *Sexualities*, 23 (5–6): 775–92.

Allen, C. (2003), *Fair Justice: The Bradford Disturbances, The Sentencing and the Impact*, London: Forum Against Islamophobia and Racism (FAIR).

Allen, C. (2005), 'From race to religion: The new face of discrimination', in T. Abbas (ed), *Muslim Britain: Communities Under Pressure*, 49–65, London: Zed Books.

Allen, C. (2017), 'The challenges facing Muslim communities and civic society', in F. Elahi and O. Khan (eds), *Islamophobia: A Challenge for Us All: 20 Years On*, 51–5, London: Runnymede Trust.

Ansari, H. (2005), 'Attitudes to Jihad, martyrdom and terrorism among British Muslims', in T. Abbas (ed), *Muslim Britain: Communities under Pressure*, 144–63, London: Zed Books.

Ansari, H. (2018), *The 'Infidel' within: Muslims in Britain since 1800*, Oxford: Oxford University Press.

Anwar, M. (1998), *Between Cultures: Continuity and Change in the Lives of Young Asians*, London: Routledge.

Aulakh, S., A. Charlwood, D. Muzio, J. Tomlinson and D. Valizade (2017), Mapping advantages and disadvantages: Diversity in the legal profession in England and Wales, *Solicitors Regulation Authority*, October 2017. https://www.sra.org.uk/sra/research-publications/diversity-legal-profession/ (accessed 13 February 2023).

Badshah, N. (2019), 'Knife crime hits record high in England and Wales', *The Guardian*, 17 October. Available online: https://www.theguardian.com/uk-news/2019/oct/17/knife-hits-new-record-high-in-england-and-wales (accessed 8 February 2023).

Bagguley, P. and Y. Hussain (2008), *Riotous Citizens: Ethnic Conflict in Multicultural Britain*, Aldershot: Ashgate.

Banerjea, K. and P. Banerjea (1996), 'Psyche and soul: A view from the "South"', in A. Sharma, J. Hutnyk and S. Sharma (eds), *Dis-Orienting Rhythms: The Politics of the New Asian Dance Music*, 105–26, London: Zed Books.

Batty, D. (2011), 'Lady Warsi claims Islamophobia is now socially acceptable in Britain', *The Guardian*, 20 January. Available online: https://www.theguardian.com/uk/2011/jan/20/lady-warsi-islamophobia-muslims-prejudice (accessed 23 October 2022).

Beckett, C. and M. Macey (2001), 'Race, gender and sexuality: The oppression of multiculturalism', *Women's Studies International Forum*, 24 (3–4): 309–19.

Behar, R. (1996), *The Vulnerable Observer: Anthropology That Breaks Your Heart*, Boston, MA: Beacon Press.

Behar, R. (2020) 'Read more, write less', in C., McGranahan (ed), *Writing Ethnography: Essays on Craft and Commitment*, 47–53, Durham: Duke University Press.

Benson, S. (1996), 'Asians have culture, West Indians have problems: Discourses of race in and out of anthropology', in T. Ranger, Y. Samad and O. Stuart (eds), *Culture, Identity and Politics*, 47–56, Aldershot: Avebury.

Berelowitz, S., C. Firmin, G. Edwards and S. Gulyurtlu (2012), *I Thought I Was the Only One in the World': The Office of the Children's Commissioner's Inquiry into Child Sexual Exploitation in Gangs and Groups*, London: Office of the Children's Commissioner. Available online: https://www.childrenscommissioner.gov.uk/wp-content/uploads/2017/07/I-thought-I-was-the-only-one-in-the-world.pdf (accessed 17 February 2023).

Berthoud, R. (2000), 'Family formation in multi-cultural Britain: Three patterns of diversity', *ISER Working Paper Series*, No. 2000–34, Colchester: University of Essex. Available online: https://www.econstor.eu/bitstream/10419/91963/1/2000-34.pdf (accessed 13 February 2023).

Bhatt, C. (2001), *Hindu Nationalism: Origins, Ideologies and Modern Myths*, London: Routledge.

Bhatt, C. (2013), *Liberation and Purity: Race, Religious Movements and the Ethics of Postmodernity*, London: UCL Press.

Bhattacharyya, G. (2008), *Dangerous Brown Men: Exploiting Sex, Violence and Feminism in the War on Terror*, London: Zed Press.

Bibi, R. (2022), 'Examining BSA Muslim women's everyday experiences of veiling through concepts of "The veil" and "Double consciousness"', *Identities: Global Studies in Culture and Power*, 29 (5): 633–51.

Bingham, J. (2012), 'Rochdale grooming case: Nothing to be gained from "shying away from" race, says Children's Minister', *The Telegraph*, 15 May. Available online: https://www.telegraph.co.uk/news/politics/9267689/Rochdale-grooming-case-nothing-to-be-gained-from-shying-away-from-race-says-Childrens-Minister.html (accessed 7 February 2023).

'Blair action pledge on gang culture' (2007), *Evening Standard*, 11 April. Available online: https://www.express.co.uk/news/uk/4167/Blair-action-pledge-on-gang-culture (accessed 8 February 2023).

Boliver, V. (2013), 'How fair is access to more prestigious UK universities?', *British Journal of Sociology*, 64 (2): 344–64.

Brennan, I. (2018), 'Knife Crime: Important new findings could help us understand why people carry weapons', *The Conversation*, 20 August.

https://theconversation.com/knife-crime-important-new-findings-could-help-us-understand-why-people-carry-weapons-101755 (accessed 13 February 2023).

Byrne, B., C. Alexander, O. Khan, J. Nazroo and W. Shankley, eds (2020), *Ethnicity, Race and Inequality in the UK*: *State of the Nation*, Bristol: Policy Press.

Callender, C. (2006), 'Access to higher education in Britain: The impact of tuition fees and financial assistance', in P. N. Teixeira, D. B. Johnstone, M. J. Rosa and H. Vossensteyn (eds) *Cost-Sharing and Accessibility in Higher Education: A Fairer Deal?*, 105–32, Dordrecht: Springer.

Cantle, T. (2001), 'Community cohesion: A report of the independent review team chaired by Ted Cantle', *Home Office*. Available online: https://www.belongnetwork.co.uk/wp-content/uploads/2019/04/communitycohesion-cantlereport.pdf (accessed 13 February 2023).

Casey, L. (2016), 'The Casey Review: A review into opportunity and integration', *Home Office*, December 2016, London: London HMSO. Available online: https://assets.publishing.service.gov.uk/government/uploads/system/uploads/attachment_data/file/575973/The_Casey_Review_Report.pdf (accessed 13 February 2023).

Centre for Contemporary Cultural Studies (1982), *The Empire Strikes Back: Race and Racism in 70's Britain*, London: Routledge.

Centre for Social Justice (2009), 'Dying to belong: An in-depth review of street gangs in Britain', *Breakthrough Britain*, February 2019, London: Centre for Social Justice. Available online: https://www.centreforsocialjustice.org.uk/wp-content/uploads/2009/02/DyingtoBelongFullReport.pdf (accessed 13 February 2023).

Centre on the Dynamics of Ethnicity (2012), 'How has ethnic diversity grown 1991–2001–2011?', *Dynamics of Diversity Series Briefing*, December 2012. Available online: http://hummedia.manchester.ac.uk/institutes/code/briefings/dynamicsofdiversity/how-has-ethnic-diversity-grown-1991-2001-2011.pdf (accessed 13 February 2023).

Chanter, K., G. Gangoli and M. Hester (2009), 'Forced marriage in the UK: Religious, cultural, economic or state violence', *Critical Social Policy*, 29 (4): 587–612.

Charsley, K., B. Storer-Church, M. Benson and N. Van Hear (2012), 'Marriage-related migration to the UK', *International Migration Review*, 46 (4): 861–90.

Charsley, K. and A. Liversage (2015), 'Silenced husbands: Muslim marriage migration and masculinity', *Men and Masculinities*, 18 (4): 489–508.

Clancy, A., M. Hough, R. Aust and C. Kershaw (2001), 'Crime, policing and justice: The experience of ethnic minorities', *Home Office Research Development and Statistics Directorate*, October 2001. Available online: https://d1wqtxts1xzle7.cloudfront.net/41502820/Crime_Policing_and_ Justice_the_Experienc (accessed 13 February 2023).

Clark, K. and S. Drinkwater (2007), 'Ethnic minorities in the labour market: Dynamics and diversity', *Joseph Rowntree Foundation*, Bristol: Policy Press. Available online: https://www.jrf.org.uk/sites/default/files/jrf/migrated/ files/1986-ethnic-minorities-employment.pdf (accessed 13 February 2023).

Clark, K. and W. Shankley (2020), 'Ethnic minorities in the labour market', in B. Byrne, C. Alexander, O. Khan, J. Nazroo and W. Shankley (eds), *Ethnicity, Race and Inequality in the UK: State of the Nation*, 127–48, Bristol: Policy Press.

Clifford, J. (1988) *The Predicament of Culture: Twentieth Century Ethnography*, Cambridge, MA: Harvard University Press.

Clifford, J. and G. Marcus (1986), *Writing Culture: The Poetics and Politics of Ethnography*, Berkeley: University of California Press.

Cockburn, E. (2013), 'Grooming and the "Asian sex gang predator": The construction of a racial crime threat', *Race and Class*, 54 (4): 22–32.

Cockbain, E. and W. Tufail (2020), 'Failing victims, fuelling hate: Challenging the harms of the "Muslim grooming gangs" narrative', *Race and Class*, 61 (3): 3–32.

Cohen, S. (1980), *Folk Devils and Moral Panics: The Creation of the Mods and Rockers*, 2nd edn, Oxford: Martin Robertson.

Cohen, B. and W. Tufail (2017), 'Prevent and the normalization of Islamophobia' in F. Elahi and O. Khan (eds) *Islamophobia: A Challenge for Us All: 20 Years on*, 41–5, London: Runnymede Trust.

Coleman, S. (2010), 'On remembering and forgetting in writing and fieldwork', in P. Collins and A. Gallinat (eds), *The Ethnographic Self as Resource: Writing Memory and Experience into Ethnography*, 215–27, Oxford: Berghahn.

Collins, P. and A. Gallinat, eds (2010), 'Introduction', *The Ethnographic Self as Resource: Writing Memory and Experience into Ethnography*, Oxford: Berghahn.

Croxford, L. and D. Raffe (2014), 'Social class, ethnicity and access to higher education in the four countries of the UK: 1996–2010', *International Journal of Lifelong Education*, 33 (1): 77–95.

Dale, A. (2002), 'Social Exclusion of Pakistani and Bangladeshi Women', *Sociological Research Online*, 7 (3): 69–81.

Dale, A. (2008), 'Migration, marriage and employment amongst Indian, Pakistani and Bangladeshi residents in the UK', *CCSR Working Paper 2008–02*, The University of Manchester. Available online: https://hummedia.manchester.ac.uk/institutes/cmist/archive-publications/working-papers/2008/2008-02-migration-marriage-and-employment.pdf (accessed 13 February 2023).

Dale, A. and S. Ahmed (2011), 'Marriage and employment patterns amongst UK-raised Indian, Pakistani and Bangladeshi women', *Ethnic and Racial Studies*, 34 (6): 902–24.

Dale, A., N. Shaheen, V. Kalra and E. Fieldhouse (2002), 'Routes into education and employment for young Pakistani and Bangladeshi women in the UK', *Ethnic and Racial Studies*, 25 (6): 942–68.

Davis, D. L. and D. I. Davis (2010), 'Dualling memories: Twinship and the disembodiment of identity', in P. Collins and A. Gallinat (eds), *The Ethnographic Self as Resource: Writing Memory and Experience into Ethnography*, 129–49, Oxford: Berghahn.

Dearden, L. (2019a), 'Islamophobic incidents rose 375% after Boris Johnson compared Muslim women to "Letterboxes", figures show', *Independent*, 2 September. Available online: https://www.independent.co.uk/news/uk/home-news/boris-johnson-muslim-women-letterboxes-burqa-islamphobia-rise-a9088476.html (accessed 7 February 2023).

Dearden, L. (2019b), 'Shamima Begum: Sajid Javid defends stripping ISIS bride of UK citizenship amid mounting pressure', *Independent*, 21 February. Available online: https://www.independent.co.uk/news/uk/home-news/shamima-begum-isis-bride-citizenship-revoked-uk-sajid-javid-home-office-a8789906.html (accessed 7 February 2023).

Dearden, L. (2019c), 'Tommy Robinson: How close EDL founder came to causing collapse of Huddersfield grooming gang trial', *Independent*, 5 July. Available online: https://www.independent.co.uk/news/uk/crime/tommy-robinson-contempt-court-case-grooming-gang-trial-huddersfield-a8990436.html (accessed 7 February 2023).

Dearden, L. (2019d), 'Far right poses as protectors of women to target Muslims, official extremism report finds', *Independent*, 7 October. Available online: https://www.independent.co.uk/news/uk/home-news/muslims-

extremism-women-far-right-tommy-robinson-rape-a9143671.html
(accessed 7 February 2023).

Denham, J. (2001), 'Building cohesive communities: A report of the ministerial group on public order and community cohesion', *Home Office*. Available online: https://ec.europa.eu/migrant-integration/library-document/building-cohesive-communities-report-ministerial-group-public-order-and-community_en (accessed 13 February 2023).

De Noronha, L. (2020) *Deporting Black Britons: Portraits of Deportation to Jamaica*, Manchester: Manchester University Press.

Dowling, K. (2016), 'The drug lords of Middle England: London's most feared criminal gangs invade England's green and pleasant shires', *Daily Mail*, 14 May. Available online: https://www.dailymail.co.uk/news/article-3590650/The-drug-lords-Middle-England.html (accessed 8 February 2023).

Doyle, J. (2012), 'Don't let PC brigade bury ethnic links to sex gangs, warns children's minister', *Daily Mail*, 3 July. Available online: https://www.dailymail.co.uk/news/article-2168365/Tim-Loughton-Political-correctness-way-police-social-workers-investigating-child-sex-abuse.html (accessed 7 February 2023).

Duggan, O. (2014), 'Cabinet splits as Gove and May point finger over extremism in Birmingham schools', *The Telegraph*. Available online: https://www.telegraph.co.uk/education/educationnews/10874020/Cabinet-splits-as-Gove-and-May-point-finger-over-extremism-in-Birmingham-schools.html (accessed 7 February 2023).

Duncan, P., C. Aguilar Garcia and L. Swan (2022), 'Census 2021 in charts: Christianity now minority religion in England and Wales', *The Guardian*, 29 November. Accessed online: Census 2021 in charts: Christianity now minority religion in England and Wales | Census | The Guardian (accessed 26 February 2023).

Eade, J. and D. Garbin (2005), *The Bangladeshi Diaspora: Community Dynamics, Transnational Politics and Islamist activities*, London: Foreign and Commonwealth Office.

Elahi, F. and O. Khan (2017), 'Introduction: What Is Islamophobia?' in F. Elaho and O. Khan (eds), *Islamophobia: A Challenge for Us All: 20 Years on*, 5–12, London: Runnymede Trust.

Evening Standard. (2012), 'Murdered teenager caught up in gangs and knife crime', *Evening Standard*, 12 April. Available online: https://www.standard.co.uk/hp/front/murdered-teenager-caught-up-in-gangs-and-knife-crime-6693228.html (accessed 8 February 2023).

Fanon, F. (1967), *Black Skin, White Masks*, New York: Grove Press.

Fassin, D., ed (2017), *If Truth Be Told: The Politics of Public Ethnography*, Durham: Duke University Press.

Finney, N. and L. Simpson (2009), *'Sleepwalking to Segregation'? Challenging Myths about Race and Migration*, Bristol: Policy Press.

Geertz, C. (2000) *Available Light: Anthropological Reflections on Philosophical Topics*, Princeton, NJ: Princeton University Press.

Gibbs, D. (2022), 'Press release – New Quilliam report on "Grooming gangs"', *Quilliam International*, 23 June. Available online: https://www.quilliaminternational.com/press-release-new-quilliam-report-on-grooming-gangs/ (accessed 7 February 2023).

Gill, A. and S. Anitha (2009), 'The illusion of protection? An analysis for forced marriage legislation and policy in the UK', *Journal of Social Welfare and Family Law*, 31 (3): 257–69.

Gill, A. K. and K. Harrison (2015), 'Child grooming and sexual exploitation: Are South Asian men the UK media's new folk devils?', *International Journal for Crime, Justice and Social Democracy*, 4 (2): 34–49.

Gill, A. K. and T. Hamed (2016), 'Muslim women and forced marriages in the UK', *Journal of Muslim Minority Affairs*, 36 (4): 540–60.

Goldstein, D. M. (2020), 'Beyond thin description: Biography, theory, ethnographic writing', in C. McGranahan (ed), *Writing Ethnography: Essays on Craft and Commitment*, 78–82, Durham: Duke University Press.

Grimshaw, R. and M. Ford (2018), 'Young people, violence and knives: Revisiting the evidence and policy discussions', *Centre for Crime and Justice Studies*, Focus (3): 1–29. Available online: https://www.crimeandjustice.org.uk/sites/crimeandjustice.org.uk/files/Knife%20crime.%20November.pdf (accessed 8 February 2023).

Hall, M. (2007), 'Black kids to blame for knife and gun murders, says Blair', *Evening Standard*, 12 April. Available online: https://www.express.co.uk/news/uk/4240/Black-kids-to-blame-for-knife-and-gun-murders-says-Blair (accessed 8 February 2023).

Hall, S. (1990) 'Cultural identity and diaspora', in J. Rutherford (ed), *Identity: Community, Culture, Difference*, 222–37, London: Lawrence & Wishart.

Hall, S. (1992), 'New ethnicities', in J. Donald and A. Rattansi (eds), *'Race', Culture and Difference*, 252–9, London: Sage.

Hall, S. (2000), 'Conclusion: The multicultural question', in B. Hesse (ed), *Un/Settled Multiculturalisms: Diasporas, Entanglements, Transruptions*, 209–41, London: Zed Press.

Hall, S. and L. Back (2009), 'Conversation: At home and not at home', *Cultural Studies*, 23 (4): 658–87.

Hall, S., C. Critcher, T. Jefferson, J. Clarke and B. Roberts (1978), *Policing the Crisis*, London: Hutchinson.

Hesse, B., ed (2000), *Un/Settled Multiculturalisms: Diasporas, Entanglements, Transruptions*, London: Zed Press.

Hickman, M., L. Thomas, S. Silvestri and H. Nickels (2011), '*Suspect Communities?*': *Counter-Terrorism Policy, the Press and the Impact on Irish and Muslim Communities*, London: London Metropolitan University.

Home Office (2000), Race Relations (Amendment) Act, London: HMSO. https://www.legislation.gov.uk/ukpga/2000/34/contents.

Home Office (2006), 'Report of the Official Account of the Bombings in London on 7ᵗʰ July 2005', 11 May, London: London HMSO. Available online: https://assets.publishing.service.gov.uk/government/uploads/system/uploads/attachment_data/file/228837/1087.pdf (accessed 7 February 2023).

Home Office (2011), *Prevent Strategy 2011*, 7 June, London: London HMSO. Available online: https://assets.publishing.service.gov.uk/government/uploads/system/uploads/attachment_data/file/97976/prevent-strategy-review.pdf (accessed 17 February 2023).

Home Office (2013), 'Advice to parents and carers on gangs', 10 July, London: London HMSO. Available online: https://assets.publishing.service.gov.uk/government/uploads/system/uploads/attachment_data/file/345337/AdviceParentsCarersGangs14.pdf (accessed 8 February 2023).

Hoque, A. (2015), *British-Islamic Identity: Third Generation Bangladeshis from East London*, London: Institute of Education Press.

Huntington, S. (1996), *The Clash of Civilisations and the Remaking of World Order*, New York: Simon & Schuster.

Husain, E. (2015), *The Islamist: Why I Joined Radical Islam in Britain, What I Saw Inside and Why I Left*, London: Penguin.

Hussain, A. (2013), 'Radio Muslims: Disparate Voices on the same wavelength', in C. Alexander, V. Redclift and A. Hussain (eds), *The New Muslims*, 26–7, London: Runnymede Trust.

Hussain, A. (2014), 'Transgressing community: The case of Muslims in a twenty-first century British city', *Ethnic and Racial Studies*, 37 (4): 621–35.

Hussain, A. (2016), 'Muslims in the metropolis: An ethnographic study of Muslim-making in a 21ˢᵗ century British city', PhD thesis, The University of Manchester, Manchester.

Hussain, A. (2022), 'Street salafism: Contingency and urbanity as religious creed', *Environment and Planning D: Society and Space*, 40 (3): 469–85.

Idriss, M. M. (2022), 'Abused by the patriarchy: Male victims, "honor"-based abuse and forced marriages', *Journal of Interpersonal Violence*, 37 (13–14): 11905–32.

Jay, A. (2014), *Independent Enquiry into Child Sexual Exploitation in Rotherham 1997–2013*, Rotherham: Rotherham Metropolitan Borough Council. Available online: https://www.rotherham.gov.uk/downloads/file/279/independent-inquiry-into-child-sexual-exploitation-in-rotherham (accessed 17 February 2023).

Jivraj, S. and L. Simpson, eds (2015), *Ethnic Identity and Inequalities in Britain: The Dunamics of Diversity*, Bristol: Policy Press.

Johal, N and K. Thompson (2022), 'Leicester one of the first cities in the UK with no ethnic group majority – data', *BBC News Online*, 29 November. Available online: Leicester one of first cities in UK with no ethnic group majority – data – BBC News (accessed 26 February 2023).

Jones, H., Y. Gunaratnam, G. Bhattacharyya, W. Davies, S. Dhaliwal, K. Forkert, E. Jackson and R. Saltus (2017), *Go Home? The Politics of Immigration Controversies*, Manchester: Manchester University Press.

Joseph, I. and A. Gunter (2011), *What's a Gang and What's Race Got to Do with It?*, London: Runnymede Trust.

Joseph-Salisbury, R. (2018), *Black Mixed-Race Men: Transatlanticity, Hybridity and 'Post-Racial' Resilience*, Bingley: Emerald Press.

Joseph-Salisbury, R. (2020), *Race and racism in English secondary schools*, London: Runnymede Trust.

Kalra, V. S. (1999), *From Textile Mills to Taxi Ranks: The Local Impact of Global Economic Change*, Aldershot: Ashgate.

Kapadia, D., J. Nazroo and K. Clark (2015), 'Have ethnic inequalities in the labour market persisted?' in S. Jivraj and L. Simpson (eds), *Ethnic Identity and Inequalities in Britain*, 161–80, Bristol: Policy Press.

Kapoor, N. (2013), 'The advancement of racial neoliberalism in Britain', *Ethnic and Racial Studies*, 36 (6): 1028–46.

Kapoor, N. (2018), *Deport, Deprive, Extradite: 21ˢᵗ Century State Extremism*, London: Verso.

Kapoor, N. and K. Narkowicz (2019), 'Unmaking citizens: Passport removals, pre-emptive policing and the reimagining of colonial governmentalities', *Ethnic and Racial Studies*, 42 (16): 45–62.

Katwala, S. (2023), 'The Prevent Review feeds a political lie: That fighting the far right lets Islamist terrorists off the hook', *The Guardian*, 8 February. Available online: https://www.theguardian.com/commentisfree/2023/feb/08/prevent-review-far-right-islamist-extremism-shawcross (accessed 26 February 2023).

Keith, M. (1995), 'Making the street visible: Placing racial violence in context', *New Community*, 21 (4): 551–65.

Keith, M. (2009), 'Urbanism and city spaces in the work of Stuart Hall', *Cultural Studies*, 23 (4): 538–58.

Kibria, N. (2011), *Muslims in Motion: Islam and National Identity in the Bangladeshi Diaspora*, New Brunswick, NJ: Rutgers University Press.

Kundnani, A. (2014), *The Muslims Are Coming!: Islamophobia, Extremism and the Domestic War on Terror*, London: Verso.

Lee, G. (2017), 'What do we know about the ethnicity of sexual abuse gangs?', *Channel 4 News FactCheck*, 18 August. Available online: https://www.channel4.com/news/factcheck/what-do-we-know-about-the-ethnicity-of-sexual-abuse-gangs (accessed 7 February 2023).

Li, Y and A. Heath (2020), 'Persisting disadvantages: A study of labour market dynamics of ethnic unemployment and earnings in the UK (2009–2015)', *Journal of Ethnic and Migration Studies*, 46 (5): 857–78.

'London's gang wars claim the first teenage victim of 2008' (2008), *Daily Mail*, 2 January. Available online: https://www.dailymail.co.uk/news/article-505627/Londons-gang-wars-claim-teenage-victim-2008.html (accessed 8 February 2023).

Macey, M. (1999), 'Religion, male violence and the control of women: Pakistani Muslim men in Bradford, UK', *Gender and Development*, 7 (1): 48–55.

Macey, M. (2009), *Multiculturalism, Religion and Women: Doing Harm by Doing Good?* Basingstoke: Palgrave Macmillan.

Macpherson, W. (1999). *The Stephen Lawrence Inquiry*, London: HMSO. Available online: https://assets.publishing.service.gov.uk/government/uploads/system/uploads/attachment_data/file/277111/4262.pdf (accessed 17 February 2023).

Mamdani, M. (2004), *Good Muslim, Bad Muslim: America, the Cold War and the Roots of Terror*, New York: Pantheon Books.

Mason, W. (2019), 'Knife crime: Folk devils and moral panics?', *Centre for Crime and Justice Studies CJS*, 7 February. Available online at: https://www.

crimeandjustice.org.uk/resources/knife-crime-folk-devils-and-moral-panics (accessed 2 February 2023).

Maznavi, N. and A. Mattu (2012), *Love, InshAllah: The Secret Love Lives of American Muslim Women*, New York: Soft Skull Press.

McCann, K. (2018), 'Rochdale grooming gang members face deportation after losing appeal', *The Telegraph*, 8 August. Available online: https://www.telegraph.co.uk/news/2018/08/08/rochdale-grooming-gang-members-face-deportation-losing-appeal/ (accessed 7 February 2023).

McGranahan, C., ed (2020), *Writing Ethnography: Essays on Craft and Commitment*, Durham: Duke University Press.

Meer, N., ed (2013), *Racialization and Religion: Race, Culture and Difference in the Study of Antisemitism and Islamophobia*, London: Routledge.

Meer, N. (2015), *Racialization and Religion: Race, Culture and Difference in the Study of Antisemitism and Islamophobia*, London: Routledge.

Metropolitan Police Service (2007), *MPS Response to Guns, Gangs and Knives in London*, 3 May. London: Metropolitan Police Authority. Available online http://policeauthority.org/metropolitan/committees/x-cop/2007/070503/05/index.html (accessed 17 February 2023).

Miah, S. (2017), *Muslims, Schooling and Security*, Basingstoke: Palgrave Macmillan.

Miles, A. (2005), 'Four pathetic young bombers', *The Times*, 13 July. Available online: https://www.thetimes.co.uk/article/four-pathetic-young-bombers-skrqz8rnmzw (accessed 7 February 2023).

Mirza, H. (1992), *Young, Female and Black*, London: Routledge.

Mirza, H. and R. Warwick (2022), 'Race and ethnicity', *IFS Deaton Review of Inequalities*, London: Institute for Fiscal Studies. Available online: https://ifs.org.uk/sites/default/files/2022-11/Race-and-ethnicity-IFS-Deaton-Review-of-Inequalities.pdf (accessed 2 February 2023).

Modood, T. (1988), '"Black", racial equality and Asian identity', *Journal of Ethnic and Migration Studies*, 14 (3): 397–404.

Modood, T. (1992), *Not Easy Being British: Colour, Culture and Citizenship*, Stoke-on-Trent: Trentham.

Modood, T., R. Berthoud, J. Lakey, J. Nazroo, P. Smith, S. Virdee and S. Beishon (1997), *Ethnic Minorities in Britain: Diversity and Disadvantage*, London: Policy Studies Institute.

'MP urges review of immigration law' (2001), *The Guardian*, 12 July. Available online: https://www.theguardian.com/world/2001/jul/12/race.immigrationpolicy (accessed 4 February 2023).

Muslim Council of Britain (2015), 'British Muslims in numbers: A demographic, socio-economic and health profile of Muslims in Britain drawing on the 2011 census', *The Muslim Council of Britain*. Available online: https://www.mcb.org.uk/wp-content/uploads/2015/02/MCBCensusReport_2015.pdf (accessed 2 February 2023).

Nicholson, K. (2022), 'Sajid Javid's perfect two-word takedown of Nigel Farage's rant about UK ethnicity', *Yahoo News*, 30 November. https://www.huffingtonpost.co.uk/entry/sajid-javid-takes-down-nigel-farage-rant-uk-ethnicity_uk_63872e6ee4b06ef4a54a1043 (accessed 26 February 2023).

Niven, J., A. Faggian and K. N. Ruwanpura (2013), 'Exploring "underachievement" among highly educated young British-Bangladeshi women', *Feminist Economics*, 19 (1): 111–36.

Orwell, G. (1984) *Why I Write*, London: Penguin.

O'Toole, T., N. Meer, D. N. DeHanas, S. Jones and T. Modood (2016), 'Governing through Prevent? Regulation and contested practice in State-Muslim engagement', *Sociology*, 50 (1): 160–77.

Ouseley, H. (2001), *Community Pride, Not Prejudice: Making Diversity Work in Bradford*, Bradford: Bradford City Council.

Parekh, B. (2000), *The Future of Multi-Ethnic Britain*, London: Runnymede Trust/Profile Books.

Paton, G. (2012), 'Asian gangs "were acting within cultural norms"', *The Telegraph*, 10 May. Available online: https://www.telegraph.co.uk/news/uknews/crime/9258403/Asian-sex-gang-were-acting-within-cultural-norms.html (accessed 7 February 2023).

Phillips, C. and B. Bowling (2017), 'Ethnicities, crime and criminal justice', in A. Liebling, S. Maruna and L. McAra (eds), *Oxford Handbook of Criminology*, 6th edn, 190–212, Oxford: Oxford University Press.

Pichler, P. (2011), 'Hybrid or in between cultures: Traditions of marriage in a group of British Bangladeshi girls', in J. Coates and P. Pichler (eds) *Language and Gender: A Reader*, 2nd edn, 236–49, Oxford: Wiley-Blackwell.

Pratchett, T. (2014) *A Slip of the Keyboard*, London: Transworld Publishers.

Prince, R. (2012), 'Jack Straw: Pakistani community must face up to grooming scandal following Rochdale case', *The Telegraph*, 27 September 2012. Available online: https://www.telegraph.co.uk/news/uknews/crime/9570189/Jack-Straw-Pakistani-community-must-face-up-to-grooming-scandal-following-Rochdale-case.html (accessed 7 February 2023).

Pulver, A. (2021), 'Riz Ahmed calls for urgent change in "toxic portrayals" of Muslims on screen', *The Guardian*, 11 June. Available online: https://www. theguardian.com/film/2021/jun/11/riz-ahmed-muslim-portrayals-screen (accessed 26 February 2023).

Puri, K. (2022), 'Leicester: Why the violent unrest was surprising to many', *BBC News Online*, 24 September. Available online: https://www.bbc.co.uk/ news/uk-63009571 (accessed 26 February 2023).

Quinn, B. (2011), 'David Starkey claims "The whites have become black"', *The Guardian*, 13 August. Available online: https://www.theguardian.com/ uk/2011/aug/13/david-starkey-claims-whites-black (accessed 8 February 2023).

Ramamurthy, A. (2013), *Black Star: Britain's Asian Youth Movements*, London: Pluto Press.

Rashid, N. (2016), *Veiled Threats: Representing the Muslim Woman in Public Policy Discourses*, Bristol: Policy Press.

Rashid, N. (2017) '"Everyone is a feminist when it comes to Muslim women": Gender and Islamophobia', in F. Elahi and O. Khan (eds), *Islamophobia: A Challenge for Us All: 20 Years on*, 61–5, London: Runnymede Trust.

Riaz, A. (2013), *Islam and Identity Politics Among British-Bangladeshis*, Manchester: Manchester University Press.

Runnymede Trust (1997), *Islamophobia: A Challenge for Us All*, London: Runnymede Trust.

Rushdie, S. (1988), *The Satanic Verses*, London: Viking Penguin.

Said, E. (1978), *Orientalism*, New York: Pantheon Books.

Salter, M. and S. Dagistanli (2015), 'Cultures of abuse: "Sex grooming", organised abuse and race in Rochdale, UK', *International Journal for Crime, Justice and Social Democracy*, 4 (2): 50–64.

Salway, S. (2007), 'Economic activity among UK Bangladeshi and Pakistani women in the 1990s: Evidence for continuity or change in the family resources survey', *Journal of Ethnic and Migration Studies*, 33 (5): 825–47.

Salway, S. (2008), 'Labour market experiences of young UK Bangladeshi men: Identity, inclusion and exclusion in inner-city London', *Ethnic and Racial Studies*, 31 (6): 1126–52.

Samad, Y. (2010), 'Forced marriage among men: An unrecognized problem', *Critical Social Policy*, 30 (2): 189–207.

Samad, Y. and J. Eade (2002), *Community Perceptions of Forced Marriage*, Community Liaison Unit, London: Foreign and Commonwealth Office.

Sarkar, M. (2019), 'In a taxi, stuck or going places? A Bourdeusian intersectional analysis of the employment habitus of Pakistani taxi drivers in the UK', PhD thesis, University of Leeds, Leeds.

Sayyid, S. (2015), *A Fundamental Fear: Eurocentrism and the Emergence of Islamism*, London: Zed Books.

Sayyid, S. and A. K. Vakil (2010), *Thinking Through Islamophobia: Global Perspectives*, London: Hurst.

Shackle, S. (2016), 'The London girls lost to ISIS: What became of the "Jihadi brides"', *The New Statesman*, 6 October. Available online: https://www.newstatesman.com/culture/observations/2016/10/london-girls-lost-isis-what-became-jihadi-brides (accessed 7 February 2023).

Shams, T. (2020), *Here, There and Elsewhere: The Making of Immigrant Identities in a Globalized World*, Stanford: Stanford University Press.

Shankley, W. and N. Finney (2020) 'Ethnic minorities and housing in Britain', in B. Byrne, C. Alexander, O. Khan, J. Nazroo and W. Shankley (eds), *Ethnicity, Race and Inequality in the UK: State of the Nation*, 149–66, Bristol: Policy Press.

Sharma, A., J. Hutnyk and S. Sharma, eds (1996), *Dis-Orienting Rhythms: The Politics of the New Asian Dance Music*, London: Zed Books.

Sian, K. P. (2013), *Unsettling Sikh and Muslim Conflict: Mistaken Identities, Forced Conversions and Postcolonial Formations*, Lanham Maryland: Lexington Books.

Siddique, H. (2023), 'Shamima Begum loses appeal against removal of British citizenship', *The Guardian*, 22 February. Available online: https://www.theguardian.com/uk-news/2023/feb/22/shamima-begum-loses-appeal-removal-british-citizenship (accessed 26 February 2023).

Sivanandan, A. (2000), 'A radical black political culture', in K. Owusu (ed), *Black British Culture and Society: A Text Reader*, 73–85, London: Routledge.

Solomos, J. and L. Back (1996), *Racism and Society*, Basingstoke: Palgrave Macmillan.

Spalek, B. and D. Wilson (2002), 'Racism and religious discrimination in prison', in B. Spalek (ed), *Islam, Crime and Criminal Justice*, 96–112, Cullompton: Willan Publishing.

Stewart, H. and R. Mason (2016), 'Nigel Farage's anti-migrant poster reported to police', *The Guardian*, 16 June. Available online: https://www.theguardian.com/politics/2016/jun/16/nigel-farage-defends-ukip-breaking-point-poster-queue-of-migrants (accessed 7 February 2023).

Stratton, Allegra & Agencies (2008), 'New crackdown on knife and gun crime', *The Guardian*, 22.

Summers, H. (2008), 'Teen killings second only to terrorism', *The London Paper*, 3 January.

Swinford, S. and K. McCann (2017), 'Sarah Champion forced out of Jeremy Corbyn's shadow cabinet after warning Pakistani men are raping white girls', *The Telegraph*, 16 August. Available online: https://www.telegraph.co.uk/news/2017/08/16/sarah-champion-quits-jeremy-corbyns-shadow-cabinet-warning-pakistani/ (accessed 7 February 2023).

Tarlo, E. (2009), *Visibly Muslim: Fashion, Politics, Faith*, Oxford: Berg.

'Teenager is stabbed to death on busy street in gang "revenge" attack' (2008), *Daily Mail*, 22 January. Available online: https://www.dailymail.co.uk/news/article-509700/Teenager-stabbed-death-busy-street-gang-revenge-attack.html (accessed 8 February 2023).

Telegraph Reporters. (2018), 'Rowan Atkinson defends Boris Johnson over burka comments', *The Telegraph*, 10 August. Available online: https://www.telegraph.co.uk/politics/2018/08/10/rowan-atkinson-defends-boris-johnson-burka-comments/ (accessed 7 February 2023).

The Times. (2011), 'Revealed: Conspiracy of silence on UK sex gangs', *The Times*, 5 January. Available online: https://www.thetimes.co.uk/article/revealed-conspiracy-of-silence-on-uk-sex-gangs-gpg5vqsqz9h (accessed 7 February 2023).

'Three-point plan to tackle gun crime' (2007), *Daily Mail*, 22 February. Available online: https://www.dailymail.co.uk/news/article-437794/Three-point-plan-tackle-gun-crime.html (accessed 8 February 2023).

Tonkiss, F. (2005), *Space, the City and Social Theory: Social Relations and Urban Forms*, Cambridge: Polity Press.

Travis, A. (2002), 'Anger at Blunkett "whining maniacs" attack', *The Guardian*, 6 September. Available online: https://www.theguardian.com/society/2002/sep/06/raceequality.politics (accessed 7 February 2023).

Tufail, W. (2015), 'Rotherham, Rochdale and the racialized threat of the "Muslim grooming gang"', *International Journal for Crime, Justice and Social Democracy*, 4 (3): 30–43.

Tufail, W. and S. Poynting (2016), 'Muslim and dangerous: "Grooming" and the politics of racialisation', in D. Pratt and R. Woodlock (eds), *Fear of Muslims? Boundaries of Religious Freedom*, 79–92, Cham: Springer.

Venkatesh, S. (2009), *Off the Books: The Underground Economy of the Urban Poor*, Boston: Harvard University Press.

Virdee, S. (2014), *Racism, Class and the Racialized Outsider*, London: Bloomsbury.

Wainwright, M., A. Perkins and A. Travis (2001), 'Bradford's "painful future"', *The Guardian*, 13 July. Available online: https://www.theguardian.com/uk/2001/jul/13/race.world1 (accessed 7 February 2023).

Wainwright, M. and V. Dodd (2002), 'Gentle fight to show unfairness of riot jailings', *The Guardian*, 31 August. Available online: https://www.theguardian.com/uk/2002/aug/31/race.world1 (accessed 7 February 2023).

Wainwright, O. (2015), 'Revealed: How developers exploit flawed planning system to minimise affordable housing', *The Guardian*, 25 June. Available online: https://www.theguardian.com/cities/2015/jun/25/london-developers-viability-planning-affordable-social-housing-regeneration-oliver-wainwright (accessed 2 February 2023).

Waite, M. (2021), *On Burnley Road*, London: Lawrence & Wishart.

Wallace, D. (2023), *The Culture Trap: Ethnic Expectations and Unequal Schooling for Black Youth*, Oxford: Oxford University Press.

Warner, S. (2018), 'How can we address gang culture in schools?', *Teacher Toolkit*, 28 October. Available online: https://www.teachertoolkit.co.uk/2018/10/28/gang-youth-violence/ (accessed 8 February 2023).

Watt, N. and M. Oliver (2009), '"Broken Britain" is like The Wire, say Tories', *The Guardian*, 25 August. Available online: https://www.theguardian.com/politics/2009/aug/25/tories-compare-britain-wire-tv (accessed 7 February 2023).

Webster, C. (1997), 'The construction of British "Asian" criminality', *International Journal of the Sociology of Law*, 25 (1): 65–86.

Werbner, P. (1990), *The Migration Process: Capital, Gifts and Offerings among British Pakistanis*, Oxford: Berg.

Williams, P. and B. Clarke (2016), 'Dangerous associations: Joint enterprise, gangs and racism: An analysis of the processes of criminalisation of Black, Asian and minority ethnic individuals', *Centre for Crime and Justice Studies*, January 2016. Available online: https://www.crimeandjustice.org.uk/sites/crimeandjustice.org.uk/files/Dangerous%20assocations%20Joint%20Enterprise%20gangs%20and%20racism.pdf (accessed 8 February 2023).

Williams, P. and B. Clarke (2018), 'The black criminal as an object of social control', *Social Sciences*, 7 (11): 234.

Willis, P. and M. Trondman (2000), 'Manifesto for Ethnography', *Ethnography*, 1 (1): 5–16.

Wintour, P. (2008), 'Smith to slash restrictions on police power', *The Guardian*, 31 January. Available online: https://www.theguardian.com/politics/2008/jan/31/uk.uknews4 (accessed 8 February 2023).

Worrall, P. (2014), 'What do we know about the grooming gangs?', *Channel 4 News FactCheck*, 28 August. Available online: https://www.channel4.com/news/factcheck/factcheck-grooming-gangs (accessed 7 February 2023).

Younge, G. (2018), 'The radical lessons of a year reporting on knife crime', *The Guardian*, 21 June. Available online: https://www.theguardian.com/membership/2018/jun/21/radical-lessons-knife-crime-beyond-the-blade (accessed 8 February 2023).

Younge, G. (2019), 'Teenagers are being killed. But more policing is too simple an answer', *The Guardian*, 6 March. Available online: https://www.theguardian.com/commentisfree/2019/mar/06/teenagers-killed-policing-knife-crime (accessed 8 February 2023).

Index

www.ingramcontent.com/pod-product-compliance
Lightning Source LLC
Chambersburg PA
CBHW070554270326
41926CB00013B/2312